THE CASE
AGAINST
THE
CONSTITUTION

THE CASE AGAINST THE CONSTITUTION

From the Antifederalists to the Present

Edited by
**John F. Manley
and Kenneth M. Dolbeare**
with a Foreword by Jackson Turner Main

M. E. Sharpe, Inc.
ARMONK, NEW YORK
LONDON, ENGLAND

To the memory of Charles A. Beard

Copyright © 1987 by M. E. Sharpe, Inc.

Available in the United Kingdom and Europe from M. E. Sharpe, Publishers, 3 Henrietta Street, London WC2E 8LU.

Library of Congress Cataloging-in-Publication Data

The Case against the Constitution.

  Contents: Introduction—The spirit of American government / J. Allen Smith—An economic interpretation of the Constitution / Charles Beard—The antifederalists / Jackson Turner Main [etc.]
  1. United States—Constitutional history. I. Manley, John F. II. Dolbeare, Kenneth M.
KF4541.C37   1987   342.73′0292   87-4640
ISBN 0-87332-432-3   347.302292
ISBN 0-87332-433-1 (pbk.)

Printed in the United States of America

Table of Contents

Documents

Foreword

The Framers of the Constitution would be astonished as well as delighted by the present adoration of their work. In their own day they had to contend with sharp differences among themselves, which led to the familiar constitutional "compromises," and with even greater disagreements within the population generally, which had somehow to be satisfied. The Framers had to seek an accommodation between the kind of government that most of them preferred, and what they thought they could actually achieve. The best they could hope for was not perfection, but improvement: a more perfect union.

For many years before 1787, American voters and their representatives had tended to divide into two major groups or blocs, or (as the word was then used) "parties." The polar nuclei can be characterized as localist vs. cosmopolitan, rural vs. urban, noncommercial vs. commercial, small property vs. large property, and farm vs. nonfarm. The first of each of these pairs valued local control and government dominated by democratic majorities, meaning themselves. The second had ideas and interests best served by a strong central government that could act vigorously in economic and political matters—and that they could control. In concrete terms, the antagonists were the somewhat isolated, rather provincial middle class and small farmers versus the educated, urban, well-to-do business and professional men and large-scale farmers. Their conflict foreshadowed that of the Populists and their opponents in the nineteenth century, and contained all the same prejudices and hostilities.

These two blocs took shape rapidly in 1774–1776 when most of the states, writing their own constitutions, had to confront a complicated series of political, military, economic, social, and religious issues. The questions that were important include the following: Should the states rely on their militias or on a permanent, national army? Should they finance the war for independence by deficit spending or by heavy taxes, and, if the latter, who should pay? Should Congress exercise extensive or limited powers? Should governments at all levels be run by "the better sort" or by ordinary people?

The debate became quite bitter in the 1780s. Many of the delegates to the Constitutional convention, such as Alexander Hamilton, had already felt the sting of popular disapproval. The reader might try to imagine what would happen today if a new constitutional convention were to meet under the domination of one of the two political parties. It would surely convene under suspicion, and it would have to reconcile not only the opposing elements within the party itself but the objectives and prejudices of the other party and of our disparate society. The new constitution would consist, surely, of some common core enveloped by expedient compromises.

The Framers of the Constitution were limited by history and by the practical circumstances of the times. Mostly lawyers, businessmen, and large land-holders—educated, cosmopolitan, and well-to-do—they sought to create a strong central government through which they could implement their political and economic program, presumably for the best interest of all. The document that they produced granted the central government less in the way of powers than they would have preferred, but more than many other Americans liked. There was a bitter struggle, ending in a narrow victory.

Because the result fully satisfied neither side, the combatants continued the struggle far into the next century and even beyond. Indeed, many of the key questions that divided the country then still divide it today. The Constitution embodied one set of answers, the Antifederalists gave another. Posterity—we, the people—must judge.

Most books about the Constitution present it as a classic to be expounded rather than evaluated. This book challenges us to think about the Constitution, to consider its flaws as well as its excellences, and perhaps even to wonder how we today might create an even more perfect union.

JACKSON TURNER MAIN
Boulder, Colorado

Introduction

The Bicentennial of the American Constitution will be celebrated from 1987 to 1991, the 200th anniversary of the ratification of the Bill of Rights. This long-planned event is, of course, only the latest in an almost unbroken series of celebrations of that document and the political genius of its Framers. Ironically, perhaps tragically, it seems likely that an uncritical, one-dimensional approach to the Constitution will prevail, and that Americans will miss an opportunity to confront the very questions about the premises and purposes of government that so vitally engaged the Framers.

Conventional wisdom holds that in the Constitution the Founding Fathers designed a system of government that would function neutrally and objectively—as if by the laws of mechanics—to produce policy in the public interest. This system is said to be so acutely attuned to human nature that it has been able to adapt to every need generated by the changing circumstances of 200 years. As such, it has more than earned the adulation of all Americans and others around the world who are truly devoted to democratic government.

However, there has always been an important body of American political thought that challenges or rejects this portrayal of the Constitution. It is a tradition that puts *democracy* first. It rejects the notion that there can be "neutral" structures of government. Values, purposes, and goals are inevitable parts of the design of any government; they should be openly debated and ultimately decided by popular majorities. It challenges the Constitution with the basic questions: who, or what interests, should be served by government, and how can control by the people be assured?

This line of thinking has its roots in seventeenth-century England. Its principal American expression is the Declaration of Independence of 1776—not the Constitution of 1787. Those who opposed ratification of the Constitution, the Anti-federalists, clearly saw the property defensiveness, centralization potential, and prospective loss of local democratic control that were implicit in the new system. They extracted grudging acquiescence to a Bill of Rights from the Constitution's advocates. Although they were defeated in their efforts to prevent adoption and implementation of the Constitution, the Antifederalists' challenge to status and property on behalf of equality and democracy has been an inspiration since first articulated in 1787.

In the face of the long survival—and indeed, the popular enshrinement—of the Constitution, the Antifederalist critique has often been misunderstood or simply dismissed. One of the major contributions of the Progressive historians, J. Allen Smith and Charles A. Beard prominent among them, was to show that their own industrial-era challenge to the system was fully anticipated by the Antifederalists. Since then, in part through the careful work of modern historians, the arguments of the Antifederalists have been examined more thoroughly.

No reputable modern historian or political theorist would argue that the Framers of the Constitution intended a democracy. Nevertheless, many assert that, as a practical political fact, democracy was accomplished in the United States sometime in the early nineteenth century and that it reigns in full flower today, warm and comfortable in the protective embrace of the Constitution. The equation of the Constitution, the government of the United States, and the treasured political principle of democracy is complete for most Americans, scholars included, and has been so for so many generations that it sometimes seems beyond dispute.

Decades of study of American politics have convinced us that, like much conventional wisdom, this conclusion simply will not stand up in the face of the facts. The Constitution was originally designed, and functions effectively today, to *permit political participation* but *prevent democracy* in the United States. Moreover, it is the Constitution that is primarily responsible for many of the failures of governance in the United States today. Americans badly need a dose of realism about the Constitution if we are to solve the serious political-economic problems heralding our third century.

Our vast bicentennial celebration is not simply a harmless patriotic extravaganza. It promises to be little more than an utterly unrealistic, and potentially tragic, exercise in self-delusion and systematic avoidance of hard political truths—and, for those very reasons, profoundly unworthy of the Framers it seeks to honor. Men like Madison and Hamilton understood their dangerous world very well. They acted in a timely fashion to create a new political-economic structure, one that met compelling needs they openly acknowledged.

We have developed this collection of classic and contemporary writings to give voice to American democracy's continuing challenge to the Constitution. We hope that it will spark serious discussion of the premises and purposes of American government as well as a realistic appraisal of the adaptation of its structures to the ends it is to serve. Readers may judge the merits of the arguments for themselves.

The plan of the collection is straightforward. Part 1 features the Progressive critique of the Constitution, the first modern, twentieth-century statement of the democratic challenge. J. Allen Smith (1907) and Charles Beard (1913) saw the issue as an industrial-era problem of corporate capitalism against democracy. The Constitution, the supposed embodiment of democracy, was the authority that was being invoked (chiefly by the courts, but by many others as well) to *legitimate* whatever economic power—in this case the corporations—wanted to do. In other words, the Constitution was being used as an instrument of economic exploitation—and the result celebrated as "democracy." In their work they sought to remove the veil of reverence that covered the Constitution, and with it the justification for allowing corporate activity to evade public control.

The Progressive historians showed that the Framers had been members of a propertied upper class determined to preserve and enhance the opportunities of their class. They showed the Constitution itself to be biased in favor of that class, and full of limitations on democratic control. Finally, they showed that many people, perhaps even a majority of all Americans at the time of ratification, were well aware of these purposes of the Constitution and the intentions of its Framers.

For this the Progressive historians were vigorously attacked. The issue was joined on two fronts: (a) the historical question of the Constitution's original biases; and (b) the contemporary question of whether the Constitution should provide corporations immunity from popular control.

In this context, the history of the Framers' actions and the Antifederalists' reactions took on new meaning. What did the Framers really intend? Which individuals, and which documents, actually championed democracy? This debate was something more than a scholarly exercise. In the United States, then as now, to argue about democracy in the present, one must be ready to take on the events, arguments, and actions of that golden age when the Constitution was fashioned. The Progressive critique is thus the hinge on which this collection turns. It is both the first statement of a continuing industrial-era challenge and a call on Americans to more clearly and realistically understand the Constitution itself.

Part 2 of our collection reaches back from the Progressive Era to the earliest challenges to the Constitution. We begin with an excerpt from the work of the leading historian of the Antifederalists, Jackson Turner Main. *The Antifederalists: Critics of the Constitution, 1781–1788* is Main's lively account of the ratification process and the class divisions that underlay the debate over adoption of the Constitution.

To give a full hearing to the Antifederalists' arguments, some immersion in their own writings is essential. We have chosen a document from the Pennsylvania dissenters, because that state had the most democratic of all the state constitutions and one of the most vigorous opposition movements to the new Constitution. Although defeated at every turn, the arguments of the Pennsylvanians were typical of the Antifederalists throughout the ratification debate.

The other document is from Richard Henry Lee, a leading Virginian whose support for the Antifederalist cause gave it significant respectability. In particular, Lee articulates the class basis of the ratification conflict that divided the country from September 1787 through June 1788.

The two principal issues raised in these documents were fundamental to the eighteenth-century concept of democracy: (a) individual liberties and (b) control by local majorities. There was no bill of rights in the Framers' Constitution. And the centralized government it proposed, far removed from voters, seemed to offer little chance for informed control. The first claim was won, at least in formal legal terms, with the adoption of the first ten amendments to the Constitution. But the second could not be allowed to succeed, if the Framers were to gain the ends that had led them to the Convention in the first place. It remains at the heart of the problem of democratic governance today.

In part 3, we come forward from the Progressives to the present. In every case, the authors of these essays first acknowledge the necessity of a clear and realistic understanding of the intents and events of the founding era. Only with such a base is it possible to see through the clouds of celebratory rhetoric and critically analyze today's Constitution in the light of present and future problems.

Our message is offered in three parts. First, John F. Manley shows that James Madison had as his primary purpose the defense of the property interests of the dominant class of his day. Rather than holding an image of many interest groups, each seeking its separate and disparate goals and following fair procedures (as the conventional wisdom would have it), Madison saw an enduring conflict between classes. These classes were based on property—the many "have-nots" against the few "haves"—and Madison was determined to provide a system that would protect the few.

The implication is that class was then, and remains today, the best analytic concept with which to understand the provisions and purposes of the Constitution. By extension, today's Constitution is biased toward control by the heirs of the ruling class of 1787—those who hold the greatest assets of power: long-established family status, institutional position, great wealth, an elite education, control of the mass media, and so forth.

Second, Kenneth Dolbeare and Linda Medcalf show that the Framers succeeded too well in their efforts to design a government in which popular majorities were prevented from becoming effective. Indeed, the authors argue, the Framers must share the responsibility for some of our present political problems. Frequent institutional "gridlock," presidential adventurism in foreign policy, and steadily declining voter turnout for national elections are only some of the contemporary problems that Dolbeare and Medcalf trace to the Framers' purposefully crafted provisions.

They show further that Alexander Hamilton's role at the Convention, during ratification, and then as Secretary of the Treasury was a crucial factor in the implementation of this design. Hamilton effectively removed two key decision-making arenas—the legal system and the financial system—from popular reach. These two systems finally crystallized in the late nineteenth century and were effectively defended in the election of 1896.

Since that time, there has been increasing popular inability to translate goals and preferences into government action. Growing frustration with the failure of elections as a way to accomplish goals has led to a widespread withdrawal from politics. The United States, celebrating the bicentennial of its Constitution, now ranks *nineteenth* among industrial democracies in the proportion of eligible voters who actually vote in national elections.

The analysis implies that substantial changes will have to be made in some basic Constitutional provisions if the United States is to resolve two pressing needs. The first need is to restore some sort of linkage between the people and their government. Popular confidence in government must be rebuilt primarily on the basis of a new capacity for popular majorities to achieve what they want from government. The second need is to become more effective in coping with economic problems. The authors sketch some illustrative changes that would, taken together, offer a chance to accomplish this end.

Third, Jeanne Hahn describes a group of modern-day Hamiltonians who share the view that the Constitution poses many problems for Americans today, but do not see democratization as a solution. Rather, they have proposed changes that would make decision making even *more* centralized and distant from voters and the possibility of democratic control. The members of this group, the Committee on the Constitutional System, are "insiders" who have found it frustratingly difficult to make the institutions of the national government work quickly and smoothly. The Committee has produced two volumes in which twelve recommended Constitutional amendments and statutory changes are presented, explained, and defended.

Hahn carefully analyzes these proposals, individually and as a package, showing that they are fully in the Hamiltonian tradition. They would enhance the capacity of the national government to act swiftly and decisively, but at the price of insulating it even more fully from any popular impact. She calls for revival of a modern version of the Antifederalist concern for democracy, with democratizing institutional changes rather than those proposed by the Committee on the Constitutional System.

Taken together, the last three essays argue the need for a realistic dialogue about the first principles of government and the manner of implementing them through a constitution. No worthy point is served by uncritical celebration; indeed, the shrewd and purposeful accomplishments of the Framers can only be dishonored by mindless rhetorical excess.

A new era of realism is needed in which some basic questions can be discussed in a serious way. What is achieved by specific constitutional provisions under today's circumstances? How does this compare with what the country wants and needs in the way of political process and governmental capability? We think that the selections in this volume lay some of the groundwork for addressing these vital questions.

1. The Progressive Critique
Capitalism vs. Democracy

J. Allen Smith
The Spirit of American Government

J. Allen Smith, late Professor of Political Science at the University of Washington, wrote a pathbreaking (1907) critique of the Constitution as a reactionary document. Smith describes the strong democratic tendencies in America that culminated in the Declaration of Independence and the Articles of Confederation. He argues that conservative elites prepared the Constitution in order to curb the power of the people and protect the property interests of the upper class. Smith's ultimate purpose was to demonstrate that the efforts of contemporary majorities to curb corporations were justified, notwithstanding the constitutional interpretations of the courts.

The American Government of the Revolutionary Period

The American colonists inherited the common law and the political institutions of the mother country. The British form of government, with its King, Lords and Commons and its checks upon the people, they accepted as a matter of course. In their political thinking they were not consciously more democratic than their kinsmen across the Atlantic. Many of them, it is true, had left England to escape what they regarded as tyranny and oppression. But to the *form* of the English government as such they had no objection. The evils which they experienced were attributed solely to the selfish spirit in which the government was administered.

The conditions, however, were more favorable for the development of a democratic spirit here than in the mother country. The immigrants to America represented the more active, enterprising and dissatisfied elements of the English people. Moreover, there was no hereditary aristocratic class in the colonies and less inequality in the distribution of wealth. This approach to industrial and social

Reprinted from J. Allen Smith, *The Spirit of American Government*, edited by Cushing Strout (Cambridge, MA: The Belknap Press of Harvard University Press, 1965), chapters 2, 3, 11, 12, and p. 331.

equality prepared the mind for the ideas of political equality which needed only the stimulus of a favorable opportunity to ensure their speedy development.

This opportunity came with the outbreak of the American Revolution which at the outset was merely an organized and armed protest against what the colonies regarded as an arbitrary and unconstitutional exercise of the taxing power. As there was no widespread or general dissatisfaction with the *form* of the English government, there is scarcely room for doubt that if England had shown a more prudent and conciliatory spirit toward the colonies, the American Revolution would have been averted. No sooner, however, had the controversy with the mother country reached the acute revolutionary stage, than the forces which had been silently and unconsciously working toward democracy, found an opportunity for political expression. The spirit of resistance to what was regarded as unconstitutional taxation rapidly assumed the form of avowed opposition to the English Constitution itself. The people were ready for a larger measure of political democracy than the English Constitution of the eighteenth century permitted. To this new and popular view of government the Declaration of Independence gave expression. It contained an emphatic, formal and solemn disavowal of the political theory embodied in the English Constitution; affirmed that "all men are created equal;" that governments derive "their just powers from the consent of the governed;" and declared the right of the people to alter or to abolish the form of the government "and to institute new government, laying its foundation on such principles and organizing its powers in such form, as to them shall seem most likely to effect their safety and happiness." This was a complete and sweeping repudiation of the English political system, which recognized the right of monarchy and aristocracy to thwart the will of the people.

To what extent the Declaration of Independence voiced the general sentiment of the colonies is largely a matter of conjecture. It is probable, however, that its specification of grievances and its vigorous arraignment of the colonial policy of the English government appealed to many who had little sympathy with its express and implied advocacy of democracy. It is doubtless true that many were carried along with the revolutionary movement who by temperament and education were strongly attached to English political traditions. It is safe to conclude that a large proportion of those who desired to see American independence established did not believe in thorough-going political democracy.

Besides those who desired independence without being in sympathy with the political views expressed in the Declaration of Independence, there were many others who were opposed to the whole Revolutionary movement. The numerical strength of the Tories can not be accurately estimated; but it is certain that a large proportion, probably not less than one-third of the total population of the colonies, did not approve of the war.[1]

In the first place, there was, prior to 1776, the official class; that is, the men holding various positions in the civil and military and naval services of the government, their immediate families, and their social connections. All such persons may be described as inclining to the Loyalist view in consequence of official bias.

Next were certain colonial politicians who, it may be admitted, took a rather selfish and an unprincipled view of the whole dispute, and who, counting on the probable, if not inevitable, success of the British arms in such a conflict, adopted the Loyalist side, not for conscience' sake, but for profit's sake, and in the expectation of being rewarded for their fidelity by offices and titles, and especially by the confiscated estates of the rebels after the rebels themselves should have been defeated, and their leaders hanged or sent into exile.

As composing still another class of Tories, may be mentioned probably a vast majority of those who stood for the commercial interests, for the capital and tangible property of the country, and who, with the instincts natural to persons who have something considerable to lose, disapproved of all measures for pushing the dispute to the point of disorder, riot and civil war.

Still another class of Loyalists was made up of people of professional training and occupation—clergymen, physicians, lawyers, teachers—a clear majority of whom seem to have been set against the ultimate measures of the Revolution.

Finally, and in general, it may be said that a majority of those who, of whatever occupation, of whatever grade of culture or of wealth, would now be described as conservative people, were Loyalists during the American Revolution.[2]

These classes prior to the Revolution had largely shaped and molded public opinion; but their opposition to the movement which they were powerless to prevent, destroyed their influence, for the time being, in American politics. The place which they had hitherto held in public esteem was filled by a new class of leaders more in sympathy with the newly born spirit of liberalism. This gave to the revolutionary movement a distinctly democratic character.

This drift toward democracy is seen in the changes made in the state constitutions after the outbreak of the Revolution. At the close of the colonial period, nearly all the state governments were modeled after the government of Great Britain. Each colony had its legislative body elected by the qualified voters and corresponding in a general way to the House of Commons. In all the colonies except Pennsylvania and Georgia there was also an upper legislative house or council whose consent was necessary before laws could be enacted. The members composing this branch of the legislature were appointed by the governor except in Massachusetts where they were elected by the lower branch of the legislature, subject to a negative by the royal governor, and in Rhode Island and Connecticut where they were chosen by the electorate.

The governor was elected by the voters only in Rhode Island and Connecticut; in all the other colonies he was appointed by the proprietaries or the Crown, and, though independent of the people, exercised many important powers. He was commander-in-chief of the armed forces of the colony; appointed the judges and all other civil and military officers; appointed and could suspend the council, which was usually the upper branch of the legislature; he could convene and dissolve the legislature and had besides an unqualified veto on all laws; he also had an unrestricted pardoning power.

The possession of these far-reaching powers gave to the irresponsible executive branch of the colonial government a position of commanding importance. This was not the case, however, in Connecticut and Rhode Island. Although the governor in these two colonies was responsible to the voters, inasmuch as he was elected by them, still he had no veto, and the appointing power was in the hands of the legislature.

The tidal-wave of democracy, which swept over the colonies during the Revolution, largely effaced the monarchical and aristocratic features of the colonial governments. Connecticut and Rhode Island, which already had democratic constitutions, were the only states which did not modify their form of government during this period. All the rest adopted new constitutions which show in a marked degree the influence of the democratic movement. In these new constitutions we see a strong tendency to subordinate the executive branch of the government and confer all important powers on the legislature. In the four New England states and in New York the governor was elected by the qualified voters; in all the rest he was chosen by the legislature. In ten states during this period his term of office was one year; in South Carolina it was two and in New York and Delaware it was three years. In addition to this the six Southern states restricted his re-election. Besides, there was in every state an executive or privy council which the governor was required to consult on all important matters. This was usually appointed by the legislature and constituted an important check on the governor.

The power to veto legislation was abolished in all but two states. In Massachusetts the governor, and in New York the Council of Revision composed of the governor and the chancellor and judges of the Supreme Court, had a qualified veto power. But a two-thirds majority in both houses of the legislature could override the veto of the governor in Massachusetts, or that of the Council of Revision in New York. The pardoning power of the governor was quite generally restricted. In five states he was allowed to exercise it only with the advice or consent of the council.[3] In three states, where the advice or consent of a council was not required, he could, subject to certain restrictions, grant pardons except where "the law shall otherwise direct."[4] The constitution of Georgia in express terms deprived the governor of all right to exercise this power.

The appointing power of the governor was also taken away or restricted. In four of the eleven states adopting new constitutions during this period he was allowed to exercise it jointly with the council.[5] In six states it was given to the legislature, or to the legislature and council.[6] The power of the governor to dissolve the legislature or either branch of it was everywhere abolished.

The supremacy of the legislature under these early state constitutions is seen also in the manner of appointment, the tenure and the powers of the judiciary. In nine states[7] the judges were elected by the state legislature, either with or without the consent of a council. In Maryland, Massachusetts, New Hampshire, and Pennsylvania they were appointed by the governor with the consent of the council. But this really amounted to indirect legislative appointment in Maryland, since both the governor and council in that state were elected annually by the legislature. The legislature also had a voice in the appointment of judges in Pennsylvania, New Hampshire and Massachusetts, since it elected the executive in the first and the council in the others. In nine states, then, the judges were elected directly by the legislature; in one indirectly by the legislature; in the other three the legislature participated in their election through an executive or a council of its own choosing.

In every state the judges could be impeached by the lower branch of the legislature and expelled from office on conviction by the senate or other tribunal, as the constitution prescribed. Moreover, in six states[8] they could be removed according to the English custom by the executive on an address from both branches of the legislature. The term of office of the judges in eight states[9] was during good behavior. In New Jersey and Pennsylvania they were appointed for seven years, and in Rhode Island, Connecticut, and Georgia they were chosen annually.

The legislature under these early state constitutions was hampered neither by the executive nor by the courts. It had all law-making power in its own hands. In no state could the courts thwart its purpose by declaring its acts null and void. Unchecked by either executive or judicial veto its supremacy was undisputed.

From the foregoing synopsis of the state constitutions of this period it is evident that their framers rejected entirely the English theory of checks and balances. The principle of separation of powers as expounded by Montesquieu and Blackstone, found little favor with those who controlled American politics at this time. Instead of trying to construct a state government composed of coordinate branches, each acting as a check upon the others, their aim was to make the legislature supreme. In this respect the early state constitutions anticipated much of the later development of the English government itself.

The checks and balances, and separation of powers, which characterized the government of England and her American colonies in the eighteenth century, resulted from the composite character of the English Constitution—its mixture of monarchy, aristocracy, and democracy. It is not surprising, then, that with the temporary ascendancy of the democratic spirit, the system of checks should have been largely discarded.

This democratic tendency is seen also in our first federal constitution, the Articles of Confederation, which was framed under the impulse of the Revolutionary movement. This document is interesting as an expression of the political philosophy of the Revolution; but like the state constitutions of that period, it has had few friendly critics among later political writers. Much emphasis has been put upon its defects, which were many, while but little attention has been given to the political theory which it imperfectly embodied. That it failed to provide a satisfactory general government may be admitted; but this result must not be accepted as conclusive proof that the principles underlying it were altogether false.

The chief feature of the Articles of Confederation was the entire absence of checks and balances. All the powers conferred upon the general government were vested in a single legislative body called the Continental Congress, which was unchecked by a distinct executive or judiciary. In this respect it bore a striking resemblance to the English government of to-day with its omnipotent House of Commons. But, unlike the English government of to-day, its powers were few and narrowly limited. Its failure was due, perhaps, not to the fact that the powers granted to the confederation were vested exclusively in a single legislative body, but to the fact that the powers thus granted were not sufficient for maintaining a strong and effective central government.

The reason for the weakness of the general government under the Articles of Confederation is obvious to the student of American history. It was only gradually, and as necessity compelled cooperation between the colonies, that the sentiment in favor of political union developed. And though some tendencies in this direction are seen more than a century before the American Revolution, the progress toward a permanent union was slow and only the pressure of political necessity finally brought it about.

As early as 1643 Massachusetts, Plymouth, Connecticut and New Haven formed a "perpetual confederation" under the name of the "United Colonies of New England." The motive for this union was mainly offence and defence against the Indian tribes and the Dutch, though provision was also made for the extradition of servants and fugitives from justice. The management of the common interests of these colonies was vested in a board of eight commissioners— two from each colony—and, in transacting the business of the confederacy, the consent of six of the eight commissioners was required. Any matter which could not be thus disposed of was to be referred to the four colonial legislatures. The general government thus provided for could not intermeddle "with the government of any of the jurisdictions." No provision was made for amending the "Articles of Confederation," and only by the unanimous consent of these colonies could any other colony be admitted to the confederacy. This union lasted for over forty years.[10]

Again in 1754 the pressure of impending war with the French and Indians brought together at Albany a convention of delegates from seven colonies north of the Potomac. A plan of union drafted by Benjamin Franklin was recommended by this convention, but it was not regarded with favor either by the colonies or by the English government. The former regarded it as going too far in the direction of subordinating the separate colonies to a central colonial authority, while for the latter it was too democratic.[11]

The union of all the colonies under the Articles of Confederation was finally brought about through the pressure of military necessity during the Revolution. Nor is it surprising, in view of the history of the American colonies, that they reluctantly yielded up any powers to a central authority. We must bear in mind that the Revolution was in a measure a democratic movement, and that democracy was then found only in local government. The general governments of all countries were at that time monarchical or aristocratic. Tyranny in the eighteenth century was associated in the minds of the people with an undue extension or abuse of the powers exercised by the undemocratic central government. It is not surprising, then, that the Revolutionary federal constitution, the Articles of Confederation, should have failed to provide a general government sufficiently strong to satisfy the needs of the country after the return of peace.

It must not be inferred, however, that the political changes which immediately followed the outbreak of the Revolution were in the nature of sweeping democratic reforms. Much that was thoroughly undemocratic remained intact. The property qualifications for the suffrage were not disturbed by the Revolutionary movement and were finally abolished only after the lapse of nearly half a century. The cruel and barbarous system of imprisonment for debt which the colonies had inherited from England, and which often made the lot of the unfortunate debtor worse than that of the chattel slave, continued in several of the states until long after the Revolution. Marked as was the democratic tendency during the first few years of our independence, it nevertheless left untouched much that the progress of democracy has since abolished.

The Constitution: A Reactionary Document

The sweeping changes made in our form of government after the Declaration of Independence were clearly revolutionary in character. The English system of checks and balances was discarded for the more democratic one under which all the important powers of government were vested in the legislature. This new scheme of government was not, however, truly representative of the political thought of the colonies. The conservative classes who in ordinary times are a powerful factor in the politics of every community had, by reason of their Loyalist views, no voice in this political reorganization; and these, as we have seen, not only on account of their wealth and intelligence, but on the basis of their numerical strength as well, were entitled to considerable influence.

With the return of peace these classes which so largely represented the wealth and culture of the colonies, regained in a measure the influence which they had lost. This tended strongly to bring about a conservative reaction. There was besides another large class which supported the Revolutionary movement without being in sympathy with its democratic tendencies. This also used its influence to undo the work of the Revolutionary radicals. Moreover, many of those who had espoused democratic doctrines during the Revolution became conservatives after the war was over. [12] These classes were naturally opposed to the new political doctrines which the Revolutionary movement had incorporated in the American government. The "hard times" and general discontent which followed the war also contributed to the reactionary movement; since many were led to believe that evils which were the natural result of other causes were due to an excess of democracy. Consequently we find the democratic tendency which manifested itself with the outbreak of the Revolution giving place a few years later to the political reaction which found expression in our present Constitution.

> The United States are the offspring of a long-past age. A hundred years, it is true, have scarcely passed since the eighteenth century came to its end, but no hundred years in the history of the world has ever before hurried it along so far over new paths and into unknown fields. The French Revolution and the First Empire were the bridge between two periods that nothing less than the remaking of European society, the recasting of European politics, could have brought so near.
>
> But back to this eighteenth century must we go to learn the forces, the national ideas, the political theories, under the domination of which the Constitution of the United States was framed and adopted. [13]

It is the general belief, nevertheless, that the Constitution of the United States is the very embodiment of democratic philosophy. The people take it for granted that the framers of that document were imbued with the spirit of political equality and sought to establish a government by the people themselves. Widely as this view is entertained, it is, however, at variance with the facts.

"Scarcely any of these men [the framers of the Constitution] entertained," says Fiske, "what we should now call extreme democratic views. Scarcely any, perhaps, had that intense faith in the ultimate good sense of the people which was the most powerful characteristic of Jefferson." [14]

Democracy—government by the people, or directly responsible to them—was not the object which the framers of the American Constitution had in view, but the very thing which they wished to avoid. In the convention which drafted that instrument it was recognized that democratic ideas had made sufficient progress among the masses to put an insurmountable obstacle in the way of any plan of government which did not confer at least the form of political power upon the people. Accordingly the efforts of the Constitutional Convention were directed to the task of devising a system of government which was just popular enough not to excite general opposition and which at the same time gave to the people as little as possible of the substance of political power.

It is somewhat strange that the American people know so little of the fundamental nature of their system of government. Their acquaintance with it extends only to its outward form and rarely includes a knowledge of the political philosophy upon which it rests. The sources of information upon which the average man relies do not furnish the data for a correct understanding of the Constitution. The ordinary text-books and popular works upon this subject leave the reader with an entirely erroneous impression. Even the writings of our constitutional lawyers deal with the outward form rather than the spirit of our government. The vital question—the extent to which, under our constitutional arrangements, the people were expected to, and as a matter of fact do, control legislation and public policy, is either not referred to, or else discussed in a superficial and unsatisfactory manner. That this feature of our Constitution should receive more attention than it does is evident when we reflect that a government works well in practice in proportion as its underlying philosophy and constitutional forms are comprehended by those who wield political power.

"It has been common," says a late Justice of the United States Supreme Court, "to designate our form of government as a democracy, but in the true sense in which that term is properly used, as defining a government in which all its acts are performed by the people, it is about as far from it as any other of which we are aware."[15]

In the United States at the present time we are trying to make an undemocratic Constitution the vehicle of democratic rule. Our Constitution embodies the political philosophy of the eighteenth century, not that of to-day. It was framed for one purpose while we are trying to use it for another. Is free government, then, being tried here under the conditions most favorable to its success? This question we can answer only when we have considered our Constitution as a means to the attainment of democratic rule.

It is difficult to understand how anyone who has read the proceedings of the Federal Convention can believe that it was the intention of that body to establish a democratic government. The evidence is overwhelming that the men who sat in that convention had no faith in the wisdom or political capacity of the people. Their aim and purpose was not to secure a larger measure of democracy, but to eliminate as far as possible the direct influence of the people on legislation and public policy. That body, it is true, contained many illustrious men who were actuated by a desire to further what they conceived to be the welfare of the country. They represented, however, the wealthy and conservative classes, and had for the most part but little sympathy with the popular theory of government.

> Hardly one among them but had sat in some famous assembly, had signed some famous document, had filled some high place, or had made himself conspicuous for learning, for scholarship, or for signal services rendered in the cause of liberty. One had framed the Albany plan of union; some had been members of the Stamp Act Congress of 1765; some had signed the Declaration of Rights in 1774; the names of others appear at the foot of the Declaration of Independence and at the foot of the Articles of Confederation; two had been presidents of Congress; seven had been, or were then, governors of states; twenty-eight had been members of Congress; one had commanded the armies of

the United States; another had been Superintendent of Finance; a third had repeatedly been sent on important missions to England, and had long been Minister to France.

Nor were the future careers of many of them to be less interesting than their past. Washington and Madison became Presidents of the United States: Elbridge Gerry became Vice-President; Charles Cotesworth Pinckney and Rufus King became candidates for the Presidency, and Jared Ingersoll, Rufus King, and John Langdon candidates for the Vice-Presidency; Hamilton became Secretary of the Treasury; Madison, Secretary of State; Randolph, Attorney-General and Secretary of State, and James McHenry, a Secretary of War; Ellsworth and Rutledge became Chief-Justices; Wilson and John Blair rose to the Supreme bench; Gouverneur Morris, and Ellsworth, and Charles C. Pinckney, and Gerry, and William Davie became Ministers abroad.[16]

The long list of distinguished men who took part in the deliberations of that body is noteworthy, however, for the absence of such names as Samuel Adams, Thomas Jefferson, Thomas Paine, Patrick Henry and other democratic leaders of that time. The Federal Convention assembled in Philadelphia only eleven years after the Declaration of Independence was signed, yet only six of the fifty-six men who signed that document were among its members.[17] Conservatism and thorough distrust of popular government characterized throughout the proceedings of that convention. Democracy, Elbridge Gerry thought, was the worst of all political evils.[18] Edmund Randolph observed that in tracing the political evils of this country to their origin, "every man [in the Convention] had found it in the turbulence and follies of democracy."[19] These views appear to reflect the general opinion of that body. Still they realized that it was not the part of wisdom to give public expression to this contempt for democracy. The doors were closed to the public and the utmost secrecy maintained with regard to the proceedings. Members were not allowed to communicate with any one outside of that body concerning the matters therein discussed, nor were they permitted, except by a vote of the Convention, to copy anything from the journals.[20]

It must be borne in mind that the Convention was called for the purpose of proposing amendments to the Articles of Confederation. The delegates were not authorized to frame a new constitution. Their appointment contemplated changes which were to perfect the Articles of Confederation without destroying the general form of government which they established. The resolution of Congress of February 21, 1787, which authorized the Federal Convention, limited its business to "the sole and express purpose of revising the Articles of Confederation," and the states of New York, Massachusetts, and Connecticut copied this in the instructions to their delegates.[21] The aim of the Convention, however, from the very start was not amendment, but a complete rejection of the system itself, which was regarded as incurably defective.

This view was well expressed by James Wilson in his speech made in favor of the ratification of the Constitution before the Pennsylvania convention.

"The business, we are told, which was entrusted to the late Convention," he said,

> was merely to amend the present Articles of Confederation. This observation has been frequently made, and has often brought to my mind a story that is related of Mr. Pope, who, it is well known, was not a little deformed. It was customary with him to use this phrase, "God mend me!" when any little accident happened. One evening a link-boy was lighting him along, and, coming to a gutter, the boy jumped nimbly over it. Mr. Pope called to him to turn, adding "God mend me!" The arch rogue, turning to light him, looked at him, and repeated, "God mend you! He would sooner make half-a-dozen new ones." This would apply to the present Confederation; for it would be easier to make another than to amend this.[22]

The popular notion that this Convention in framing the Constitution was actuated solely by a desire to impart more vigor and efficiency to the general government is but a part of the truth. The Convention desired to establish not only a strong and vigorous central government, but one which would at the same time possess great stability or freedom from change. This last reason is seldom mentioned in our constitutional literature, yet it had a most important bearing on the work of the Convention. This desired stability the government under the Confederation did not possess, since it was, in the opinion of the members of the Convention, dangerously responsive to public opinion; hence their desire to supplant it with an elaborate system of constitutional checks. The adoption of this system was the triumph of a skillfully directed reactionary movement.

Of course the spirit and intention of the Convention must be gathered not from the statements and arguments addressed to the general public in favor of the ratification of the Constitution, but from what occurred in the Convention itself. The discussions which took place in that body indicate the real motives and purposes of those who framed the Constitution. These were carefully withheld from the people and it was not until long afterward that they were accessible to students of the American Constitution. The preamble began with, "We, the people," but it was the almost unanimous sentiment of the Convention that the less the people had to do with the government the better. Hamilton wanted to give the rich and well born "a distinct, permanent share in the government."[23] Madison thought the government ought "to protect the minority of the opulent against the majority."[24] The prevalence of such views in this Convention reminds one of Adam Smith's statement, made a few years before in his "Wealth of Nations," that "civil government, so far as it is instituted for the security of property, is in reality instituted for the defence of the rich against the poor, or of those who have some property against those who have none at all."[25] The solicitude shown by the members of this convention for the interests of the well-to-do certainly tends to justify Adam Smith's observation.

The framers of the Constitution realized, however, that it would not do to carry this system of checks upon the people too far. It was necessary that the government should retain something of the *form* of democracy, if it was to command the respect and confidence of the people. For this reason Gerry thought that "the people should appoint one branch of the government in order to inspire them with the necessary confidence."[26] Madison also saw that the necessary sympathy between the people and their rulers and officers must be maintained and that "the policy of refining popular appointments by successive filtrations" might be pushed too far.[27] These discussions, which took place behind closed doors and under pledge of secrecy, may be taken as fairly representing what the framers of our Constitution really thought of popular government. Their public utterances, on the other hand, influenced as they necessarily were, by considerations of public policy, are of little value. From all the evidence which we have, the conclusion is irresistible that they sought to establish a form of government which would effectually curb and restrain democracy. They engrafted upon the Constitution just so much of the features of popular government as was, in their opinion, necessary to ensure its adoption.

Individual Liberty and the Constitution

The eighteenth-century conception of liberty was the outgrowth of the political conditions of that time. Government was largely in the hands of a ruling class who were able to further their own interests at the expense of the many who were unrepresented. It was but natural under these circumstances that the people should seek to limit the exercise of political authority, since every check imposed upon the government lessened the dangers of class rule. The problem which the advocates of political reform had to solve was how to secure the largest measure of individual liberty compatible with an irresponsible government. They were right in believing that this could be accomplished only by building up an elaborate system of constitutional restraints which would narrowly limit the exercise of irresponsible authority. Individual liberty as they understood the term was immunity from unjust interference at the hands of a minority.

This was a purely negative conception. It involved nothing more than the idea of protection against the evils of irresponsible government. It was a view of liberty adapted, however, to the needs of the time and served a useful purpose in aiding the movement to curb without destroying the power of the ruling class. Any attempt to push the doctrine of liberty farther than this and make it include more than mere immunity from governmental interference would have been revolutionary. The seventeenth and eighteenth century demand was not for the abolition, but for the limitation of irresponsible authority. It was not for popular government based upon universal suffrage, but for such modifications of the system as would give to the commercial and industrial classes the power to resist all encroachments upon their rights at the hands of the hereditary branches of the government. The basis and guarantee of individual liberty, as the term was then understood, was the popular veto such as was exercised through the House of Commons. This conception of liberty was realized for those represented in any coordinate branch of the government wherever the check and balance stage of political development had been reached.

The American revolution, which supplanted hereditary by popular rule, worked a fundamental change in the relation of the individual to the government. So far at least as the voters were concerned the government was no longer an alien institution—an authority imposed upon them from above, but an organization emanating from them—one in which they had and felt a direct proprietary interest. It was no longer a government in which the active principle was irresponsible authority, but one which rested upon the safe and trustworthy basis of popular control.

The overthrow of monarchy and aristocracy necessitated a corresponding change in the idea of liberty to make it fit the new political conditions which had emerged. In so far as government had now passed into the hands of the people there was no longer any reason to fear that it would encroach upon what they regarded as their rights. With the transition, then, from class to popular sovereignty there was a corresponding change in the attitude of the people toward the government. They naturally desired to limit the authority and restrict the activity of the government as long as they felt that it was irresponsible; but as soon as they acquired an active control over it, the reason which formerly actuated them in desiring to limit its powers was no longer operative. Their ends could now be accomplished and their interests best furthered by unhampered political activity. They would now desire to remove the checks upon the government for the same reason that they formerly sought to impose them—viz., to promote their own welfare.

This tendency is seen in the changes made in the state constitutions at the beginning of the American revolution. As shown in a previous chapter, they established the supremacy of the legislative body and through this branch of the government, the supremacy of the majority of the qualified voters. We have here a new conception of liberty. We see a tendency in these constitutional changes to reject the old passive view of state interference as limited by the consent of the governed and take the view that real liberty implies much more than the mere power of constitutional resistance—that it is something positive, that its essence is the power to actively control and direct the policy of the state. The early state constitutions thus represent a long step in the direction of unlimited responsible government.

This, as we have seen, was the chief danger which the conservative classes saw in the form of government established at the outbreak of the Revolution. They were afraid that the power of the numerical majority would be employed to further the interests of the many at the expense of the few, and to guard against such a use of the government they sought to re-establish the system of checks. The Constitution which restored the old scheme of government in a new garb also revived the old conception of individual liberty. There is, however, one important difference between the eighteenth-century conception of liberty and that which finds expression in our constitutional literature. Formerly it was because of the lack of popular control that the people generally desired to limit the authority of the government, but the framers of the Constitution wished to bring about the limitation of governmental functions because they feared the consequences of majority rule. Formerly the many advocated the limitation of the power of king and aristocracy in the interest of liberty; now the few advocate the limitation of the power of the many for their own protection. With the abolition of monarchy and aristocracy the attitude of the few and the many has been reversed. The aristocratic and special interests that formerly opposed the limitation of political activity when they were predominant in the government, now favor it as a protection against the growing power of the masses, while the latter, who formerly favored, now oppose it. The conservative classes now regard the popular majority with the same distrust which the liberals formerly felt toward the king and aristocracy. In fact, the present-day conservative goes even farther than this and would have us believe that the popular majority is a much greater menace to liberty than king or aristocracy has ever been in the past.

"There can be no tyranny of a monarch so intolerable," says a recent American writer, "as that of the multitude, for it has the power behind it that no king can sway."[28] This is and has all along been the attitude of the conservative classes who never lose an opportunity to bring the theory of democracy into disrepute. The defenders of the American Constitution clearly see that unless the fundamental principle of popular government is discredited the system of checks can not survive.

There is no liberty, we are told by the present-day followers of Alexander Hamilton, where the majority is supreme. The American political system realizes this conception of liberty mainly through the Supreme Court—an organ of government which interprets the Constitution and laws of Congress and which may forbid the carrying out of the expressed will of the popular majority. It necessarily follows that the authority which can thus overrule the majority and enforce its own views of the system is an authority greater than the majority. All governments must belong to one or the other of two classes according as the ultimate basis of political power is the many or the few. There is, in fact, no middle ground. We must either recognize the many as supreme, with no checks upon their authority except such as are implied in their own intelligence, sense of justice and spirit of fair play, or we must accept the view that the ultimate authority is in the hands of the few. Every scheme under which the power of the majority is limited means in its practical operation the subordination of the majority to the minority. This inevitable consequence of the limitation of popular rule is not alluded to by the advocates of checks and balances, though it is obvious to any careful student of the system.

I would, however, do injustice to the intelligence of those who champion the scheme of checks and balances to give them credit for any real sympathy with the aims and purposes of democracy. Individual liberty as guaranteed by majority rule was not the end which the framers of the Constitution had in view, nor is it the reason why the present-day conservative defends their work. The Constitution as originally adopted did not contain that highly prized guarantee of personal liberty which democracy everywhere insists upon. The failure to make any provision for freedom of the press should be regarded as a significant omission. This, however, was not an essential part of the Federalists' scheme of government, which aimed rather to protect the property and privileges of the few than to guarantee personal liberty to the masses. This omission is the more noteworthy in view of the fact that this guarantee was at that time expressly included in a majority of the state constitutions, and that the temper of the people was such as to compel its speedy adoption as an amendment to the Federal Constitution itself.

Liberty, as the framers of the Constitution understood the term, had to do primarily with property and property rights. The chief danger which they saw in the Revolutionary state governments was the opportunity afforded to the majority to legislate upon matters which the well-to-do classes wished to place beyond the reach of popular interference. The unlimited authority which the state government had over taxation and its power to restrict or abridge property rights were viewed with alarm by the wealthy classes, who felt that any considerable measure of democracy would be likely to deprive them of their time-honored prerogatives. To guard against this danger the Constitution sought, in the interest of the classes which dominated the Federal Convention, to give the widest possible scope to private property. It prohibited private property in nothing—permitting it, as originally adopted, even in human beings. It may be said without exaggeration that the American scheme of government was planned and set up to perpetuate the ascendency of the property-holding class in a society leavened with democratic ideas. Those who framed it were fully alive to the fact that their economic advantages could be retained only by maintaining their class ascendency in the government. They understood the economic significance of democracy. They realized that if the supremacy of the majority were once fully established the entire policy of the government would be profoundly changed. They foresaw that it would mean the abolition of all private monopoly and the abridgment and regulation of property rights in the interest of the general public.

The Constitution was in form a political document, but its significance was mainly economic. It was the outcome of an organized movement on the part of a class to surround themselves with legal and constitutional guarantees which would check the tendency toward democratic legislation. These were made effective through the attitude of the United States courts which, as Professor Burgess says, ''have never declined jurisdiction where private property was immediately affected on the ground that the question was political.''[29]

There can be no question that the national government has given to the minority a greater protection than it has enjoyed anywhere else in the world, save in those countries where the minority is a specially privileged aristocracy and the right of suffrage is limited. So absolute have property rights been held by the Supreme Court, that it even, by the Dred Scott decision, in effect made the whole country a land of slavery, because the slave was property, and the rights of property were sacred.[30]

In carrying out the original intent of the Constitution with reference to property the courts have developed and applied the doctrine of vested rights—a doctrine which has been used with telling effect for the purpose of defeating democratic reforms. This doctrine briefly stated is that property rights once granted are sacred and inviolable. A rigid adherence to this policy would effectually deprive the government of the power to make the laws governing private property conform to social and economic changes. It would disregard the fact that vested rights are often vested wrongs, and that one important, if not indeed the most important, task which a government by and for the people has to perform is to rectify past mistakes and correct the evils growing out of corruption and class rule. A government without authority to interfere with vested rights would have little power to promote the general welfare through legislation.

The adoption of the Constitution brought this doctrine from the realm of political speculation into the arena of practical politics. The men who framed and set up our Federal government were shrewd enough to see that if the interests of the property-holding classes were to be given effective protection, it was necessary that political power should rest ultimately upon a class basis. This they expected to accomplish largely through the judicial veto and the power and influence of the Supreme Court. The effect of establishing the supremacy of this branch of the government was to make the legal profession virtually a ruling class. To their charge was committed under our system of government the final authority in all matters of legislation. They largely represent by virtue of their training and by reason of the interests with which they are affiliated, the conservative as opposed to the democratic influences. The power and influence exerted by lawyers in this country are the natural outgrowth of the constitutional position of our Supreme Court. Its supremacy is in the last analysis the supremacy of lawyers as a class and through them of the various interests which they represent and from which they derive their support. This explains the fact so often commented on by foreign critics, that in this country lawyers exert a predominant influence in political matters.

We are still keeping alive in our legal and constitutional literature the eighteenth-century notion of liberty. Our future lawyers and judges are still trained in the old conception of government—that the chief purpose of a constitution is to limit the power of the majority. In the meantime all other democratic countries have outgrown this early conception which characterized the infancy of democracy. They have in theory at least repudiated the eighteenth-century doctrine that the few have a right to thwart the will of the many. The majority has in such countries become the only recognized source of legitimate authority. "There is no fulcrum *outside* of the majority, and therefore there is nothing on which, as *against* the majority resistance or lengthened opposition can lean."[31] This statement was made with reference to France, but it would apply as well to England, Switzerland, and all other countries in which the principle of majority rule has received full recognition.

On the other hand American constitutional and legal literature still inculcates and keeps alive fear and distrust of majority rule. The official and ruling class in this country has been profoundly influenced by political ideas which have long been discarded in the countries which have made the most rapid strides in the direction of popular government. The influence which our constitutional and legal literature, based as it is upon a profound distrust of majority rule, has had upon the lawyers, politicians, and public men of this country can hardly be overestimated. It is true that many who have been most influenced by this spirit of distrust toward popular government would be unwilling to admit that they are opposed to majority rule—in fact, they may regard themselves as sincere believers in democracy. This is not to be wondered at when we consider that throughout our history under the Constitution the old and the new have been systematically jumbled in our political literature. In fact, the main effort of our constitutional writers would appear to be to give to the undemocratic eighteenth-century political ideas a garb and setting that would in a measure reconcile them with the democratic point of view. The natural and inevitable result has followed. The students of American political literature have imbibed the fundamental idea of the old system—its distrust of majority rule—along with a certain sentimental attachment to and acceptance of the outward forms of democracy. This irreconcilable contradiction between the form and the substance, the body and the spirit of our political institutions is not generally recognized even by the American students of government. Constitutional writers have been too much preoccupied with the thought of defending and glorifying the work of the fathers and not enough interested in disclosing its true relation to present-day thought and tendencies. As a consequence of this, the political ideas of our education classes represent a curious admixture of democratic beliefs superimposed upon a hardly conscious substratum of eighteenth-century doctrines. It is this contradiction in our thinking that has been one of our chief sources of difficulty in dealing with political problems. While honestly believing that we have been endeavoring to make democracy a success, we have at the same time tenaciously held on to the essential features of a political system designed for the purpose of defeating the ends of popular government.

Individual Liberty and the Economic System

The American doctrine of individual liberty had its origin in economic conditions widely different from those which prevail to-day. The tools of production were simple and inexpensive and their ownership widely diffused. There was no capital-owning class in the modern sense. Business was carried on upon a small scale. The individual was his own employer, or, if working for another, could look forward to the time when, by the exercise of ordinary ability and thrift, he might become an independent producer. The way was open by which every intelligent and industrious wage-earner could become his own master. Industrially society was democratic to a degree which it is difficult for us to realize at the present day. This economic independence which the industrial classes enjoyed ensured a large measure of individual liberty in spite of the fact that political control was in the hands of a class.

The degree of individual freedom and initiative which a community may enjoy is not wholly, or even mainly, a matter of constitutional forms. The actual liberty of the individual may vary greatly without any change in the legal or constitutional organization of society. A political system essentially undemocratic would be much less destructive of individual liberty in a society where the economic life was simple and ownership widely diffused than in a community possessing a wealthy capitalist class on the one hand and an army of wage-earners on the other. The political system reacts, it is true, upon the economic organization, but the influence of the latter upon the individual is more direct and immediate than that of the former. The control exerted over the individual directly by the government may, as a matter of fact, be slight in comparison with that which is exercised through the various agencies which control the economic system. But the close interdependence between the political and the business organization of society can not be overlooked. Each is limited and conditioned by the other, though constitutional forms are always largely the product and expression of economic conditions.

Individual liberty in any real sense implies much more than the restriction of governmental authority. In fact, true liberty consists, as we have seen, not in divesting the government of effective power, but in making it an instrument for the unhampered expression and prompt enforcement of public opinion. The old negative conception of liberty would in practice merely result in limiting the power of the government to control social conditions. This would not necessarily mean, however, the immunity of the individual from external control. To limit the power of the government may permit the extension over the individual of some other form of control even more irresponsible than that of the government itself— the control which inevitably results from the economic supremacy of a class who own the land and the capital.

The introduction of the factory system forced the great majority of small independent producers down into the ranks of mere wage-earners, and subjected them in their daily work to a class rule under which everything was subordinated to the controlling purpose of the employers—the desire for profits.

The significance of this change from the old handicraft system of industry to present-day capitalistic production is fully understood by all students of modern industry. Even Herbert Spencer, the great expounder of individualism, admitted that the so-called liberty of the laborer "amounts in practice to little more than the ability to exchange one slavery for another" and that "the coercion of circumstances often bears more hardly on him than the coercion of a master does on one in bondage."[32] This dependence of the laborer, however, he regarded as unfortunate, and looked forward to the gradual amelioration of present conditions through the growth of cooperation in production.

Individualism as an economic doctrine was advocated in the eighteenth century by those who believed in a larger measure of freedom for the industrial classes. The small business which was then the rule meant the wide diffusion of economic power. A *laissez faire* policy would have furthered the interests of that large body of small independent producers who had but little representation in and but little influence upon the government. It would have contributed materially to the progress of the democratic movement by enlarging the sphere of industrial freedom for all independent producers. It does not follow, however, that this doctrine which served a useful purpose in connection with the eighteenth-century movement to limit the power of the ruling class is sound in view of the political and economic conditions which exist to-day. The so-called industrial revolution has accomplished sweeping and far-reaching changes in economic organization. It has resulted in a transfer of industrial power from the many to the few, who now exercise in all matters relating to production an authority as absolute and irresponsible as that which the ruling class exercised in the middle of the eighteenth century over the state itself. The simple decentralized and more democratic system of production which formerly prevailed has thus been supplanted by a highly centralized and thoroughly oligarchic form of industrial organization. At the same time political development has been tending strongly in the direction of democracy. The few have been losing their hold upon the state, which has come to rest, in theory at least, upon the will of the many. A political transformation amounting to a revolution has placed the many in the same position in relation to the government which was formerly held by the favored few.

As a result of these political and economic changes the policy of government regulation of industry is likely to be regarded by the masses with increasing favor. A society organized as a political democracy can not be expected to tolerate an industrial aristocracy. As soon, then, as the masses come to feel that they really control the political machinery, the irresponsible power which the few now exercise in the management of industry will be limited or destroyed as it has already been largely overthrown in the state itself. In fact the doctrine of *laissez faire* no longer expresses the generally accepted view of state functions, but merely the selfish view of that relatively small class which, though it controls the industrial system, feels the reins of political control slipping out of its hands. The limitation of governmental functions which was the rallying-cry of the liberals a century ago has thus become the motto of the present-day conservative.

The opponents of government regulation of industry claim that it will retard or arrest progress by restricting the right of individual initiative. They profess to believe that the best results for society as a whole are obtained when every corporation or industrial combination is allowed to manage its business with a free hand. It is assumed by those who advocate this policy that there is no real conflict of interests between the capitalists who control the present-day aggregations of corporate wealth and the general public. No argument is needed, however, to convince any one familiar with the facts of recent industrial development that this assumption is not true.

The change in the attitude of the people toward the let-alone theory of government is, as a matter of fact, the outcome of an intelligently directed effort to enlarge and democratize—not abridge—the right of initiative in its relation to the management of industry. The right of individual initiative in the sense of the right to exercise a real control over production was lost by the masses when the substitution of machinery for tools made them directly dependent upon a class of capital-owning employers. The subsequent growth of large scale production has centralized the actual control of industry in the hands of a small class of large capitalists. The small capitalists as separate and independent producers are being rapidly crushed or absorbed by the great corporation. They may still belong to the capitalist class in that they live upon an income derived from the ownership of stock or bonds. But they have no real control over the business in which their capital is invested. They no longer have the power to organize and direct any part of the industrial process. They enjoy the benefits which accrue from the ownership of wealth, but they can no longer take an active part in the management of industry. For them individual initiative in the sense of an effective control over the industrial process has disappeared almost as completely as it has in the case of the mere wage-earner. Individual initiative even for the capital-owning class has thus largely disappeared. It has been superseded by corporate initiative which means the extinguishment of individual initiative except in those cases where it is secured to the large capitalist through the ownership of a controlling interest in the business.

The abandonment of the *laissez faire* policy, then, in favor of the principle of government regulation of industry is the outgrowth, not of any hostility to individual initiative, but of the conviction that the monopoly of industrial power by the few is a serious evil. It is manifestly impossible to restore to the masses the right of individual initiative. Industry is too complex and too highly organized to permit a return to the old system of decentralized control. And since the only substitute for the old system of individual control is collective control, it appears to be inevitable that government regulation of business will become a fixed policy in all democratic states.

The *laissez faire* policy is supposed to favor progress by allowing producers to make such changes in business methods as may be prompted by the desire for larger profits. The doctrine as ordinarily accepted contains at least two erroneous assumptions, viz., (1) that any innovation in production which makes it possible for the capitalist to secure a larger return is necessarily an improvement in the sense of augmenting the average efficiency of labor, and (2) that policies are to be judged solely by their economic effects. Even if non-interference resulted in industrial changes which in all cases increase the efficiency of labor, it would not follow that such changes are, broadly considered, always beneficial. Before drawing any sweeping conclusion we must consider all the consequences direct and indirect, immediate and remote, political and social as well as economic. Hence the ordinary test—the direct and immediate effect upon productive efficiency—is not a satisfactory one. Moreover, many changes in the methods or organization of business are designed primarily to alter distribution in the interest of the capitalist by decreasing wages or by raising prices. In so far as a policy of non-interference permits changes of this sort, it is clearly harmful to the community at large, though advantageous to a small class.

In all democratic countries the conservative classes are beginning to realize that their ascendency in production is imperiled by the ascendency of the masses in the state. It thus happens that in the hope of checking or retarding the movement toward regulation of business in the interest of the people generally, they have taken refuge behind that abandoned tenet of democracy, the doctrine of non-interference.

.   .   .

The limitation of governmental powers in the Constitution of the United States was not designed to prevent all interference in business, but only such as was conceived to be harmful to the dominant class. The nature of these limitations as well as the means of enforcing them indicate their purpose. The provision relating to direct taxes is a good example. The framers of the Constitution were desirous of preventing any use of the taxing power by the general government that would be prejudicial to the interests of the well-to-do classes. This is the significance of the provision that no direct taxes shall be laid unless in proportion to population.[33] The only kind of a direct tax which the framers intended that the general government should have power to levy was the poll tax which would demand as much from the poor man as from the rich. This was indeed one of the reasons for opposing the ratification of the Constitution.

"Many specters," said Hamilton,

> have been raised out of this power of internal taxation to excite the apprehensions of the people: double sets of revenue officers, a duplication of their burdens by double taxations, and the frightful forms of odious and oppressive poll-taxes,

have been played off with all the ingenious dexterity of political legerde-
main. . . .

As little friendly as I am to the species of imposition [poll-taxes], I still feel a
thorough conviction that the power of having recourse to it ought to exist in the
Federal government. There are certain emergencies of nations, in which expedients, that in the ordinary state of things ought to be forborne, become essential
to the public weal. And the government, from the possibility of such emergencies, ought ever to have the option of making use of them.[34]

It is interesting to observe that Hamilton's argument in defense of the power to
levy poll-taxes would have been much more effective if it had been urged in
support of the power to levy a direct tax laid in proportion to wealth. But this kind
of a tax would, in the opinion of the framers, have placed too heavy a burden upon
the well-to-do. Hence they were willing to deprive the general government of the
power to levy it even at the risk of crippling it in some great emergency when
there might be urgent need of a large revenue.

This is not strange, however, when we remember that it was the property-
owning class that framed and secured the adoption of the Constitution. That they
had their own interests in view when they confined the general government
practically to indirect taxes levied upon articles of general consumption, and
forbade direct taxes levied in proportion to wealth, seems highly probable. It
appears, then, that the recent decision of the United States Supreme Court
declaring the Federal Income Tax unconstitutional merely gave effect to the
original spirit and purpose of this provision.

The disposition to guard the interests of the property-holding class rather than
to prevent legislation for their advantage is also seen in the interpretation which
has been given to the provision forbidding the states to pass any laws impairing
the obligation of contracts. The framers of the Constitution probably did not have
in mind the extended application which the courts have since made of this
limitation on the power of the states. Perhaps they intended nothing more than
that the states should be prevented from repudiating their just debts. But whatever
may have been the intention of the framers themselves, the reactionary movement
in which they were the recognized leaders, finally brought about a much broader
and, from the point of view of the capitalist class, more desirable interpretation of
this provision.

There is evidence of a desire to limit the power of the states in this direction
even before the Constitutional Convention of 1787 assembled. The legislature of
Pennsylvania in 1785 passed a bill repealing an act of 1782 which granted a
charter to the Bank of North America. James Wilson, who is said to have
suggested the above-mentioned clause of the Federal Constitution, made an
argument against the repeal of the charter, in which he claimed that the power, or
at least the right of the legislature, to modify or repeal did not apply to all kinds of
legislation. It could safely be exercised, he thought, in the case of "a law

respecting the rights and properties of all the citizens of the state."
"Very different," he says,

> is the case with regard to a law, by which the state grants privileges to a
> congregation or other society. . . . Still more different is the case with regard to a
> law by which an estate is vested or confirmed in an individual: if, in this case, the
> legislature may, at discretion, and without any reason assigned, divest or destroy
> his estate, then a person seized of an estate in fee-simple, under legislative
> sanction, is, in truth, nothing more than a solemn tenant at will. . . .
>
> To receive the legislative stamp of stability and permanency, acts of incorpor-
> ation are applied for from the legislature. If these acts may be repealed without
> notice, without accusation, without hearing, without proof, without forfeiture,
> where is the stamp of their stability? . . . If the act for incorporating the subscrib-
> ers to the Bank of North America shall be repealed in this manner, a precedent
> will be established for repealing, in the same manner, every other legislative
> charter in Pennsylvania. . . . Those acts of the state, which have hitherto been
> considered as the sure anchors of privilege and of property, will become the sport
> of every varying gust of politics, and will float wildly backwards and forwards on
> the irregular and impetuous tides of party and faction.[35]

In 1810 the case of Fletcher v. Peck[36] was decided in the Supreme Court of
the United States. Chief Justice Marshall, in delivering the opinion of the court,
said:

> The principle asserted is that one legislature is competent to repeal any act
> which a former legislature was competent to pass; and that one legislature can not
> abridge the powers of a succeeding legislature. The correctness of this principle,
> so far as respects general legislation, can never be controverted. But if an act be
> done under a law, a succeeding legislature can not undo it. . . .
>
> When then a law is in the nature of a contract, when absolute rights have
> vested under that contract, a repeal of the law can not devest those rights; . . .
>
> It may well be doubted whether the nature of society and of government does
> not prescribe some limits to the legislative power; . . .
>
> It is, then, the unanimous opinion of the court, that, in this case, the estate
> having passed into the hands of a purchaser for a valuable consideration, without
> notice, the state of Georgia was restrained, either by general principles, which
> are common to our free institutions, or by the particular provisions of the
> Constitution of the United States, from passing a law whereby the estate of the
> plaintiff in the premises so purchased could be constitutionally and legally
> impaired and rendered null and void.

It is evident from this opinion that the court would have been disposed at that
time to declare state laws impairing property rights null and void, even if there

had been nothing in the Constitution of the United States to justify the exercise of such a power. Justice Johnson, in a separate opinion, said:

> I do not hesitate to declare that a state does not possess the power of revoking its own grants. But I do it on a general principle, on the reason and nature of things: a principle which will impose laws even on the Deity. . . .
>
> I have thrown out these ideas that I may have it distinctly understood that my opinion on this point is not founded on the provision in the Constitution of the United States, relative to laws impairing the obligation of contracts.

It was contended in this case that the state of Georgia had the right to revoke the grant on the ground that it was secured by corrupt means. This argument evidently failed to appeal to the court. It was referred to by Justice Johnson who said "as to the idea that the grants of a legislature may be void because the legislature are corrupt, it appears to me to be subject to insuperable difficulties. . . . The acts of the supreme power of a country must be considered pure. . . ."

It is interesting to observe that the Federalist judges in the early years of our history under the Constitution did not deem it necessary to find a constitutional ground for decisions of this sort. But with the overthrow of the Federalist party and the progress of belief in popular government, there is an evident disposition on the part of the court to extend the protection of the Federal Constitution to all the powers which it claimed the right to exercise. Thus in the Dartmouth College case, decided in 1819, the United States Supreme Court appears to have abandoned its earlier position and to have recognized the Constitution as the source of its power to annul state laws.

"It is under the protection of the decision in the Dartmouth College case," says Judge Cooley,

> that the most enormous and threatening powers in our country have been created; some of the great and wealthy corporations actually having greater influence in the country at large, and upon the legislation of the country than the states to which they owe their corporate existence. Every privilege granted or right conferred—no matter by what means or on what pretence—being made inviolable by the Constitution, the government is frequently found stripped of its authority in very important particulars, by unwise, careless, or corrupt legislation; and a clause of the Federal Constitution, whose purpose was to preclude the repudiation of debts and just contracts, protects and perpetuates the evil.[37]

Any government framed and set up to guard and promote the interests of the people generally ought to have full power to modify or revoke all rights or privileges granted in disregard of the public welfare. But the Supreme Court, while permitting the creation or extension of property rights, has prevented the subsequent abridgment of such rights, even when the interests of the general public demanded it. The effect of this has been to make the corporations take an active part in corrupting state politics. Special legislation was not prohibited. In fact, it was a common way of creating property rights. If a bank, an insurance company, or a railway corporation was organized, it was necessary to obtain a charter from the legislature which defined its powers and privileges. The corporation came into existence by virtue of a special act of the legislature and could exercise only such powers and enjoy only such rights and privileges as that body saw fit to confer upon it. The legislature might refuse to grant a charter, but having granted it, it became a vested right which could not be revoked. The charter thus granted by the legislature was a special privilege. In many instances it was secured as a reward for political services by favorites of the party machine, or through the corrupt expenditure of money or the equally corrupt distribution of stock in the proposed corporation among those who controlled legislation. Not only did this system invite corruption in the granting of such charters, but it also created a motive for the further use of corrupt means to keep possible competitors from securing like privileges. It was worth the while to spend money to secure a valuable privilege if when once obtained the legislature could not revoke it. And it was also worth the while to spend more money to keep dangerous competitors out of the field if by so doing it could enjoy some of the benefits of monopoly. By thus holding that a privilege granted to an individual or a private corporation by special act of the legislature was a contract which could not be revoked by that body, the courts in their effort to protect property rights opened the door which allowed corporation funds to be brought into our state legislatures early in our history for purposes of corruption.

But little attention has been given as yet to this early species of corruption which in some of the states at least assumed the proportions of a serious political evil.

"During the first half century, banking in New York," says Horace White,

> was an integral part of the spoils of politics. Federalists would grant no charters to Republicans, and Republicans none to Federalists. After a few banks had been established they united, regardless of politics, to create a monopoly by preventing other persons from getting charters. When charters were applied for and refused, the applicants began business on the common-law plan. Then, at the instigation of the favored ones, the politicians passed a law to suppress all unchartered banks. The latter went to Albany and bribed the legislature. In short, politics, monopoly, and bribery constitute the key to banking in the early history of the state.[38]

The intervention of the courts which made the conditions above described possible, while ostensibly limiting the power of the state legislature, in reality enlarged and extended it in the interest of the capital-owning class. It gave to the state legislature a power which up to that time it had not possessed—the power to grant rights and privileges of which the grantees could not be deprived by subsequent legislation. Before the adoption of the Federal Constitution no act of the legislature could permanently override the will of the qualified voters. It was subject to modification or repeal at the hands of any succeeding legislature. The voters of the state thus had what was in effect an indirect veto on all legislative acts—a power which they might exercise through a subsequent legislature or constitutional convention. But with the adoption of the Constitution of the United States the Federal courts were able to deprive them of this power where it was most needed. This removed the only effective check on corruption and class legislation, thus placing the people at the mercy of their state legislatures and any private interests that might temporarily control them.

The power which the legislatures thus acquired to grant charters which could not be amended or repealed made it necessary for the people to devise some new method of protecting themselves against this abuse of legislative authority. The outcome of this movement to re-establish some effective popular check on the legislature has taken the form in a majority of the states of a constitutional amendment by which the right is reserved to amend or repeal all laws conferring corporate powers. Such constitutional changes provide no remedy, however, for the evils resulting from legislative grants made previous to their adoption. The granting of special charters is now also prohibited in many states, the constitution requiring that all corporations shall be formed under general laws. These constitutional changes may be regarded as in the interest of the capitalist class as a whole, whose demand was for a broader and more liberal policy—one which would extend the advantages of the corporate form of organization to all capitalists in every line of business. But even our general corporation laws have been enacted too largely in the interest of those who control our business undertakings and without due regard to the rights of the general public.

A study of our political history shows that the attitude of the courts has been responsible for much of our political immorality. By protecting the capitalist in the possession and enjoyment of privileges unwisely and even corruptly granted, they have greatly strengthened the motive for employing bribery and other corrupt means in securing the grant of special privileges. If the courts had all along held that any proof of fraud or corruption in obtaining a franchise or other legislative grant was sufficient to justify its revocation, the lobbyist, the bribe-giver, and the "innocent purchaser" of rights and privileges stolen from the people would have found the traffic in legislative favors a precarious and much less profitable mode of acquiring wealth.

[Conclusions]

The distinguishing feature of the Constitution, as shown in the preceding chapters of this book, was the elaborate provisions which it contained for limiting the power of the majority. The direction of its development, however, has in many respects been quite different from that for which the more conservative of its framers hoped.[39] The checks upon democracy which it contained were nevertheless so skilfully contrived and so effective that the progress of the popular movement has been more seriously hampered and retarded here than in any other country where the belief in majority rule has come to be widely accepted. In some important respects the system as originally set up has yielded to the pressure of present-day tendencies in political thought; but many of its features are at variance with what has come to be regarded as essential in any well-organized democracy.

Notes

1. Tyler, *The Literary History of the American Revolution*, Vol. I, p. 300.
2. Tyler, *The Literary History of the American Revolution*, Vol. I, p. 301.
3. Massachusetts, New Hampshire, New Jersey, Pennsylvania and Virginia.
4. Delaware, Maryland and North Carolina.
5. Massachusetts, New Hampshire, Pennsylvania and Maryland.
6. Delaware, New York, New Jersey, North Carolina, South Carolina and Virginia.
7. Connecticut, Rhode Island, New Jersey, Virginia, North Carolina, South Carolina, Georgia, New York and Delaware.
8. Massachusetts, New Hampshire, Maryland, Delaware, South Carolina and Pennsylvania.
9. Massachusetts, New Hampshire, New York, Delaware, Maryland, North Carolina, South Carolina and Virginia.
10. Macdonald, ed., *Select Charters*, Vol. I, pp. 94–101.
11. [James] Schouler, *Constitutional Studies: State and Federal*, [1896], pp. 70–78, Macdonald, *Select Charters*, Vol. I.
12. "Who would have thought, ten years ago, that the very men who risked their lives and fortunes in support of republican principles, would now treat them as the fictions of fancy?" M. Smith in the New York Convention held to ratify the Constitution, Elliot, *Debates*, Second Edition, Vol. II, p. 250.
13. Simeon E. Baldwin, *Modern Political Institutions*, pp. 83 and 84.
14. [John Fiske], *Critical Period of American History*, [1901], p. 226.
15. S.F. Miller, *Lectures on the Constitution of the United States*, pp. 84–85.
16. McMaster, *With the Fathers*, pp. 112–113.
17. "They [the framers of the Constitution] represented the conservative intelligence of the country very exactly; from this class there is hardly a name, except that of Jay, which could be suggested to complete the list." Article by Alexander Johnston on the Convention of 1787 in Lalor's *Cyclopaedia of Pol. Science, Pol. Econ. and U.S. Hist.*
18. Elliot, *Debates*, Vol. V, p. 557.
19. Ibid., p. 138.
20. "By another [rule] the doors were to be shut, and the whole proceedings were to be kept secret; and so far did this rule extend, that we were thereby prevented from corresponding with gentlemen in the different states upon the subjects under our discussion. . . . So *extremely solicitous* were they that their proceedings should not transpire, that the members were prohibited even from taking copies of resolutions, on which the Convention were deliberating, or extracts of any kind from the Journals without formally moving for and obtaining permission, by a vote of the Convention for that purpose." Luther Martin's Address to the Maryland House of Delegates. Ibid., Vol. I, p. 345.

"The doors were locked, and an injunction of strict secrecy was put upon everyone. The results of their work were known in the following September, when the draft of the Federal Constitution was published. But just what was said and done in this secret conclave was not revealed until fifty years had passed, and the aged James Madison, the last survivor of those who sat there, had been gathered to his fathers." Fiske, *The Critical Period of American History*, p. 229, McMaster, *With the Fathers*, p. 112.

21. Elliot, *Debates*, Vol. I, pp. 119–127.
22. Elliot, *Debates*, Vol. II, p. 470.
23. Elliot, *Debates*, Vol. I, p. 422.
24. Ibid., p. 450.
25. Book, 5, Ch. I, Part II.
26. Elliot, *Debates*, Vol. V, p. 160.
27. Ibid., p. 137.
28. Willoughby, *The Nature of the State*, p. 416.
29. *Political Science and Constitutional Law*, Vol. I, p. 197.
30. Ford, ed., *The Federalist*, Introduction, p. xiii.
31. Boutmy, *Studies in Constitutional Law*, p. 155.
32. *Principles of Sociology*, Vol. III, p. 525.
33. Art. I, sec. 9.
34. *Federalist*, No. 36.
35. Considerations, on the Power to Incorporate the Bank of North America, *Works*, Vol. I.
36. 6 Cranch 87.
37. *Constitutional Limitations*, 6th ed., pp. 335–336, n.
38. *Money and Banking*, p. 327. See also Myers, *The History of Tammany Hall*, pp. 113–116.
39. "Over and over again our government has been saved from complete breakdown only by an absolute disregard of the Constitution, and most of the very men who framed the compact would have refused to sign it, could they have foreseen its eventual development." Ford, ed., *Federalist*, Introduction, p. vii.

Charles A. Beard
An Economic Interpretation of the Constitution

Charles A. Beard's classic, An Economic Interpretation of the Constitution, *created
a national sensation when it appeared in 1913. Beard was denounced for defiling the
memory of the Founding Fathers. In time, historians came to accept Beard's thesis
that the prime force behind the Constitution was economic interest, but his work
continues to generate controversy today. See John P. Diggins, "Power and Authority
in American History: The Case of Charles A. Beard and His Critics,"* American
Historical Review, *86 (October 1981), 701–30; and Henry Steele Commager, "The
Constitution: Was It an Economic Document?"* American Heritage, *December 1958.*

Introduction to the 1935 Edition
(Beard's Reply to His Critics)

This volume was first issued in 1913 during the tumult of discussion that accompanied the advent of the Progressive party, the split in Republican ranks, and the
conflict over the popular election of United States Senators, workmen's compensation, and other social legislation. At that time Theodore Roosevelt had raised
fundamental questions under the head of "the New Nationalism" and proposed
to make the Federal Government adequate to the exigencies created by railways,
the consolidation of industries, the closure of free land on the frontier, and the
new position of labor in American economy. In the course of developing his
conceptions, Mr. Roosevelt drew into consideration the place of the judiciary in
the American system. While expressing high regard for that branch of govern-

ment, he proposed to place limitations on its authority. He contended that "by the abuse of the power to declare laws unconstitutional the courts have become a law-making instead of a law-enforcing agency." As a check upon judicial proclivities, he proposed a scheme for "the recall of judicial decisions." This project he justified by the assertion that "when a court decides a constitutional question, when it decides what the people as a whole can or cannot do, the people should have the right to recall that decision when they think it wrong." Owing to such declarations, and to the counter-declarations, the "climate of opinion" was profoundly disturbed when *An Economic Interpretation of the Constitution* originally appeared.

Yet in no sense was the volume a work of the occasion, written with reference to immediate controversies. Doubtless I was, in common with all other students, influenced more or less by "the spirit of the times," but I had in mind no thought of forwarding the interests of the Progressive party or of its conservative critics and opponents. I had taken up the study of the Constitution many years before the publication of my work, while a profound calm rested on the sea of constitutional opinion. In that study I had occasion to read voluminous writings by the Fathers, and I was struck by the emphasis which so many of them placed upon economic interests as forces in politics and in the formulation of laws and constitutions. In particular I was impressed by the philosophy of politics set forth by James Madison in Number X of the *Federalist* (below, page 14), which seemed to furnish a clue to practical operations connected with the formation of the Constitution—operations in which Madison himself took a leading part.

Madison's view of the Constitution seemed in flat contradiction to most of the theorizing about the Constitution to which I had been accustomed in colleges, universities, and legal circles. It is true, older historians, such as Hildreth, had pointed out that there had been a sharp struggle over the formation and adoption of the Constitution, and that in the struggle an alignment of economic interests had taken place. It is true that Chief Justice Marshall, in his life of George Washington, had sketched the economic conflict out of which the Constitution sprang. But during the closing years of the nineteenth century this realistic view of the Constitution had been largely submerged in abstract discussions of states' rights and national sovereignty and in formal, logical, and discriminative analyses of judicial opinions. It was admitted, of course, that there had been a bitter conflict over the formation and adoption of the Constitution; but the struggle was usually explained, if explained at all, by reference to the fact that some men cherished states' rights and others favored a strong central government. At the time I began my inquiries the generally prevailing view was that expressed recently by Professor Theodore Clarke Smith: "Former historians had described the struggle over the formation and adoption of the document as a contest between sections ending in a victory of straight-thinking national-minded men over narrower and more local opponents." How some men got to be "national-minded" and "straight-thinking," and others became narrow and local in their ideas did not disturb the thought of scholars who presided over historical writing at the turn of the nineteenth century. Nor were those scholars at much pains to explain whether the term "section," which they freely used, meant a segment of physical geography or a set of social and economic arrangements within a geographic area, conditioned by physical circumstances.

One thing, however, my masters taught me, and that was to go behind the pages of history written by my contemporaries and read "the sources." In applying this method, I read the letters, papers, and documents pertaining to the Constitution written by the men who took part in framing and adopting it. And to my surprise I found that many Fathers of the Republic regarded the conflict over the Constitution as springing essentially out of conflicts of economic interests, which had a certain geographical or sectional distribution. This discovery, coming at a time when such conceptions of history were neglected by writers on history, gave me "the shock of my life." And since this aspect of the Constitution had been so long disregarded, I sought to redress the balance by emphasis, "naturally" perhaps. At all events I called my volume "an economic interpretation of the Constitution." I did not call it "the" economic interpretation, or "the only" interpretation possible to thought. Nor did I pretend that it was "the history" of the formation and adoption of the Constitution. The reader was warned in advance of the theory and the emphasis. No attempt was made to take him off his guard by some plausible formula of completeness and comprehensiveness. I simply sought to bring back into the mental picture of the Constitution those realistic features of economic conflict, stress, and strain, which my masters had, for some reason, left out of it, or thrust far into the background as incidental rather than fundamental.

When my book appeared, it was roundly condemned by conservative Republicans, including ex-President Taft, and praised, with about the same amount of discrimination, by Progressives and others on the left wing. Perhaps no other book on the Constitution has been more severely criticized, and so little read. Perhaps no other book on the subject has been used to justify opinions and projects so utterly beyond its necessary implications. It was employed by a socialist writer to support a plea for an entirely new constitution and by a conservative judge of the United States Supreme Court to justify an attack on a new piece of "social legislation." Some members of the New York Bar Association became so alarmed by the book that they formed a committee and summoned me to appear before it; and, when I declined on the ground that I was not engaged in legal politics or political politics, they treated my reply as a kind of contempt of court. Few took the position occupied by Justice Oliver Wendell Holmes, who once remarked to me that he had not got excited about the book, like some of his colleagues, but had supposed that it was intended to throw light on the nature of the Constitution, and, in his opinion, did so in fact.

Among my historical colleagues the reception accorded the volume varied. Professor William A. Dunning wrote me that he regarded it as "the pure milk of the word," although it would "make the heathen rage." Professor Albert Bushnell Hart declared that it was little short of indecent. Others sought to classify it by calling it "Marxian." Even as late as the year 1934, Professor Theodore Clarke Smith, in an address before the American Historical Association, expressed this view of the volume, in making it illustrative of a type of historical writing, which is "doctrinaire" and "excludes anything like impartiality." He said: "This is the view that American history, like all history, can and must be explained in economic terms. . . . This idea has its origin, of course, in the Marxian theories."[1] Having made this assertion, Professor Smith turned his scholarly battery upon *An Economic Interpretation of the Constitution.*

Now as a matter of fact there is no reason why an economic interpretation of the Constitution should be more partisan than any other interpretation. It may be employed, to be sure, to condemn one interest in the conflict or another interest, but no such use of it is imposed upon an author by the nature of the interpretation. Indeed an economic analysis may be coldly neutral, and in the pages of this volume no words of condemnation are pronounced upon the men enlisted upon either side of the great controversy which accompanied the formation and adoption of the Constitution. Are the security holders who sought to collect principal and interest through the formation of a stronger government to be treated as guilty of impropriety or praised? That is a question to which the following inquiry is not addressed. An answer to that question belongs to moralists and philosophers, not to students of history as such. If partiality is taken in the customary and accepted sense, it means "leaning to one party or another." Impartiality means the opposite. Then this volume is, strictly speaking, impartial. It supports the conclusion that in the main the men who favored the Constitution were affiliated with certain types of property and economic interest, and that the men who opposed it were affiliated with other types. It does not say that the former were "straight-thinking" and that the latter were "narrow." It applies no moralistic epithets to either party.

On the other hand Professor Smith's statement about the conflict over the constitution is his *interpretation* of the nature of things, in that it makes the conflict over the Constitution purely psychological in character, unless some economic content is to be given to the term "section." In any event it assumes that straight-thinking and national-mindedness are entities, particularities, or forces, apparently independent of all earthly considerations coming under the head of "economic." It does not say how these entities, particularities, or forces got into American heads. It does not show whether they were imported into the colonies from Europe or sprang up after the colonial epoch closed. It arbitrarily excludes the possibilities that their existence may have been conditioned if not determined by economic interests and activities. It is firm in its exclusion of other interpretations and conceptions. Whoever does not believe that the struggle over the Constitution was a simple contest between the straight-thinking men and narrower and local men of the respective sections is to be cast into outer darkness as "Marxian" or lacking in "impartiality." Is that not a doctrinaire position?

Not only is Professor Smith's position exclusive. It is highly partial. The men who favored the Constitution were "straight-thinking" men. Those who opposed it were "narrower" men. These words certainly may be taken to mean that advocates of the Constitution were wiser men, men of a higher type of mind, than the "narrower" men who opposed it. In a strict sense, of course, straight-thinking may be interpreted as thinking logically. In that case no praise or partiality is necessarily involved. A trained burglar who applies his science to cracking a safe may be more logical than an impulsive night watchman who sacrifices his life in the performance of duty. But in common academic acceptance a logical man is supposed to be superior to the institutional and emotional man.

Nor is there exactness in such an antithesis as "straight-thinking" and narrowness. Narrowness does not, of necessity, mean lack of straight-thinking. Straight-thinking may be done in a narrow field of thought as well as in a large domain. But there is a true opposition in national-mindedness and local-mindedness, and the student of economic history merely inquires whether the antithesis does not correspond in the main to an economic antagonism. He may accept Professor Smith's psychological antithesis and go beyond it to inquire into its origins. But in so doing he need not ascribe any superior quality of intellect to the one party or the other. To ascribe qualities of mind—high or low—to either party is partiality, dogmatic and doctrinaire partiality. It arbitrarily introduces virtues of intellectual superiority and inferiority into an examination of matters of fact.

In the minds of some, the term "Marxian," imported into the discussion by Professor Smith, means an epithet; and in the minds of others, praise. With neither of these views have I the least concern. For myself I can say that I have never believed that "all history" can or must be "explained" in economic terms, or any other terms. He who really "explains" history must have the attributes ascribed by the theologians to God. It can be "explained," no doubt, to the satisfaction of certain mentalities at certain times, but such explanations are not universally accepted and approved. I confess to have hoped in my youth to find "the causes of things," but I never thought that I had found them. Yet it has seemed to me, and does now, that in the great transformations in society, such as was brought about by the formation and adoption of the Constitution, economic "forces" are primordial or fundamental, and come nearer "explaining" events than any other "forces." Where the configurations and pressures of economic interests are brought into an immediate relation to the event or series of events under consideration, an economic interpretation is effected. Yet, as I said in 1913, on page 18, "It may be that some larger world process is working through each series of historical events; but ultimate causes lie beyond our horizon." If anywhere I have said or written that "all history" can be "explained" in economic terms, I was then suffering from an aberration of the mind.

Nor can I accept as a historical fact Professor Smith's assertion that the economic interpretation of history or my volume on the Constitution had its origin in "Marxian theories." As I point out in Chapter I of my *Economic Basis of Politics*, the germinal idea of class and group conflicts in history appeared in the writings of Aristotle, long before the Christian era, and was known to great writers on politics during the middle ages and modern times. It was expounded by James Madison in Number X of the *Federalist*, written in defense of the Constitution of the United States, long before Karl Marx was born. Marx seized upon the idea, applied it with rigor, and based predictions upon it, but he did not originate it. Fathers of the American Constitution were well aware of the idea, operated on the hypothesis that it had at least a considerable validity, and expressed it in numerous writings. Whether conflicting economic interests bulk large in contemporary debates over protective tariffs, foreign trade, transportation, industry, commerce, labor, agriculture, and the nature of the Constitution itself, each of our contemporaries may decide on the basis of his experience and knowledge.

Yet at the time this volume was written, I was, in common with all students who professed even a modest competence in modern history, conversant with the theories and writings of Marx. Having read extensively among the writings of the Fathers of the Constitution of the United States and studied Aristotle, Machiavelli, Locke, and other political philosophers, I became all the more interested in Marx when I discovered in his works the ideas which had been cogently expressed by outstanding thinkers and statesmen in the preceding centuries. That interest was deepened when I learned from an inquiry into his student life that he himself had been acquainted with the works of Aristotle, Montesquieu, and other writers of the positive bent before he began to work out his own historical hypothesis. By those who use his name to rally political parties or to frighten Daughters of the American Revolution, students of history concerned with the origins of theories need not be disturbed.

For the reason that this volume was not written for any particular political occasion but designed to illuminate all occasions in which discussion of the Constitution appears, I venture to re-issue it in its original form. It does not "explain" the Constitution. It does not exclude other explanations deemed more satisfactory to the explainers. Whatever its short-comings, the volume does, however, present some indubitable facts pertaining to that great document which will be useful to students of the Constitution and to practitioners engaged in interpreting it. The Constitution was of human origin, immediately at least, and it is now discussed and applied by human beings who find themselves engaged in certain callings, occupations, professions, and interests.

.   .   .

It has also been lightly assumed that this volume pretends to show that the form of government established and powers conferred were "determined" in every detail by the conflict of economic interests. Such pretension was never in my mind; nor do I think that it is explicit or implicit in the pages which follow. I have never been able to discover all-pervading determinism in history. In that field of study I find, what Machiavelli found, *virtu, fortuna*, and *necessita*, although the boundaries between them cannot be sharply delimited. There is determinism, necessity, in the world of political affairs; and it bears a relation to economic interests; otherwise Congress might vote $25,000 a year in present values to every family in the United States, and the Soviet Government might make every Russian rich; but this is not saying that every event, every institution, every personal decision is "determined" by discoverable "causes."

Nevertheless, whoever leaves economic pressures out of history or out of the discussion of public questions is in mortal peril of substituting mythology for reality and confusing issues instead of clarifying them. It was largely by recognizing the power of economic interests in the field of politics and making skillful use of them that the Fathers of the American Constitution placed themselves among the great practicing statesmen of all ages and gave instructions to succeeding generations in the art of government. By the assiduous study of their works and by displaying their courage and their insight into the economic interests underlying all constitutional formalities, men and women of our generation may guarantee the perpetuity of government under law, as distinguished from the arbitrament of force. It is for us, recipients of their heritage, to inquire constantly and persistently, when theories of national power or states' rights are propounded: "What interests are behind them and to whose advantage will changes or the maintenance of old forms accrue?" By refusing to do this we become victims of history—clay in the hands of its makers.

Historical Interpretation in the United States

. . . [T]he inquiry which follows is based upon the political science of James Madison, the father of the Constitution and later President of the Union he had done so much to create. This political science runs through all of his really serious writings and is formulated in its most precise fashion in *The Federalist*[2] as follows: "The diversity in the faculties of men, from which the rights of property originate, is not less an insuperable obstacle to a uniformity of interests. The protection of these faculties is the first object of government. From the protection of different and unequal faculties of acquiring property, the possession of different degrees and kinds of property immediately results; and from the influence of these on the sentiments and views of the respective proprietors, ensues a division of society into different interests and parties. . . . The most common and durable source of factions has been the various and unequal distribution of property. Those who hold and those who are without property have ever formed distinct interests in society. Those who are creditors, and those who are debtors, fall under a like discrimination. A landed interest, a manufacturing interest, a mercantile interest, a moneyed interest, with many lesser interests, grow up of necessity in civilized nations and divide them into different classes, actuated by different sentiments and views. The regulation of these various and interfering interests forms the principal task of modern legislation, and involves the spirit of party and faction in the necessary and ordinary operations of the government.''

Here we have a masterly statement of the theory of economic determinism in politics.[3] Different degrees and kinds of property inevitably exist in modern society; party doctrines and "principles" originate in the sentiments and views which the possession of various kinds of property creates in the minds of the possessors; class and group divisions based on property lie at the basis of modern government; and politics and constitutional law are inevitably a reflex of these contending interests. Those who are inclined to repudiate the hypothesis of economic determinism as a European importation must, therefore, revise their views, on learning that one of the earliest, and certainly one of the clearest, statements of it came from a profound student of politics who sat in the Convention that framed our fundamental law.

The requirements for an economic interpretation of the formation and adoption of the Constitution may be stated in a hypothetical proposition which, although it cannot be verified absolutely from ascertainable data, will at once illustrate the problem and furnish a guide to research and generalization.

It will be admitted without controversy that the Constitution was the creation of a certain number of men, and it was opposed by a certain number of men. Now, if it were possible to have an economic biography of all of those connected with its framing and adoption,—perhaps about 160,000 men altogether,—the materials for scientific analysis and classification would be available. Such an economic biography would include a list of the real and personal property owned by all of these men and their families; lands and houses, with incumbrances, money at interest, slaves, capital invested in shipping and manufacturing, and in state and continental securities.

Suppose it could be shown from the classification of the men who supported and opposed the Constitution that there was no line of property division at all; that is, that men owning substantially the same amounts of the same kinds of property were equally divided on the matter of adoption or rejection—it would then become apparent that the Constitution had no ascertainable relation to economic groups or classes, but was the product of some abstract causes remote from the chief business of life—gaining a livelihood.

Suppose, on the other hand, that substantially all of the merchants, money lenders, security holders, manufacturers, shippers, capitalists, and financiers and their professional associates are to be found on one side in support of the Constitution and that substantially all or the major portion of the opposition came from the non-slaveholding farmers and the debtors—would it not be pretty conclusively demonstrated that our fundamental law was not the product of an abstraction known as "the whole people," but of a group of economic interests which must have expected beneficial results from its adoption? Obviously all the facts here desired cannot be discovered, but the data presented in the following chapters bear out the latter hypothesis, and thus a reasonable presumption in favor of the theory is created.

Of course, it may be shown (and perhaps can be shown) that the farmers and debtors who opposed the Constitution were, in fact, benefited by the general improvement which resulted from its adoption. It may likewise be shown, to take an extreme case, that the English nation derived immense advantages from the Norman Conquest and the orderly administrative processes which were introduced, as it undoubtedly did; nevertheless, it does not follow that the vague thing known as "the advancement of general welfare" or some abstraction known as "justice" was the immediate, guiding purpose of the leaders in either of these great historic changes. The point is, that the direct, impelling motive in both cases was the economic advantages which the beneficiaries expected would accrue to themselves first, from their action. Further than this, economic interpretation cannot go. It may be that some larger world-process is working through each series of historical events; but ultimate causes lie beyond our horizon.

A Survey of Economic Interests in 1787

. . . A survey of the economic interests of the members of the Convention presents certain conclusions:

A majority of the members were lawyers by profession.

Most of the members came from towns, on or near the coast, that is, from the regions in which personalty was largely concentrated.

Not one member represented in his immediate personal economic interests the small farming or mechanic classes.

The overwhelming majority of members, at least five-sixths, were immediately, directly, and personally interested in the outcome of their labors at Philadelphia, and were to a greater or less extent economic beneficiaries from the adoption of the Constitution.

1. Public security interests were extensively represented in the Convention.[4] Of the fifty-five members who attended no less than forty appear on the Records of the Treasury Department for sums varying from a few dollars up to more than one hundred thousand dollars. Among the minor holders were Basset, Blount, Brearley, Broom, Butler, Carroll, Few, Hamilton, L. Martin, Mason, Mercer, Mifflin, Read, Spaight, Wilson, and Wythe. Among the larger holders (taking the sum of about $5000 as the criterion) were Baldwin, Blair, Clymer, Dayton, Ellsworth, Fitzsimons, Gilman, Gerry, Gorham, Jenifer, Johnson, King, Langdon, Lansing, Livingston,[5] McClurg, R. Morris, C.C. Pinckney, C. Pinckney, Randolph, Sherman, Strong, Washington, and Williamson.

It is interesting to note that, with the exception of New York, and possibly Delaware, each state had one or more prominent representatives in the Convention who held more than a negligible amount of securities, and who could therefore speak with feeling and authority on the question of providing in the new Constitution for the full discharge of the public debt:

Langdon and Gilman, of New Hampshire.
Gerry, Strong, and King, of Massachusetts.
Ellsworth, Sherman, and Johnson, of Connecticut.

Hamilton, of New York. Although he held no large amount personally, he was the special pleader for the holders of public securities and the maintenance of public faith.

Dayton, of New Jersey.

Robert Morris, Clymer, and Fitzsimons, of Pennsylvania.

Mercer and Carroll, of Maryland.

Blair, McClurg, and Randolph, of Virginia.

Williamson, of North Carolina.

The two Pinckneys, of South Carolina.

Few and Baldwin, of Georgia.

2. Personalty invested in lands for speculation was represented by at least fourteen members: Blount, Dayton, Few, Fitzsimons, Franklin, Gilman, Gerry, Gorham, Hamilton, Mason, R. Morris, Washington, Williamson, and Wilson.

3. Personalty in the form of money loaned at interest was represented by at least twenty-four members: Bassett, Broom, Butler, Carroll, Clymer, Davie, Dickinson, Ellsworth, Few, Fitzsimons, Franklin, Gilman, Ingersoll, Johnson, King, Langdon, Mason, McHenry, C.C. Pinckney, C. Pinckney, Randolph, Read, Washington, and Williamson.

4. Personalty in mercantile, manufacturing, and shipping lines was represented by at least eleven members: Broom, Clymer, Ellsworth, Fitzsimons, Gerry, King, Langdon, McHenry, Mifflin, G. Morris, and R. Morris.

5. Personalty in slaves was represented by at least fifteen members: Butler, Davis, Jenifer, A. Martin, L. Martin, Mason, Mercer, C.C. Pinckney, C. Pinckney, Randolph, Read, Rutledge, Spaight, Washington, and Wythe.

It cannot be said, therefore, that the members of the Convention were "disinterested." On the contrary, we are forced to accept the profoundly significant conclusion that they knew through their personal experiences in economic affairs the precise results which the new government that they were setting up was designed to attain. As a group of doctrinaires, like the Frankfort assembly of 1848, they would have failed miserably; but as practical men they were able to build the new government upon the only foundations which could be stable: fundamental economic interests.[6] The fact that a few members of the Convention, who had considerable economic interests at stake, refused to support the Constitution does not invalidate the general conclusions here presented. In the cases of Yates, Lansing, Luther Martin, and Mason, definite economic reasons for their action are forthcoming; but this is a minor detail.

The Constitution as an Economic Document

It is difficult for the superficial student of the Constitution, who has read only the commentaries of the legists, to conceive of that instrument as an economic document. It places no property qualifications on voters or officers; it gives no outward recognition of any economic groups in society; it mentions no special privileges to be conferred upon any class. It betrays no feeling, such as vibrates through the French constitution of 1791; its language is cold, formal, and severe.

The true inwardness of the Constitution is not revealed by an examination of its provisions as simple propositions of law; but by a long and careful study of the voluminous correspondence of the period,[7] contemporary newspapers and pamphlets, the records of the debates in the Convention at Philadelphia and in the several state conventions, and particularly, *The Federalist*, which was widely circulated during the struggle over ratification. The correspondence shows the exact character of the evils which the Constitution was intended to remedy; the records of the proceedings in the Philadelphia Convention reveal the successive steps in the building of the framework of the government under the pressure of economic interests; the pamphlets and newspapers disclose the ideas of the contestants over the ratification; and *The Federalist* presents the political science of the new system as conceived by three of the profoundest thinkers of the period, Hamilton, Madison, and Jay.

Doubtless, the most illuminating of these sources on the economic character of the Constitution are the records of the debates in the Convention, which have come down to us in fragmentary form; and a thorough treatment of material forces reflected in the several clauses of the instrument of government created by the grave assembly at Philadelphia would require a rewriting of the history of the proceedings in the light of the great interests represented there.[8] But an entire volume would scarcely suffice to present the results of such a survey, and an undertaking of this character is accordingly impossible here.

The Federalist, on the other hand, presents in a relatively brief and systematic form an economic interpretation of the Constitution by the men best fitted, through an intimate knowledge of the ideals of the framers, to expound the political science of the new government. This wonderful piece of argumentation by Hamilton, Madison, and Jay is in fact the finest study in the economic interpretation of politics which exists in any language; and whoever would understand the Constitution as an economic document need hardly go beyond it. It is true that the tone of the writers is somewhat modified on account of the fact that they are appealing to the voters to ratify the Constitution, but at the same time they are, by the force of circumstances, compelled to convince large economic groups that safety and strength lie in the adoption of the new system.

Indeed, every fundamental appeal in it is to some material and substantial interest. Sometimes it is to the people at large in the name of protection against invading armies and European coalitions. Sometimes it is to the commercial classes whose business is represented as prostrate before the follies of the Confederation. Now it is to creditors seeking relief against paper money and the assaults of the agrarians in general; now it is to the holders of federal securities which are depreciating toward the vanishing point. But above all, it is to the owners of personalty anxious to find a foil against the attacks of levelling democracy, that the authors of *The Federalist* address their most cogent arguments in favor of ratification. It is true there is much discussion of the details of the new frame-work of government, to which even some friends of reform took exceptions; but Madison and Hamilton both knew that these were incidental matters when compared with the sound basis upon which the superstructure rested.

In reading the pages of this remarkable work as a study in political economy, it is important to bear in mind that the system, which the authors are describing, consisted of two fundamental parts—one positive, the other negative:

I. A government endowed with certain positive powers, but so constructed as to break the force of majority rule and prevent invasions of the property rights of minorities.

II. Restrictions on the state legislatures which had been so vigorous in their attacks on capital.

Under some circumstances, action is the immediate interest of the dominant party; and whenever it desires to make an economic gain through governmental functioning, it must have, of course, a system endowed with the requisite powers.

Examples of this are to be found in protective tariffs, in ship subsidies, in railway land grants, in river and harbor improvements, and so on through the catalogue of so-called ''paternalistic'' legislation. Of course it may be shown that the ''general good'' is the ostensible object of any particular act; but the general good is a passive force, and unless we know who are the several individuals that benefit in its name, it has no meaning. When it is so analyzed, immediate and remote beneficiaries are discovered; and the former are usually found to have been the dynamic element in securing the legislation. Take for example, the economic interests of the advocates who appear in tariff hearings at Washington.

On the obverse side, dominant interests quite as often benefit from the prevention of governmental action as from positive assistance. They are able to take care of themselves if let alone within the circle of protection created by the law. Indeed, most owners of property have as much to fear from positive governmental action as from their inability to secure advantageous legislation. Particularly is this true where the field of private property is already extended to cover practically every form of tangible and intangible wealth. This was clearly set forth by Hamilton:

> It may perhaps be said that the power of preventing bad laws includes that of preventing good ones. . . . But this objection will have little weight with those who can properly estimate the mischiefs of that inconstancy and mutability in the laws which form the greatest blemish in the character and genius of our governments. They will consider every institution calculated to restrain the excess of law-making, and to keep things in the same state in which they happen to be at any given period, as more likely to do good than harm. . . . The injury which may possibly be done by defeating a few good laws will be amply compensated by the advantage of preventing a number of bad ones.[9]

The Underlying Political Science of the Constitution[10]

Before taking up the economic implications of the structure of the federal government, it is important to ascertain what, in the opinion of *The Federalist*, is the basis of all government. The most philosophical examination of the foundations of political science is made by Madison in the tenth number. Here he lays down, in no uncertain language, the principle that the first and elemental concern of every government is economic.

1. "The first object of government," he declares, is the protection of "the diversity in the faculties of men, from which the rights of property originate." The chief business of government, from which, perforce, its essential nature must be derived, consists in the control and adjustment of conflicting economic interests. After enumerating the various forms of propertied interests which spring up inevitably in modern society, he adds: "The regulation of these various and interfering interests forms the principal task of modern legislation, and involves the spirit of party and faction in the ordinary operations of the government."[11]

2. What are the chief causes of these conflicting political forces with which the government must concern itself? Madison answers. Of course fanciful and frivolous distinctions have sometimes been the cause of violent conflicts; "but the most common and durable source of factions has been the various and unequal distribution of property. Those who hold and those who are without property have ever formed distinct interests in society. Those who are creditors, and those who are debtors, fall under a like discrimination. A landed interest, a manufacturing interest, a mercantile interest, a moneyed interest, with many lesser interests grow up of necessity in civilized nations, and divide them into different classes actuated by different sentiments and views."

3. The theories of government which men entertain are emotional reactions to their property interests. "From the protection of different and unequal faculties of acquiring property, the possession of different degrees and kinds of property immediately results; *and from the influence of these on the sentiments and views of the respective proprietors, ensues a division of society into different interests and parties.*" Legislatures reflect these interests. "What," he asks, "are the different classes of legislators but advocates and parties to the causes which they determine." There is no help for it. "The causes of faction cannot be removed," and "we well know that neither moral nor religious motives can be relied on as an adequate control."

4. Unequal distribution of property is inevitable, and from it contending factions will rise in the state. The government will reflect them, for they will have their separate principles and "sentiments"; but the supreme danger will arise from the fusion of certain interests into an overbearing majority, which Madison, in another place, prophesied would be the landless proletariat,[12]—an overbearing majority which will make its "rights" paramount, and sacrifice the "rights" of the minority. "To secure the public good," he declares, "and private rights against the danger of such a faction and at the same time preserve the spirit and the form of popular government is then the great object to which our inquiries are directed."

5. How is this to be done? Since the contending classes cannot be eliminated and their interests are bound to be reflected in politics, the only way out lies in making it difficult for enough contending interests to fuse into a majority, and in balancing one over against another. The machinery for doing this is created by the new Constitution and by the Union. (a) Public views are to be refined and enlarged "by passing them through the medium of a chosen body of citizens." (b) The very size of the Union will enable the inclusion of more interests so that the danger of an overbearing majority is not so great. "The smaller the society, the fewer probably will be the distinct parties and interests composing it; the fewer the distinct parties and interests, the more frequently will a majority be found of the same party. . . . Extend the sphere, and you take in a greater variety of parties and interests; you

make it less probable that a majority of the whole will have a common motive to invade the rights of other citizens; or if such a common motive exists, it will be more difficult for all who feel it to discover their strength and to act in unison with each other.''

Q.E.D., ''in the extent and proper structure of the Union, therefore, we behold a republican remedy for the diseases most incident to republican government.''[13]

The Structure of Government or the Balance of Powers

The fundamental theory of political economy thus stated by Madison was the basis of the original American conception of the balance of powers which is formulated at length in four numbers of *The Federalist* and consists of the following elements:

1. No mere parchment separation of departments of government will be effective. ''The legislative department is everywhere extending the sphere of its activity, and drawing all power into its impetuous vortex. The founders of our republic . . . seem never for a moment to have turned their eyes from the danger to liberty from the overgrown and all-grasping prerogative of an hereditary magistrate, supported and fortified by an hereditary branch of the legislative authority. They seem never to have recollected the danger from legislative usurpations, which, by assembling all power in the same hands, must lead to the same tyranny as is threatened by executive usurpations.''[14]

2. Some sure mode of checking usurpations in the government must be provided, other than frequent appeals to the people. ''There appear to be insuperable objections against the proposed recurrence to the people as a provision in all cases for keeping the several departments of power within their constitutional limits.''[15] In a contest between the legislature and the other branches of the government, the former would doubtless be victorious on account of the ability of the legislators to plead their cause with the people.

3. What then can be depended upon to keep the government in close rein? ''The only answer that can be given is, that as all these exterior provisions are found to be inadequate, the defect must be supplied by so contriving the interior structure of the government as that its several constituent parts may, by their mutual relations, be the means of keeping each other in their proper places. . . . It is of great importance in a republic not only to guard the society against the oppression of its rulers, but to guard one part of the society against the injustice of the other part. Different interests necessarily exist in different classes of citizens. If a majority be united by a common interest, the rights of the minority will be insecure.''[16] There are two ways of obviating this danger: one is by establishing a monarch independent of popular will, and the other is by reflecting these contending interests (so far as their representatives may be enfranchised) in the very structure of the government itself so that a majority cannot dominate the minority—which minority is of course composed of those who possess property that may be attacked. ''Society itself will be broken into so many parts, interests, and classes of citizens, that the rights of individuals, or of the minority, will be in little danger from interested combinations of the majority.''[17]

4. The structure of the government as devised at Philadelphia reflects these several interests and makes improbable any danger to the minority from the majority. ''The House of Representatives being to be elected immediately by the people, the Senate by the State legislatures, the President by electors chosen for that purpose by the people, there would be little probability of a common interest to cement these different branches in a predilection for any particular class of electors.''[18]

5. All of these diverse interests appear in the amending process but they are further reinforced against majorities. An amendment must receive a two-thirds vote in each of the two houses so constituted and the approval of three-fourths of the states.

6. The economic corollary of this system is as follows: Property interests may, through their superior weight in power and intelligence, secure advantageous legislation whenever necessary, and they may at the same time obtain immunity from control by parliamentary majorities.

If we examine carefully the delicate instrument by which the framers sought to check certain kinds of positive action that might be advocated to the detriment of established and acquired rights, we cannot help marvelling at their skill. Their leading idea was to break up the attacking forces at the starting point: the source of political authority for the several branches of the government. This disintegration of positive action at the source was further facilitated by the differentiation in the terms given to the respective departments of the government. And the crowning counterweight to "an interested and over-bearing majority," as Madison phrased it, was secured in the peculiar position assigned to the judiciary, and the use of the sanctity and mystery of the law as a foil to democratic attacks.

It will be seen on examination that no two of the leading branches of the government are derived from the same source. The House of Representatives springs from the mass of the people whom the states may see fit to enfranchise. The Senate is elected by the legislatures of the states, which were, in 1787, almost uniformly based on property qualifications, sometimes with a differentiation between the sources of the upper and lower houses. The President is to be chosen by electors selected as the legislatures of the states may determine—at all events by an authority one degree removed from the voters at large. The judiciary is to be chosen by the President and the Senate, both removed from direct popular control and holding for longer terms than the House.

A sharp differentiation is made in the terms of the several authorities, so that a complete renewal of the government at one stroke is impossible. The House of Representatives is chosen for two years; the Senators for six, but not at one election, for one-third go out every two years. The President is chosen for four years. The judges of the Supreme Court hold for life. Thus "popular distempers," as eighteenth century publicists called them, are not only restrained from working their havoc through direct elections, but they are further checked by the requirement that they must last six years in order to make their effects felt in the political department of the government, providing they can break through the barriers imposed by the indirect election of the Senate and the President. Finally, there is the check of judicial control that can be overcome only through the manipulation of the appointing power which requires time, or through the operation of a cumbersome amending system.

The keystone of the whole structure is, in fact, the system provided for judicial control—the most unique contribution to the science of government which has been made by American political genius. It is claimed by some recent writers that it was not the intention of the framers of the Constitution to confer upon the

Supreme Court the power of passing upon the constitutionality of statutes enacted by Congress; but in view of the evidence on the other side, it is incumbent upon those who make this assertion to bring forward positive evidence to the effect that judicial control was not a part of the Philadelphia programme.[19] Certainly, the authors of *The Federalist* entertained no doubts on the point, and they conceived it to be such an excellent principle that they were careful to explain it to the electors to whom they addressed their arguments.

After elaborating fully the principle of judicial control over legislation under the Constitution, Hamilton enumerates the advantages to be derived from it. Speaking on the point of tenure during good behavior, he says:

> In a monarchy it is an excellent barrier to the despotism of the prince; in a republic it is no less an excellent barrier to the encroachments and oppressions of the representative body. . . . If, then, the courts of justice are to be considered as the bulwarks of a limited Constitution against legislative encroachments, this consideration will afford a strong argument for the permanent tenure of judicial offices, since nothing will contribute so much as this to that independent spirit in the judges which must be essential to the faithful performance of so arduous a duty. . . . But it is not with a view to infractions of the Constitution only that the independence of the judges may be an essential safeguard against the effects of occasional ill humors in the society. These sometimes extend no farther than to the injury of private rights of particular classes of citizens, by unjust and partial laws. Here also the firmness of the judicial magistracy is of vast importance in mitigating the severity and confining the operation of such laws. It not only serves to moderate the immediate mischiefs of those which may have been passed, but it operates as a check upon the legislative body in passing them; who, perceiving that obstacles to the success of iniquitous intention are to be expected from the scruples of the courts, are in a manner compelled, by the very motives of injustice they meditate, to qualify their attempts. This is a circumstance calculated to have more influence upon the character of our governments than but few may be aware of.[20]

.   .   .

The Economic Conflict over Ratification as Viewed by Contemporaries

Having discovered the nature of the social conflict connected with the formation and adoption of the Constitution, and having shown the probable proportion of the people who participated in the conflict and the several group-interests into which they fell, it is interesting, though not fundamentally important, to inquire whether the leading thinkers of the time observed the nature of the antagonisms present in the process. A full statement of the results of such an inquiry would require far more space than is at command in this volume; and consequently only a few illustrative and representative opinions can be given.

No one can pore for weeks over the letters, newspapers, and pamphlets of the years 1787–1789 without coming to the conclusion that there was a deep-seated conflict between a popular party based on paper money and agrarian interests, and a conservative party centred in the towns and resting on financial, mercantile, and personal property interests generally. It is true that much of the fulmination in pamphlets was concerned with controversies over various features of the Constitution; but those writers who went to the bottom of matters, such as the authors of *The Federalist*, and the more serious Anti-Federalists, gave careful attention to the basic elements in the struggle as well as to the incidental controversial details.

. . .

It is in the literature of the contest in the states where the battle over ratification was hottest that we find the most frank recognition of the fact that one class of property interests was in conflict with another. This recognition appears not so much in attacks on opponents as in appeals to the groups which have the most at stake in the outcome of the struggle, although virulent abuse of debtors and paper money advocates is quite common. Merchants, money lenders, public creditors are constantly urged to support the Constitution on the ground that their economic security depends upon the establishment of the new national government.

Perhaps the spirit of the battle over ratification is best reflected in the creed ironically attributed to each of the contending parties by its opponents. The recipe for an Anti-Federalist essay, which indicates in a very concise way the class-bias that actuated the opponents of the Constitution, ran in this manner:

> Wellborn, nine times—Aristocracy, eighteen times—Liberty of the Press, thirteen times repeated—Liberty of Conscience, once—Negro slavery, once mentioned—Trial by jury, seven times—Great Men, six times repeated—Mr. Wilson, forty times. . . .—put them altogether and dish them up at pleasure.[21]

To this sarcastic statement of their doctrines, the Anti-Federalists replied by formulating the ''Political Creed of Every Federalist'' as follows:

> I believe in the infallibility, all-sufficient wisdom, and infinite goodness of the late convention; or in other words, I believe that some men are of so perfect a nature that it is absolutely impossible for them to commit errors or design villainy. I believe that the great body of the people are incapable of judging in their nearest concerns, and that, therefore, they ought to be guided by the opinions of their superiors. . . . I believe that aristocracy is the best form of government. . . . I believe that trial by jury and the freedom of the press ought to be exploded from every wise government. . . . I believe that the new constitution will prove the bulwark of liberty—the balm of misery—the essence of justice—and the astonishment of all mankind. In short, I believe that it is the best form of

government which has ever been offered to the world. I believe that to speak, write, read, think, or hear any thing against the proposed government is damnable heresy, execrable rebellion, and high treason against the sovereign majority of the convention—And lastly I believe that every person who differs from me in belief is an infernal villain. AMEN.[22]

.   .   .

Conclusions

At the close of this long and arid survey—partaking of the nature of catalogue—it seems worth while to bring together the important conclusions for political science which the data presented appear to warrant.

The movement for the Constitution of the United States was originated and carried through principally by four groups of personalty interests which had been adversely affected under the Articles of Confederation: money, public securities, manufactures, and trade and shipping.

The first firm steps toward the formation of the Constitution were taken by a small and active group of men immediately interested through their personal possessions in the outcome of their labors.

No popular vote was taken directly or indirectly on the proposition to call the Convention which drafted the Constitution.

A large propertyless mass was, under the prevailing suffrage qualifications, excluded at the outset from participation (through representatives) in the work of framing the Constitution.

The members of the Philadelphia Convention which drafted the Constitution were, with a few exceptions, immediately, directly, and personally interested in, and derived economic advantages from, the establishment of the new system.

The Constitution was essentially an economic document based upon the concept that the fundamental private rights of property are anterior to government and morally beyond the reach of popular majorities.

The major portion of the members of the Convention are on record as recognizing the claim of property to a special and defensive position in the Constitution.

In the ratification of the Constitution, about three-fourths of the adult males failed to vote on the question, having abstained from the elections at which delegates to the state conventions were chosen, either on account of their indifference or their disfranchisement by property qualifications.

The Constitution was ratified by a vote of probably not more than one-sixth of the adult males.

It is questionable whether a majority of the voters participating in the elections for the state conventions in New York, Massachusetts, New Hampshire, Virginia, and South Carolina, actually approved the ratification of the Constitution.

The leaders who supported the Constitution in the ratifying convention represented the same economic groups as the members of the Philadelphia Convention; and in a large number of instances they were also directly and personally interested in the outcome of their efforts.

In the ratification, it became manifest that the line of cleavage for and against the Constitution was between substantial personalty interests on the one hand and the small farming and debtor interests on the other.

The Constitution was not created by "the whole people" as the jurists have said; neither was it created by "the states" as Southern nullifiers long contended; but it was the work of a consolidated group whose interests knew no state boundaries and were truly national in their scope.

Notes

1. *American Historical Review*, April, 1935, p. 447.

2. Number 10.

3. The theory of the economic interpretation of history as stated by professor Seligman seems as nearly axiomatic as any proposition in social science can be: "The existence of man depends upon his ability to sustain himself; the economic life is therefore the fundamental condition of all life. Since human life, however, is the life of man in society, individual existence moves within the framework of the social structure and is modified by it. What the conditions of maintenance are to the individual, the similar relations of production and consumption are to the community. To economic causes, therefore, must be traced in the last instance those transformations in the structure of society which themselves condition the relations of social classes and the various manifestations of social life." *The Economic Interpretation of History*, p. 3.

4. See [Beard, *An Economic Interpretation of the Constitution*], p. 75, n. 3.

5. See [ibid.], p. 124. Livingston's holdings are problematical.

6. The fact that a few members of the Convention, who had considerable economic interests at stake, refused to support the Constitution does not invalidate the general conclusions here presented. In the cases of Yates, Lansing, Luther Martin, and Mason, definite economic reasons for their action are forthcoming; but this is a minor detail.

7. A great deal of this valuable material has been printed in the *Documentary History of the Constitution*, Vols. IV and V; a considerable amount has been published in the letters and papers of the eminent men of the period; but an enormous mass still remains in manuscript form. Fortunately, such important papers as those of Washington, Hamilton, Madison, and others are in the Library of Congress; but they are not complete, of course.

8. From this point of view, the old conception of the battle at Philadelphia as a contest between small and large states—as political entities—will have to be severely modified. See Professor Farrand's illuminating paper on the so-called compromises of the Constitution in the *Report of the American Historical Association, 1903*, Vol. I, pp. 73 ff. J.C. Welling, "States' Rights Conflict over the Public Lands," *ibid.* (1888), pp. 184 ff.

9. *The Federalist*, No. 73.

10. See J.A. Smith, *The Spirit of American Government*.

11. See Noah Webster's consideration of the subject of government and property; [Paul Leicester] Ford, ed., *Pamphlets on the Constitution of the United States*, [1888], pp. 57 ff.

12. [M.] Farrand, ed., *The Records of the Federal Convention of 1787*, Vol. II, p. 203.

13. This view was set forth by Madison in a letter to Jefferson in 1788. "Wherever the real power in a Government lies, there is the danger of oppression. In our Governments the

real power lies in the majority of the Community, and the invasion of private rights is *chiefly* to be apprehended, not from acts of Government contrary to the sense of its constituents, but from acts in which the Government is the mere instrument of the major number of the constituents. This is a truth of great importance, but not yet sufficiently attended to, and is probably more strongly impressed upon my mind by facts, and reflections suggested by them, than on yours which has contemplated abuses of power issuing from a very different quarter. Wherever there is an interest and power to do wrong, wrong will generally be done, and not less readily by a powerful and interested party than by a powerful and interested prince.'' *Documentary History of the Constitution*, Vol. V, p. 88.

14. *The Federalist*, No. 48.

15. *Ibid.*, No. 49.

16. *The Federalist*, No. 51.

17. *Ibid.*, No. 51.

18. *Ibid.*, No. 60.

19. Beard, *The Supreme Court and the Constitution*. See also the criticisms of this work by Professor W.F. Dodd, in the *American Historical Review* for January, 1913.

20. Number 78.

21. *New Hampshire Spy*, November 30, 1787.

22. *American Museum*, July, 1788, Vol. IV, p. 85.

2. The Antifederalist Critique
Democracy Denied

Jackson Turner Main
The Antifederalists
Critics of the Constitution

Jackson Turner Main deepens the analyses of Smith and Beard by examining the class structure of America in the 1780s. He presents evidence that the Antifederalists were defenders of popular democracy, and that the division over the Constitution followed class lines. He concludes that class conflict, while not the exclusive explanation for the character of the Constitution, nevertheless had a major influence on it.

Social and Political Background

The United States consisted in the 1780s of a number of sections and subsections, each with a distinctive social structure, economy, and set of political objectives. From Maine to Georgia, by way of Vermont, the Wyoming Valley, the Alleghany district, and the Wateree, stretched the frontier. Except where great landholders with their tenants and slaves pursued the retreating supply of topsoil, frontier society did not include extremes of wealth and poverty. There was an embryonic class structure but it was potential only; property was, in comparison with other sections, equally distributed, and from the bottom to the top was but a short step. The men of the frontier wanted to keep it that way: thus the first Kentucky convention, meeting in the winter of 1784–85, declared: "That to grant any Person a larger quantity of Land than he designs Bona Fide to seat himself or his Family on, is a greevance, Because it is subversive of the fundamental Principles of a free republican Government to allow any individual, or Company or Body of Men to possess such large tracts of Country in their own

From *The Antifederalists: Critics of the Constitution, 1781–1788*, by Jackson Turner Main, © 1962 The University of North Carolina Press, pp. 1–13, 261–69, and 279–81 (with deletions). Published for the Institute of Early American History and Culture, Williamsburg. Reprinted by permission.

right as may at a future Day give them undue influence.''[1] Along the whole arc of the frontier, expansion was the essential need—expansion of geographical area, of available capital, of facilities for transportation, and of political organization.

What frontier society became, once the frontier had passed on, depended upon a number of circumstances, of which two were particularly important during the 1780's: soil and transportation facilities. If the soil was fertile and easily worked, a surplus could be produced; if this surplus could be marketed, farming on a commercial basis was possible. But if the soil was not fertile, or if transportation facilities were poor, it was more difficult to raise produce for market and the farmer was limited to a near-subsistence level. One or the other of these inhibiting factors was present over wide areas. In most of New England, for example, the soil precluded raising a surplus; in most of North Carolina, lack of transportation facilities rendered a surplus of little value. In the great stretches of uplands, between the river valleys, there existed a society of subsistence or subsistence-plus farmers—a frontier in arrested development. Here, as on the frontier itself, no wealthy class existed because there was little chance to accumulate wealth; property was widely distributed, and although it was easy to acquire land, upward social mobility was limited by the ceiling which rivers and soil imposed.

Those who achieved riches usually lived on the valley lands, not the uplands. Here farming was profitable, and the subsistence farmer could become a wealthy planter. He could, that is, so long as the region was undergoing development; for after a period during which wealth was accumulated rapidly, large estates were formed, and then the newcomer was confronted with expensive land, which he could perhaps rent but hardly buy. In contrast with the social structure of the frontier and uplands, the society of the valley was characterized by greater class distinctions. The emergence of an aristocracy of wealth was balanced by the growth of a far larger lower class, and between these groups the small property holders were proportionately less numerous. Although agricultural, the interest of such a region was also commercial, for its prosperity depended upon selling the surplus overseas or in a nearby city. The city developed still another type of class structure, but this society is not of such importance to us because Antifederalism was rural rather than urban.

In referring to a class structure of society during the Revolutionary era one might be accused of interpreting the past with words of the present. The existence of classes, however, was clearly recognized in the eighteenth century. Usually three were distinguished. These were, as Patrick Henry expressed it, the well-born, the middle, and the lower "ranks."[2] There is, and was, no clear dividing line between the first two. The term "well born" implied a hereditary aristocracy, and it is true that by the 1780's such a thing did exist in America, but its basis was pecuniary; property, not birth, was the major factor in determining class structure. Phrases such as "the rich," "men of wealth and ability," "men of Sense and Property" describe the upper class as the Revolutionary generation saw it. John Jay defined this class as "the better kind of people, by which I mean the people who are orderly and industrious, who are content with their situation and not uneasy in their circumstances."[3] Such men were frequently termed "gentlemen," a word which usually implied superior wealth as well as superior status and behavior, as the phrase "gentlemen of property" suggests.[4] Indeed, wealth was essential in order to acquire the attributes of a gentleman: to dress fashionably, become educated, patronize arts, purchase luxuries, and conduct oneself in society as gentlemen were supposed to do.

The distinction between gentlemen and other sorts of men existed everywhere in some degree. John Adams pretended that it was a phenomenon known only outside New England. In 1775 he wrote to Joseph Hawley from Philadelphia: "Gentlemen in other colonies have large plantations of slaves, and the common people among them are very ignorant and very poor. These gentlemen are [more] . . . habituated to higher notions of themselves, and the distinction between them and the common people, than we are."[5] But Hawley could have set him right, for a decade earlier he had pleaded that a writ was defective because it designated the defendant as a yeoman when he was really a gentleman![6] It is undoubtedly true, however, that the upper class was larger and more conspicuous in the South than in most parts of the North.

There were obviously great variations among the well-to-do. They were persons of different degrees of wealth and, above all, of varying interests. Greater and lesser planters, debtors and creditors, merchants in towns and in cities, speculators and landlords, lawyers and shipowners, "River Gods" and "manor lords"—each had particular economic and political aspirations. They did not always agree with one another, yet they did share similar attitudes toward property and politics. In 1787, gentlemen of property provided the Antifederalists with many of their ablest leaders, but the great majority gave the Federalists vigorous support.

In contrast with the better sort, the rest of the people were sometimes simply lumped together and identified as "common" or "lower."[7] As a rule, however, a distinction was made between those who had property and those who had not. The former were referred to as the "middle" or "middling" classes (or sorts, or ranks), and the latter were designated as "lower," or "inferior."[8] The number of men who belonged to this latter group varied from only 25 or 30 per cent of the total in rural New England to well over half in some Southern counties.[9] Their political influence was as slight as their prestige.

Most significant was the middle class, from which the Antifederalists drew their greatest strength. The majority of white Americans, and by far the largest number of voters, were farmers who owned their land and who lived at a subsistence-plus level.[10] It is difficult to generalize about their economic status, but two major groups can be distinguished. First, many lived on the good soil of the river valleys, in well-established communities, where transportation facilities made marketing easy. Such farmers were fairly well-to-do. They might contract debts in order to improve their holdings or, like the rich, to purchase luxuries, but they were generally solvent. Their prosperity depended upon commerce, and they were interested in stability. Hence they were often allied politically with the mercantile interest and the conservative elements of society in defense of a favorable status quo. On the other hand many farmers were poor. In North Carolina a few surviving tax records reveal that the median amount of cash in hand held by landowners was £17—this at a time when large quantities of paper money had been issued.[11] One of the best farms in Rhode Island made a profit of only £31½ cash in 1785 while another made just over £5½.[12] The income of farmers in Worcester County, Massachusetts, during the depression year 1786 was about £9 per poll.[13] The great variation in farm value is suggested by the fact that the legislature of Connecticut estimated that the annual income from land ranged from 7ᶜ to $1.67 per acre.[14] Many farmers must have been living near the margin, with little cash income, so that they were obliged to obtain necessities by barter or credit. They had little left over for taxes and were especially vulnerable if there was a depression or a scarcity of money.

It appears that a large proportion of the farmers, especially of this second type, were in debt. To acquire a farm often demanded a fairly large capital investment. Even 100 acres would cost not far from £50 to £100 in the South, and much more than that in the North, unless one sought out poor, discarded, or isolated land and thereby sentenced oneself to permanent penury. The purchase of essential farm animals, equipment, and supplies would raise the cost still higher. Since wages were not high enough to enable laborers to save such a sum easily, the number of landless men and of tenant farmers was increasing, while those who owned land often had to borrow in order to pay for it.[15] Suits for debt were everywhere numerous, as were complaints concerning debts. The situation was most serious during the period of money shortage that followed the Revolution. During the 1780's there were riots among debtors in Massachusetts, New Hampshire, Connecticut, Rhode Island, New Jersey, Maryland, Virginia, and South Carolina; paper money laws were passed or strongly supported in every state.

Debts were a factor which motivated farmers to take an interest in politics; they were also vitally concerned about tax policy and the payment of the state debts. Seeking to transfer their tax burdens to different shoulders, farmers and other small property holders opposed poll taxes and heavy taxes on cultivated land. They tried to reduce government expenses and official salaries in order to keep taxes low. To ease the burden of discharging public debts, they variously tried to delay payment, to depreciate the value of public securities, to levy taxes payable in securities, or to pay the interest in paper money or in certificates created for the purpose. When taxes were levied, they preferred payment in kind, and in depression years they tried to postpone payment of the whole or part of the tax. Unwilling to grant Congress as much money as it asked, they adopted various expedients to lower the amount to be paid, and tried to avoid any form of payment which would require state taxes to be collected in hard money. It would not be fair to say that they refused to support their governments, but a considerable gap sometimes separated what the governments thought was needed and what the farmers were willing to give. The isolation of many farmers, their lack of formal education, and the limited horizons of their experience, also made them unwilling to surrender local advantages for the more general good.

An attractive solution to the farmers' financial problems was paper money. It could be issued to pay the expenses of government, discharge public debts, and reduce the hardship of paying taxes. Private debts could also be more easily paid. As a debtor, the farmer also hoped that the judicial process might be made more favorable to him. He demanded the more convenient location of courts, lower court costs and lawyer fees, laws obliging creditors to accept property at a "fair" value, the abolition of imprisonment for debt, and laws delaying the recovery of debts. Such measures as these occasionally attracted the support of larger property holders, especially during the years 1784–86 when the complex of debts involved both rich and poor; but the principal support came from the small farmers.

Everywhere the small farmers, like all other economic and social groups, tried to increase their political power in order to achieve their objectives. In doing so, they could draw upon their experience as colonials and revolutionists, and they could also select out of the great body of the world's political literature those doctrines which were most useful. These doctrines, though their origins were doubtless unknown to the rank and file of Americans, were their common property, and had been made familiar first during the pre-Revolutionary years, when they were incorporated into sermons, pamphlets, and newspaper articles, and then extended into the first period of constitution-making after independence.

Different aspects of this experience and different parts of this literature appealed to different groups. Future Federalists as well as future Antifederalists accepted the great body of English political thought incorporated into the Whig tradition, which emphasized individual liberty and the ultimate authority of the people. The Antifederalists, however, advanced much further toward democratic political ideas, so that the background of their thought is to be found in what might be called the left wing of Whiggism. Two works in particular are relevant to their ideas. *Cato's Letters*, the joint product of Thomas Gordon and John Trenchard, was written during 1720–23 and had passed through a number of English editions by the time of the Revolution.[16] Although it was never published in America, it was widely read in the colonies and became "a favorite textbook of the patriots."[17] The writers who adopted "Cato" as their nom de plumes were probably thinking as often of the British authors as of the Roman original. The other major source of Antifederal thought was James Burgh's *Political Disquisitions*. An American edition, published in 1775, was "encouraged" by some seventy-five prominent Americans.[18]

The basic concept stressed in both of these works was the evil effect of power. "The love of power is natural," wrote Burgh, "it is insatiable; it is whetted, not cloyed, by possession."[19] Gordon and Trenchard observed that "Power renders men wanton, insolent to others, and fond of themselves. . . . All history affords but few Instances of Men trusted with great Power without abusing it, when with Security they could.'' The people must retain power in their own hands, grant it but sparingly, and then only under the strictest supervision.[20] ''The people can never be too jealous of their liberties,'' warned Burgh. ''Power is of an elastic nature, ever extending itself and encroaching on the liberties of the subjects.''[21] ''Cato'' also believed that ''Political Jealousy, . . . in the People, is a necessary and laudable Passion.'' Therefore the people must select their rulers with care, and these must be ''narrowly watched, and checked with Restraints stronger than their Temptation to break them.''[22]

This mistrust of power was characteristic of American political thought during this period. Long before the doctrine was applied to the Constitution, it was frequently expressed by men who became Antifederalists. For example, Samuel Adams asserted that ''there is a Degree of Watchfulness over all Men possessed of Power or Influence upon which the Liberties of Mankind much depend. It is necessary to guard against the Infirmities of the best as well as the Wickedness of the worst of Men.'' Therefore, ''Jealousy is the best Security of publick Liberty.''[23] So also Hugh Hughes, a New York City Antifederalist, warned, ''From the Conduct of our Church and the Senate, we see how *absolutely requisite* it is, to continually guard against Power; for, when once Bodies of Men, in authority, get Possession of, or become invested with, Property or Prerogative, whether it be by Intrigue, Mistake, or Chance, they scarcely ever relinquish their Claim, even if founded in Iniquity itself.''[24]

The power to govern must therefore be retained by the people, who alone can be trusted to know their own will, and who, as ''Cato'' believed, ''generally, if not always, judge well.'' Since all men are equal, there is no reason to grant power to the ''Great Men,'' who indeed are most apt to be oppressors.[25] ''Democritus'' warned the Massachusetts voters that even if the well-educated and well-to-do had good intentions, they have been taught to look upon their inferiors as their property, so that they would have ''very little compassion.'' Only those could be trusted who earned their living by ''honest industry'' and who were men ''in middling circumstances.''[26]

Still another condition was necessary to ensure that the government would express the popular will. Such a government, wrote ''Cato,'' required a relatively equal division of property. Since ''Dominion follows Property, . . . An Equality of Estate will give an Equality of Power; and an Equality of Power is a Commonwealth, or Democracy,'' whereas ''Very great Riches in private Men . . . destroy, amongst the Commons, that Balance of Property and Power, which is necessary to a Democracy.'' If property is thus equally divided, ''there is no hindering a popular Form of Government, unless sudden Violence takes away all Liberty, and to preserve itself, alters the Distribution of Property again.''[27]

Years before, James Harrington had written that where an equality of estates existed there must be equality of power.[28] This doctrine contained radical implications which few followed to the logical conclusion, yet the relationship between power and property was observed in America, and among the Antifederalists there were at least some who attacked any trend toward the inequality of wealth as being dangerous to democracy. They recognized, as Thomson Mason wrote in 1783, that "power is the constant, the necessary attendant on property."[29] Connecticut, as Captain Welton observed, had a government that was "popular or democratical," which God had given as the best system, and "for this purpose an equal distribution of property was necessary."[30] It followed that where property was widely distributed, a democratic or popular government was most agreeable. Joseph Reed in Pennsylvania and Joseph Warren in Massachusetts were two who noted that a democracy would be congenial to Americans only so long as an excessive concentration of wealth was avoided.[31]

In order to guard against the tyranny of power and preserve popular rule, the men entrusted with power had to be kept responsive to public opinion. If they were allowed to act independently, history proved that the results were evil, and the former colonials did not have to look far into the past to perceive this truth. The Revolutionary generation needed only to recall events out of their own experiences: the behavior of the royal governors or of officials appointed by them; the failure of councilors and even of elective officers to heed the people's will. The corruption of power, the oppression of strong government, had been vital, immediate dangers to those who waged the Revolution because of them. How could responsibility be maintained?

Frequent and regular elections were certainly essential. In England and in many colonies, elections had been held only at long intervals and might be delayed by the executive, so that when an important new issue arose, the vote of the legislators did not always reflect a changing public opinion. It was therefore recognized that to preserve popular rule, elections must be held every year. "Where annual elections end, slavery begins," Burgh declared, and the Pennsylvania democrat William Findley agreed: "Annual Elections are an annual Recognition of the Sovereignty of the People."[32] In addition, there was the danger that an official might remain in office so long that he ceased to sympathize with the people. Rotation in office, according to "Cato," was "essentially necessary to a free Government: It is indeed the Thing itself; and constitutes, animates, and informs it, as much as the Soul institutes the Man. It is a Thing sacred and inviolable, where-ever Liberty is thought sacred."[33] This principle was forcibly expressed by the Pennsylvania constitution of 1776, which required a rotation in office in order that "the danger of establishing an inconvenient aristocracy will be effectually prevented."[34]

The Antifederalists, like most Americans, believed that if the government were truly to represent the people, the principal power should rest in the popular branch. There was, however, some disagreement as to whether this branch of government should be all-powerful or restrained by a coequal upper house and executive. "Cato" had favored a political system of three parts: the magistracy, to prevent confusion; the people, to prevent oppression; and the senate, consisting of men distinguished for their fortunes and abilities. Such an arrangement was made familiar by many other writers, including Locke. On the other hand, Burgh argued that there ought to be no checks whatever on the people's representatives by king or lords.[35] Certainly the trend in America had consistently been toward the elevation of the lower house at the expense of the upper house and the governor. The citizens of Ashfield, Massachusetts, represent the extreme: they wished no governor except God, as they said, and under him a states general. They envisaged the state legislature as a unicameral body, annually elected; any acts pertaining to the towns were to be approved by the towns. Even the judiciary was to be under popular control, for each town was to choose its own judges.[36] Antifederal thought did not always insist on the complete elimination of the senate, as in this instance, but it did require a readjustment of power in favor of the more democratic lower house. A reduction in the executive authority was almost universally demanded after 1776 because of a reaction against the royal governors.

Many Antifederalists also wished to reduce the high property qualifications for holding office. Arguing against any special requirement for the election of the governor, the town of Petersham, Massachusetts (soon to be a Shaysite center and then Antifederal), resolved "Riches and Dignity neither make the head wiser nor the heart better. The overgrown Rich we consider the most dangerous to the Liberties of a free State."[37] Orange County in the North Carolina uplands, various little New Hampshire towns, and other spokesmen of democracy demanded that the suffrage be extended.[38]

.   .   .

Conclusion

. . . [T]here is a good deal of evidence to show that the division followed on class lines. There was no working class to any extent, but there did exist an antagonism between small and large property holders. It is true that such conflicts were tempered by exceptionally high vertical mobility, but there were nevertheless significant economic and social differences, well recognized at the time, that were continually reflected in political disputes. In the debate over the Constitution, several types of evidence are available to prove the existence of a division along class lines. First, there is the testimony of contemporaries. In Massachusetts the statements of King, Knox, Jackson, Thatcher, Sewall, Minot, Singletary, Lewis Morris, and Randal have been cited. Both East and Harding give other examples.[39] In New Hampshire, Sullivan, Madison, Atherton, and Tobias Lear testified that the Federalists were men of greater wealth. Hugh Ledlie referred to the Connecticut Federalists as men of "superior rank" while David Humphreys listed clergy, lawyers, physicians, merchants, and army officers. In Rhode Island, General Varnum observed that "the wealth and resources of this state are chiefly in the possession of the well-affected."[40] Similarly in New York, both sides noted a difference, the Federalists with pride, the Antifederalists with alarm.[41] The Pennsylvanian George Bryan discussed class differences, while Benjamin Rush contrasted the "people" and "their rulers." Observers in the South noted the same distinction, as Arthur Bryan did when he discovered that in South Carolina the "second class of people" were especially inclined to Antifederalism; Burke contrasted the "rich leading men" with "the Multitude." Timothy Bloodworth felt that the aristocracy favored adoption in North Carolina. Lord Dorchester was informed that "the partizans in favour of the new system hold the greater share of landed and personal property." John Quincy Adams also felt that there was a general class division over the Constitution. Even in Maryland, John Francis Mercer believed that the contest was between "wealthy men" or "the *few*" and "the People" or "the *many*," and another observer there believed that ratification was secured by the aristocracy, not the "common class."[42] Some proof by implication may be drawn from the fact that Antifederalists generally criticized the Constitution for its undemocratic features,[43] while in contrast a considerable number of Federalists did not approve of the upsurge of the democracy and praised the constitution as a check on popular majorities.

Another type of evidence is based on a study of individuals whose politics are known, especially members of the ratifying conventions. Such a study clearly reveals a class alignment. If it be conceded that there was some sort of a difference between "Esq." and "Mr." as used in New England, then it is evident that the Federalists outranked their opponents by a significant margin; they constituted nearly three and one-half times as many esquires. Second, it is probably true in New England and certainly true in the south that there was a correlation between socio-economic status and army rank. In every state for which information is available, except New York, the higher ranking officers were Federal by a margin of more than two to one.[44] On the other hand there were about the same number of lesser ranking officers on either side, lieutenants tending toward Antifederalism. Third, the holders of a college degree almost always came from the upper income groups and they were Federal by a margin of more than three to one. Fourth, certain professions carried with them superior prestige and usually higher income. Merchants were Federal by a five to one margin, lawyers and judges by well over two to one, shipowners, ship captains, and large manufacturers by over seven to one.

The highest political offices were at that time principally held by men of wealth and status (even aside from the property qualifications), and taking as representative of these offices the governors, state senators, and members of Congress, it appears that the Federalists held well over twice as many such posts in states where close contests occurred. Among the governors and former governors whose political opinions are known, twenty-seven were Federal and eleven were Antifederal, and of the latter, five changed sides. Men who had served in Congress were Federal by a four to one margin.

The political preference of the members of state senates is of particular interest. They were numerous (over eight hundred served at various times from 1775 to 1788) and influential because their approval was essential for the passage of all laws. The great majority of them were well-to-do merchants, lawyers, or large landholders. Among those whose opinions are known, nearly two-thirds voted for ratification. This may be attributed to their superior education and wider experience, or to the fact that as men of political knowledge they recognized the need for change. But economic status had something to do with it too. The wealthier senators supported the Constitution by a margin of over three to one; those who were merely well-to-do favored it two to one; but those of only moderate means opposed it by a small margin. The wealthier the senator, the more apt he was to be a Federalist.[45]

Indeed, men of wealth in general, in or out of the conventions, were usually Federalists. Almost all of them in New Jersey, Delaware, and Georgia apparently favored ratification, and nearly all in Connecticut and Maryland. In the remaining eight states, among almost three hundred men definitely known to have possessed considerable fortunes, nearly three-fourths were Federal. Yet in these states the majority of the population was against the Constitution.[46]

Other evidence to the same effect may be stated briefly. In Pennsylvania, the Federalist delegates to the ratifying convention owned, on the average, half again as much land and other taxable property as the Antifederalists. In Massachusetts, Federal towns were wealthier. In Rhode Island, Federal towns contained far more slaves than did the Antifederal. Another type of property, public securities, was also unequally distributed, for much of the debt, worth millions of dollars, was concentrated in centers of Federalist strength.[47] Observers agreed that creditors, both public and private, tended to be Federal, while debtors were ordinarily Antifederal. Finally, the areas which supported Federalism, including the towns and rich river valleys, contained most of the men who were well-to-do and a great proportion of the whole wealth of the country.

Still a third type of evidence in support of a class division is based upon a correlation between the alignment on ratification and that on earlier issues which involved conflicts between rich and poor, large and small property owners. Allowing for the inevitable exceptions, the Antifederalists had in the past supported the more democratic state constitutions which increased the political power of the majority, whereas the Federalists had preferred to restrain or "manage" the democracy; the Antifederalists had supported paper money, lower interest rates, legal tender clauses, valuation and instalment and stay laws, and other measures favorable to debtors; they had attempted also to reduce the state debts so as to render taxes less burdensome to the majority, while the Federalists upheld the creditor interest and favored the taxes necessary to pay the debts at par. Similarly the Antifederalists, in combating the loyalists, opposing the Bank of North America, obstructing enforcement of the British treaty, striving for lower court fees, and checking the increase of power in government, had defended the interest of the many against the few. The struggle over the Constitution was in part a continuation of a long history of social conflicts which extended far back into colonial times.

All of this evidence proves that there was a division along lines of class. It does not, however, prove that the struggle over ratification can be explained exclusively in terms of class conflict. There are several states in which the concept obviously does not hold. In Georgia both wealthy planters and yeomen farmers agreed on ratification. In North Carolina and Virginia a large number of planters were Antifederal, and in the interior of the latter state, two large sections inhabited by small farmers favored ratification. Maryland does not fit the theory, nor do Delaware and New Jersey. Delegates from small farmer strongholds in Connecticut, New Hampshire, Pennsylvania, and even Massachusetts (parts of Hampshire County) were Federal.

But the most serious of all objections to an interpretation based exclusively on an alignment along class lines is the complete absence of a division of opinion in the towns. Where there should have been the most feeling, the least existed. This is a fact of such significance that it deserves fuller discussion.

In Charleston a solidly Federal delegation was elected without any sign of opposition. Alexander Gillon, who had been anti-Morris, skeptical of the impost, pro-debtor, and spokesman for the common man, was Federal. His ally Dr. John Budd voted for ratification. Aedanus Burke noted that everyone in the city, rich and poor alike, was "boisterous to drive it down."[48] In neighboring North Carolina, the towns of Wilmington, Halifax, and Salisbury, all situated in Antifederal areas, were themselves Federal, as was an unrepresented town (Tarborough) in Antifederal Edgecomb County. Edenton and New Bern likewise supported ratification. Only Hillsborough, farther west, did not. Both Williamsburg and Norfolk in Virginia elected Federal delegates; Fredericksburg was Federal in an Antifederal county (Spotsylvania); the freeholders of Alexandria voted for ratification, as did the inhabitants of Winchester (unanimously) and Petersburgh.[49] The town of Baltimore in Maryland was not unanimous, but the Federalists polled over 70 per cent of the vote,[50] whereas in the county they were defeated. In Annapolis, too, Federal candidates won in an Antifederal county.

Pennsylvania towns united in support of the Constitution. The Antifederalists could gain only an average of 150 votes per candidate in Philadelphia, scarcely one-eighth as many as the Federalists; George Bryan declared that "most townsmen were for it," and far to the west the residents of Pittsburgh favored ratification.[51] A hopeful letter written the next spring reviewed Antifederal gains in Pennsylvania, but admitted that the town of Carlisle had many Federalists and that Lancaster was Federal; Northampton and Easton also approved of their delegates' vote for ratification.[52]

In New York City a few former leaders of the Sons of Liberty days, headed by General John Lamb, tried to organize the artisans as of old; but even Governor Clinton could get only 134 votes; Federalists polled well over 90 per cent of the votes cast in the city. Moreover they carried the city of Albany, at a time when all of the upstate counties were lost, and were victorious in Lansingburgh and Hudson too.[53] In Rhode Island there were only two towns with more than a thousand inhabitants, and in these the Antifederalists managed to poll exactly twelve votes. The mass meeting of the Boston mechanics to hail the Constitution has been previously noted, and other Massachusetts towns with populations of over nine hundred favored ratification, twenty-four to four. Portsmouth, Dover, and other large New Hampshire towns were centers of Federalist strength. Indeed in the entire United States there was scarcely a town that was not Federal.[54] Was this perhaps due to the absence of any class conflict during this period? Far from it; throughout the 1780's there were numerous clashes within the cities along class lines. The history of Charleston, for example, reveals important internal disputes. But there was no such contest between urban classes over the ratification of the Constitution.

If urban classes were not divided, was there not a class division implicit in a sectional alignment over the Constitution? This thesis, which was most fully developed by Libby, set east versus west, or, to be more accurate, seacoast versus backcountry. Libby's protagonists were the debtor areas of the interior and the creditor, mercantile centers near the coast. Emphasizing the issues which separated the two general regions, he stressed the correlation between Antifederalism and paper money as a proof of his hypothesis.

This interpretation has much truth. There had most certainly been just such a division all during the colonial period, and it continued to be of great importance for many decades. There is an abundance of evidence to support this explanation; as a matter of fact, the contrast between seacoast and interior was in some cases even more marked than Libby believed. The strength of Antifederalism was greater in upstate New York and backcountry South Carolina than he appreciated, and he did not fully exploit the possibilities of Rhode Island or of Maine. It is also true, as he contended, that paper money was a factor in the contest. In Massachusetts, towns opposing paper were Federal by about four to one, while pro-paper money towns were Antifederal by an even wider margin.[55] The hard (or less soft) money towns in New Hampshire were Federal; most of the Antifederal strength in Connecticut was found in paper money districts; and the case of Rhode Island is sufficiently familiar. In New York it was the Clinton party which favored bills of credit in 1784, 1785, and 1786. Delegates from the Federal counties of New York, Kings, and Richmond, had voted against such issues; and when Suffolk and Queens counties finally changed sides and voted for ratification, they joined long-time allies on the paper money question. The same was true of the individuals involved: New York's Federalists had opposed paper money, whereas Antifederal members of the convention had voted for it, twenty-one to eleven; of the eleven Antifederalists who had opposed paper money, no less than seven were among those who ultimately changed sides on the Constitution or refrained from voting. Thus the advocates of hard money drew together in support of the Constitution. In Maryland and in Virginia the paper money forces opposed ratification. This was also the case in North Carolina, while in South Carolina, Antifederal strength lay in the backcountry, which had favored inflation.

.   .   .

When a question so complex as the ratification of the Constitution is examined, it is to be expected that any generalization will be surrounded by exceptions. If too much attention is devoted to these exceptions, the generalization may become obscured or disguised, if not entirely hidden, so that one may even be mistaken for the other. On the other hand, if the over-all view is to be successfully maintained, and the generalization proved valid, the exceptions must be account-ed for. In the case we are considering, it would be too much to contend that the division between commercial and non-commercial elements entirely accounts for the alignment over the Constitution, and even when it is added that a division along class lines is also evident, much remains unexplained.

Along the great arc of the frontier, for example, were two areas which were Federal because of their peculiar circumstances. These are, first, backcountry Georgia, which wanted protection from the Indians, and second, a region includ-ing West Virginia, the Shenandoah Valley, and western Pennsylvania, which hoped that a strong central government could drive out the British and Indians. In these areas, military and diplomatic considerations, rather than socio-economic factors, determined a preference for the Constitution. There were also several instances in which the influence of prominent local leaders brought Federalism to unlikely spots. Such was probably the case in northern New Hampshire, Hunting-don and Luzerne counties in Pennsylvania, and parts of Berkshire County in Massachusetts. Another exceptional instance is the strength of Federalism in the interior of Connecticut, which is especially surprising when contrasted with the Antifederalism of Rhode Island; the reasons are to be found in the quite different economic, political, and perhaps even cultural backgrounds of the two areas.[56]

The magnitude of the Antifederalists' victory in New York and their quick defeat in Pennsylvania are equally puzzling; the Hudson was a great commercial highway which should have recruited strength for Federalism in the interior, whereas much of the Quaker state was backcountry and should have adhered to Antifederalism. Here the major explanation lies in contrasting political trends in the two states. In Pennsylvania, the conservative Republicans were increasing in strength, whereas in New York the Clintonian party had governed so successfully that it had never lost control. Special circumstances, like those we have already noted, governed the situation in other states, such as New Jersey, Delaware, and Maryland.

But after all of these facts have been taken into account, we can return to the major generalization: that the struggle over the ratification of the Constitution was primarily a contest between the commercial and non-commercial elements in the population. This is the most significant fact, to which all else is elaboration, amplification, or exception. The Federalists included the merchants and the other town dwellers, farmers depending on the major cities, and those who produced a surplus for export. The Antifederalists were primarily those who were not so concerned with, or who did not recognize a dependence upon, the mercantile community and foreign markets. Such people were often isolated from the major paths of commerce and usually were less well-to-do because they produced only enough for their own purposes. Because of this basic situation, a majority of the large property holders were Federal, but this division along class lines did not exist in the towns and not everywhere in the country. It was real enough however to find reflections in the political ideas of both sides. Because the Federalists dominated the towns and the rich valleys, they included most of the public and private creditors, great landowners, lawyers and judges, manufacturers and ship-owners, higher ranking civil and military officials, and college graduates. Although the Antifederalists derived their leadership from such men, the rank and file were men of moderate means, with little social prestige, farmers often in debt, obscure men for the most part.

Antifederalist thought was shaped by the composition and objectives of the party, but was modified by the social and political attitudes of the articulate leaders through whom it was expressed. Only a few of these leaders came from the small farmers or truly represented them. They frequently defended views somewhat less democratic than those of their constituents, and they were often out of sympathy with the economic demands of the rank and file, especially in the case of paper money and debtor relief legislation. As a result, Antifederalism as formulated by its most prominent spokesmen sometimes lacks the democratic overtones we have attributed to it.

But the democratic implication existed. As a body of political thought, Antifederalism had a background in English and American political theory long before the Constitution was drafted. Its principles were embodied in the Articles of Confederation; later they were elaborated in the controversy over the impost. Always the emphasis was on local rule and the retention of power by the people, which were democratic tenets in that age. Such a body of thought could of course be used by special interest groups; its bare political doctrine was put forth in opposition to the impost by the merchants of Rhode Island and Massachusetts. But it was always more congenial to the many than the few. Throughout the 1780's, whenever the question of sovereignty arose, the same men representing the same interests rehearsed the arguments they were to employ in debating the Constitution. Although the Antifederalist position was employed to mask special interests, it was fundamentally anti-aristocratic; whoever used its arguments had to speak in terms which implied, if they did not clearly define, a democratic content. It was therefore peculiarly congenial to those who were tending toward democracy, most of whom were soon to rally around Jefferson. The Antifederalists, who lost their only major battle, are forgotten while the victors are remembered, but it is not so certain which is the more memorable.

Notes

1. Quoted in Thomas Perkins Abernethy, *Western Lands and the American Revolution* (New York, 1937), 305.
2. Elliot, ed., *Debates*, III, 140; Richard Henry Lee in Paul Leicester Ford, ed., *Pamphlets on the Constitution of the United States* (Brooklyn, N.Y., 1888), 295.
3. To George Washington, June 27, 1786, in Henry P. Johnston, ed., *The Correspondence and Public Papers of John Jay*, 4 vols. (New York, 1890–1893), III, 205; Melancton Smith in Elliot, ed., *Debates*, II, 248; "Sydney," in Paul Leicester Ford, ed., *Essays on the Constitution of the United States* (Brooklyn, N.Y., 1892), 307.
4. For example, John Lloyd, quoted in Ulrich B. Phillips, "The South Carolina Federalists, I," *American Historical Review*, 14 (1908–1909), 537; Robert Livingston, quoted in E. Wilder Spaulding, *New York in the Critical Period, 1783–1789* (New York, 1932), 146–47.
5. November 25, 1775 in Edmund Cody Burnett, ed., *Letters of Members of the Continental Congress*, 8 vols. (Washington, 1921–1936), I, 260.
6. Ernest F. Brown, *Joseph Hawley, Colonial Radical* (New York, 1931), 55.
7. Samuel Osgood to John Adams, December 7, 1783, Burnett, ed., *Letters*, VII, 378; Peter Tappen to George Clinton, Sept. 29, 1787, Clinton Papers, Bancroft Transcripts, New York Public. Library; *Maryland Journal and Baltimore Advertise*, May 16, 1788; Louis B. Wright and Marion Tinling, eds., *Quebec to Caroline in 1785–1786. Being the Travel Diary and Observations of Robert Hunter, Jr., a Young Merchant of London* (San Marino, Calif., 1943), 119.
8. James M. Hughes to General Gates, November 20, 1787, Emmett Coll., No. H, New York Public Library; Edmund Pendleton in Elliot, ed., *Debates*, III, 295; William Findley in McMaster and Stone, *Pennsylvania and the Constitution*, 778; Aedanus Burke, quoted in Charles Gregg Singer, *South Carolina in the Confederation* (Philadelphia, 1941), 32.
9. This material on social structure is drawn from a wide variety of sources. Especially worth noting are the tax records for North Carolina, available on microfilm as listed in William S. Jenkins and Lillian A. Hamrick, eds., *Guide to the Microfilm Collection of Early State Records* (Washington, 1950), 73–74; discussion and sources cited in Jackson Turner Main, "The Distribution of Property in Post-Revolutionary Virginia," *Mississippi Valley Historical Review*, 41 (1954–55), 241–58, and "The One Hundred," *William and Mary Quarterly*, 3rd Ser., 11 (1954), 354–84; Francis G. and Phyllis May Morris, "Economic Conditions in North Carolina about 1780," *North Carolina Historical Review*, 16 (1939), 107–33, 296–327; Charles A. Barker, *The Background of the Revolution in Maryland* (New Haven, 1940), Appendix I; Chilton Williamson, "The Connecticut Property Test and the East Guilford Voter: 1800," Connecticut Historical Society, *Bulletin*, 19 (1954), 101–4; Stella Sutherland, *Population Distribution in Colonial America* (New York, 1936); United States Bureau of the Census, *A Century of Population Growth from the first census of the United States to the twelfth, 1790–1900* (Washington, 1909); Evarts B. Greene and Virginia D. Harrington, *American Population before the Federal Census of 1790* (New York, 1932).
10. What percentage of the men could vote is a moot point. In the South, where it was usually necessary to own land, about half were disenfranchised, but in New England probably between 60 and 90 per cent had the suffrage. At present not enough research has been done. See A.E. McKinley, *The Suffrage Franchise in the Thirteen English Colonies in America* (Philadelphia, 1905); Charles S. Sydnor, *Gentlemen Freeholders: Political Practices in Washington's Virginia* (Chapel Hill, 1952); Robert E. Brown, *Middle-Class*

Democracy and the Revolution in Massachusetts, 1691–1780 (Ithaca, 1955); Richard P. McCormick, *Experiment in Independence: New Jersey in the Critical Period, 1783–1789* (New Brunswick, 1950); Williamson, "Connecticut Property Test," Connecticut Historical Society, *Bulletin*, 19 (1954).

11. Tax lists cited in *n*. 9, above.

12. Douglas S. Robertson, ed., *An Englishman in America in 1785 being the Diary of Joseph Hadfield* (Toronto, 1933), 219; Wright and Tinling, eds., *Quebec to Caroline*, 127–28.

13. John G. Metcalf, *Annals of the Town of Mendon, from 1659 to 1880* (Providence, 1880), 432.

14. Williamson, "Connecticut Property Test," Connecticut Historical Society, *Bulletin*, 19 (1954), 103.

15. The extent of rural indebtedness is suggested by a recent article which indicates that Virginians of the Piedmont owed a good deal of money to Scotch merchants. See Jacob M. Price, "The Rise of Glasgow in the Chesapeake Tobacco Trade, 1707–1775," *William and Mary Quarterly.*, 3rd Ser., 11 (1954), 179–99. That land was hard to obtain, as a freehold, in the longer settled parts of New York, is made clear by the article of E. Marie Becker, "The 801 Westchester County Freeholders of 1763," New York Historical Society, *Quarterly*, 35 (1951), 283–321.

16. [Thomas Gordon and John Trenchard], *Cato's Letters: or, Essays on Liberty, Civil, and Religious, and other important Subjects*, 4 vols., 5th Ed. (London, 1748).

17. Arthur M. Schlesinger, *Prelude to Independence* (New York, 1958), 96, 137. Among those who consulted "Cato" were Joseph Hawley, Benjamin Franklin, Josiah Quincy, Jr., John Adams, and Thomas Jefferson. Brown, *Hawley*, 93; Sidney Kobre, *The Development of the Colonial Newspaper* (Pittsburgh, 1944), 32; Caroline Robbins, "Algernon Sidney's *Discourses Concerning Government*: Textbook of Revolution," *William and Mary Quarterly.*, 3rd Ser., 4 (1947), 269–70; H. Trevor Colbourn, "Thomas Jefferson's Use of the Past," *ibid.*, 15 (1958), 65.

18. James Burgh, *Political Disquisitions; or, an Enquiry into public Errors, Defects, and Abuses. Illustrated by, and established upon Facts and Remarks, extracted from a Variety of Authors, Ancient and Modern*, 3 vols. (Philadelphia, 1775). Caroline Robbins has discussed the English Whig background of political thought in *The Eighteenth-Century Commonwealthman* (Cambridge, Mass., 1959).

19. Burgh, *Disquisitions*, I, 106.

20. *Ibid.*, II, 36, 230.

21. *Ibid.*, III, 311.

22. *Ibid.*, I, 260, III, 82. See also on power, [Gordon and Trenchard], *Cato's Letters*, I, 184, 225, II, 233, III, 80–81, IV, 82; Burgh, *Disquisitions*, I, 112 (where he refers to Harrington).

23. To Elbridge Gerry, April 23, 1784, in Harry Alonzo Cushing, ed., *The Writings of Samuel Adams*, 4 vols. (New York, 1904–1908), IV, 302; to John Winthrop, December 21, 1778, Burnett, ed., *Letters*, III, 545.

24. To Charles Tillinghast, March 7, 1787, John Lamb Papers, New York Historical Society. See also, for example, "Cassius," In the *Hudson Weekly Gazette* (N.Y.), Dec. 14, 1786.

25. [Gordon and Trenchard], *Cato's Letters*, I, 156, 177–79, II, 85, 88.

26. Quoted in Ralph Volney Harlow, *Samuel Adams* (New York, 1923), 281.

27. [Gordon and Trenchard], *Cato's Letters*, I, 113, III, 161, 207. See also III, 151. The authors note the necessity of a law prohibiting entail.

28. James Harrington, *The Commonwealth of Oceana*, ed. Henry Morley (London, 1887), 64. See also Robbins, *Commonwealthman*, 38–39, 190–92, 207–8, 353.

29. To the Freeholders of Stafford County, June 10, 1783, in Kate Mason Rowland,

The Life of George Mason, 2 vols. (New York, 1892), II, 53. Thomson Mason was the father of Stevens Thomson Mason and the brother of George Mason.

30. *Middlesex Gazette* (Middletown, Conn.), June 18, 1787. Welton, who was speaking in the House of Representatives, came from Woodbridge, a town which opposed the Constitution. He was an advocate of paper money.

31. Reed to Anthony Wayne, June 13, 1781, in John F. Roche, *Joseph Reed: A Moderate in the American Revolution* (New York, 1957), 187; Warren to Edmund Dana, March 19, 1766, Richard Frothingham, *Life and Times of Joseph Warren* (Boston, 1865), 20–21. On the relation between power and property and democracy, see also "A Spartan," *New York Packet and American Advertiser*, February 16, 1786; petition of Albemarle County, November 3, 1787, *William and Mary Quarterly*, 2nd Ser., 2 (1922), 213–216; Samuel Adams to Elbridge Gerry, September 9, 1783, in Cushing, ed., *Writings of Adams*, IV, 287; John Francis Mercer in Worthington Chauncey Ford, ed., *Journals of the Continental Congress, 1774–1789*, 34 Vols. (Washington, 1904–1937), XXV, 916; James Otis, *The Rights of the British Colonies Asserted and Proved* (Boston, 1764), 8; Philadelphia convention of 1776 and Mecklenburg instructions of 1776 quoted in Elisha P. Douglass, *Rebels and Democrats* (Chapel Hill, 1955), 226, 127; *Hampshire Herald: Or, Weekly Advertiser* (Springfield), May 7, 1785; *Cumberland Gazette* (Falmouth, Maine), June 8, 1786; "Brutus," in the *Boston Gazette*, April 2, 1787. At an earlier date Governor Tryon of New York had seen the same point and advocated large grants as a means of preventing democracy. Virginia D. Harrington, *New York Merchants on the Eve of the Revolution* (New York, 1935), 142. The success of his policy caused a New Yorker later to regret the separation of Vermont, for had that not occurred he saw that the "Democratic Spirit" would have been strengthened against the aristocracy which, he recognized, had resulted from an unequal distribution of property. Chilton Williamson, *Vermont in Quandary: 1763–1825* (Montpelier, 1949), 67. For an extremely interesting discussion of the economic basis of politics, see "The Free Republican" in the *Boston Magazine*, August 1784, 420–23.

32. Burgh, *Disquisitions*, I, 83, 87; McMaster and Stone, *Pennsylvania and the Constitution*, 776.

33. [Gordon and Trenchard], *Cato's Letters*, II, 240; see also Burgh, *Disquisitions*, I, 175–76.

34. Francis Newton Thorpe, comp., *The Federal and State Constitutions, Colonial Charters, and other Organize Laws of the States, Territories, and Colonies Now or Heretofore Forming the United States of America*, 7 vols. (Washington, 1909), V, 3087.

35. [Gordon and Trenchard], *Cato's Letters*, III, 12–14; Burgh, *Disquisitions*, I, 116.

36. Resolutions of Oct. 4, 1776, in Harlow, *Adams*, 282–83. See also, for example, the *Cumberland Gazette* (Falmouth), May 11, 1786.

37. Quoted in Douglass, *Rebels and Democrats*, 207. For other objections to property qualifications for the governor in Massachusetts, see Samuel Eliot Morison, "The Struggle over the Adoption of the Constitution of Massachusetts, 1780," Massachusetts Historical Society, *Proceedings*, 50 (1916–1917), 385. Most of the towns mentioned were Antifederal.

38. Instructions to Thomas Burke, in Elisha P. Douglass, "Thomas Burke, Disillusioned Democrat," *North Carolina Historical Review*, 26 (1949), 160; Richard Francis Upton, *Revolutionary New Hampshire* (Hanover, 1936), 184, 190; Peter Force, ed., *American Archives . . . a Documentary History of . . . the North American Colonies*, 4th Ser., 6 vols. (Washington, 1837–53), V, 1119; discussion and references given in Merrill Jensen, "Democracy and the American Revolution," *Huntington Library Quarterly*, 20 (1957), 328–38.

39. See especially "Atticus," quoted in Harding, *Ratification in Massachusetts*, 11. East gives many commentaries on this fact. "Massachusetts Conservatives," Morris, ed.,

Era of the American Revolution.

40. Quoted in Bates, *Rhode Island and the Union*, 158.

41. In addition to previous citations see "A Citizen of America," in the *Daily Advertiser* (N.Y.), copied in the *Columbian Herald* (Charleston), March 24, 1788.

42. *Maryland Journal* (Baltimore), May 16, 1788.

43. Especially "Agrarius," in the *Independent Gazetteer* (Phila.), February 29, 1788; "Lycurgus," in *ibid.*, October 17, 1787; "John Humble," in *ibid.*, October 29, 1787; "Rusticus," in the *New York Journal*, September 13, 1787.

44. By available I mean available to me, but this means fairly complete information in states where Antifederalism existed, and exhaustive research would probably not change the generalization. Specific figures for members of the ratifying conventions are, generals, 30–12, colonels, 70–37, majors, 28–13.

45. Among 209 delegates to Congress living in 1788 whose attitude is known, 161 favored ratification from the start, and 9 more joined them eventually. The political ideas of about half of the senators are not known, but although further research may add a few, the generalizations will remain. The figures below include among the Federalists those who started as Antifederalists and then changed.

	Federal	*Antifederal*
wealthy	98	22
well-to-do	83	45
moderate means	28	39
unknown wealth	11	6
Total	220	112

46. Since my research was directed primarily toward discovering Antifederalists, the error here, if it exists, probably lies in understating the proportion of wealthy Federalists. The exact figures are: Federalists, 209, Antifederalists, 79, of whom 6 changed sides. Where exact figures concerning property were available the standard for admission into this class was 50 slaves and 5,000 acres, or the equivalent, or an estate valued at £10,000. "Well-to-do" indicates an estate of £2,000. Usually it was necessary to rely on general statements in biographies, genealogies, or local histories; their tendency to exaggerate was allowed for. The union of rich men in support of the Constitution was more striking in the North (nearly 80 per cent) than in the South (barely 70 per cent). The only state in which the division was nearly equal was North Carolina. If *all* the states were included, then it would surely be safe to say that well over three-fourths of the economic elite were Federalists.

47. Again I am indebted to the work of E. James Ferguson. Detailed research into the question of private debts and into the distribution of other types of property is essential. Until this is done, all generalizations must remain tentative.

48. See also Phillips, "South Carolina Federalists," *Am. Hist. Rev.*, 14 (1908–1909), 542.

49. Monroe to Madison, Fredericksburgh, Feb. 7, 1788, Hamilton, ed., *Writings of Monroe*, I, 181; *Pa. Packet* (Phila.), Oct. 18, Nov. 6, 1787; Hart, *Valley of Virginia*, 172–73.

50. Crowl, *Maryland During the Revolution*, 165.

51. Konkle, *Bryan*, 305; *Pa. Packet* (Phila.), Dec. 13, 1787; *Pittsburgh Gazette*, *passim.*

52. *N.Y. Journal*, Apr. 18, 1788; *Pa. Packet* (Phila.), Jan. 3, 31, 1788.

53. Spaulding, *New York in the Critical Period*, 9, 220, 228–29.

54. Excluding, of course, the rural New England towns.

55. Based on scattered sources. Pro-paper money towns cast only 3 votes for and 22

votes against ratification; anti-paper money towns favored ratification 29 to 7.

56. Connecticut and Rhode Island did not share quite the same cultural background: orthodox Congregationalism and Episcopalianism in Connecticut exerted a different influence than the more heterodox faiths of Rhode Island. Economically, the farmers of Connecticut seem to have been more prosperous than those of Rhode Island. In Rhode Island, the great anti-impost feeling stimulated by the merchants had predisposed opinion against the Constitution. The merchants, who were changing their minds about centralization, secured political power in 1786, but passed some unpopular measures and were promptly repudiated with resultant loss of prestige. In Connecticut, on the other hand, the future Federalists managed to retain the respect of the majority. In Rhode Island the commercial towns were therefore left isolated, whereas they had much backcountry support in Connecticut.

The Address and Reasons of Dissent of the Minority of the Convention of Pennsylvania to Their Constituents

The Pennsylvania dissenters included several men closely associated with the remarkably democratic Pennsylvania Constitution of 1776. Their story is one of having been subjected to physical coercion to produce and maintain the necessary quorum of members of the legislature, in order that the body could issue the required call for a ratifying convention. Their rejection of the new Constitution was also quite substantive, having to do with the lack of a bill of rights and what they saw as inevitable centralizing potential. It was published in the Pennsylvania Packet and Daily Advertiser *on 18 December 1787.*

It was not until after the termination of the late glorious contest, which made the people of the United States, an independent nation, that any defect was discovered in the present confederation. It was formed by some of the ablest patriots in America. It carried us successfully through the war; and the virtue and patriotism of the people, with their disposition to promote the common cause, supplied the want of power in Congress.

The requisition of Congress for the five *per cent* impost was made before the peace, so early as the first of February, 1781, but was prevented taking effect by the refusal of one state; yet it is probable every state in the union would have agreed to this measure at that period, had it not been for the extravagant terms in which it was demanded. The requisition was new moulded in the year 1783, and accompanied with an additional demand of certain supplementary funds for 25 years. Peace had now taken place, and the United States found themselves labouring under a considerable foreign and domestic debt, incurred during the war. The requisition of 1783 was commensurate with the interest of the debt, as it was then calculated; but it has been more accurately ascertained since that time. The domestic debt has been found to fall several millions of dollars short of the calculation, and it has lately been considerably diminished by large sales of the western lands. The states have been called on by Congress annually for supplies until the general system of finance proposed in 1783 should take place.

It was at this time that the want of an efficient federal government was first complained of, and that the powers vested in Congress were found to be inadequate to the procuring of the benefits that should result from the union. The impost was granted by most of the states, but many refused the supplementary funds; the annual requisitions were set at nought by some of the states, while others complied with them by legislative acts, but were tardy in their payments, and Congress found themselves incapable of complying with their engagements, and supporting the federal government. It was found that our national character was sinking in the opinion of foreign nations. The Congress could make treaties of commerce, but could not enforce the observance of them. We were suffering from the restrictions of foreign nations, who had shackled our commerce, while we were unable to retaliate; and all now agreed that it would be advantageous to the union to enlarge the powers of Congress; that they should be enabled in the amplest manner to regulate commerce, and to lay and collect duties on the imports throughout the United States. With this view a convention was first proposed by Virginia, and finally recommended by Congress for the different states to appoint deputies to meet in convention, "for the purposes of revising and amending the present articles of confederation, so as to make them adequate to the exigencies of the union." This recommendation the legislatures of twelve states complied with so hastily as not to consult their constituents on the subject; and though the different legislatures had no authority from their constituents for the purpose, they probably apprehended the necessity would justify the measure; and none of them extended their ideas at that time further than "revising and amending the present articles of confederation." Pennsylvania by the act appointing deputies expressly confined their powers to this object; and though it is probable that some of the members of the assembly of this state had at that time in contemplation to annihilate the present confederation, as well as the constitution of Pennsylvania, yet the plan was not sufficiently matured to communicate it to the public.

The majority of the legislature of this commonwealth, were at that time under the influence of the members from the city of Philadelphia. They agreed that the deputies sent by them to convention should have no compensation for their services, which determination was calculated to prevent the election of any member who resided at a distance from the city. It was in vain for the minority to attempt electing delegates to the convention, who understood the circumstances, and the feelings of the people, and had a common interest with them. They found a disposition in the leaders of the majority of the house to chuse themselves and some of their dependants. The minority attempted to prevent this by agreeing to vote for some of the leading members, who they knew had influence enough to be appointed at any rate, in hopes of carrying with them some respectable citizens of Philadelphia, in whose principles and integrity they could have more confidence; but even in this they were disappointed, except in one member: the eighth member was added at a subsequent session of the assembly.

The Continental convention met in the city of Philadelphia at the time appointed. It was composed of some men of excellent characters; of others who were more remarkable for their ambition and cunning, than their patriotism; and of some who had been opponents to the independence of the United States. The delegates from Pennsylvania were, six of them, uniform and decided opponents to the constitution of this commonwealth. The convention sat upwards of four months. The doors were kept shut, and the members brought under the most solemn engagements of secrecy.[1] Some of those who opposed their going so far beyond their powers, retired, hopeless, from the convention, others had the firmness to refuse signing the plan altogether; and many who did sign it, did it not as a system they wholly approved, but as the best that could be then obtained, and notwithstanding the time spent on this subject, it is agreed on all hands to be a work of haste and accommodation.

Whilst the gilded chains were forging in the secret conclave, the meaner instruments of despotism without, were busily employed in alarming the fears of the people with dangers which did not exist, and exciting their hopes of greater advantages from the expected plan than even the best government on earth could produce.

The proposed plan had not many hours issued forth from the womb of suspicious secrecy, until such as were prepared for the purpose, were carrying about petitions for people to sign, signifying their approbation of the system, and requesting the legislature to call a convention. While every measure was taken to intimidate the people against opposing it, the public papers teemed with the most violent threats against those who should dare to think for themselves, and *tar and feathers* were liberally promised to all those who would not immediately join in supporting the proposed government be it what it would. Under such circumstances petitions in favour of calling a convention were signed by great numbers in and about the city, before they had leisure to read and examine the system, many of whom, now they are better acquainted with it, and have had time to investigate its principles, are heartily opposed to it. The petitions were speedily handed into the legislature.

Affairs were in this situation when on the 28th of September last a resolution was proposed to the assembly by a member of the house who had been also a member of the federal convention, for calling a state convention, to be elected within *ten* days for the purpose of examining and adopting the proposed constitution of the United States, though at this time the house had not received it from Congress. This attempt was opposed by a minority, who after offering every argument in their power to prevent the precipitate measure, without effect, absented themselves from the house as the only alternative left them, to prevent the measure taking place previous to their constituents being acquainted with the business—That violence and outrage which had been so often threatened was now practised; some of the members were seized the next day by a mob collected for the purpose, and forcibly dragged to the house, and there detained by force whilst the quorum of the legislature, *so formed*, compleated their resolution. We shall dwell no longer on this subject, the people of Pennsylvania have been already acquainted therewith. We would only further observe that every member of the legislature, previously to taking his seat, by solemn oath or affirmation, declares, "that he will not do or consent to any act or thing whatever that shall have a tendency to lessen or abridge their rights and privileges, as declared in the constitution of this state." And that constitution which they are so solemnly sworn to support cannot legally be altered but by a recommendation of a council of censors, who alone are authorised to propose alterations and amendments, and even these must be published at least *six months*, for the consideration of the people. —The proposed system of government for the United States, if adopted, will alter and may annihilate the constitution of Pennsylvania; and therefore the legislature had no authority whatever to recommend the calling a convention for that purpose. This proceeding could not be considered as binding on the people of this commonwealth. The house was formed by violence, some of the members composing it were detained there by force, which alone would have vitiated any proceedings, to which they were otherwise competent; but had the legislature been legally formed, this business was absolutely without their power.

In this situation of affairs were the subscribers elected members of the convention of Pennsylvania. A convention called by a legislature in direct violation of their duty, and composed in part of members, who were compelled to attend for that purpose, to consider of a constitution proposed by a convention of the United States, who were not appointed for the purpose of framing a new form of government, but whose powers were expressly confined to altering and amending the present articles of confederation. —Therefore the members of the continental convention in proposing the plan acted as individuals, and not as deputies from Pennsylvania.[2] The assembly who called the state convention acted as individuals, and not as the legislature of Pennsylvania; nor could they or the convention chosen on their recommendation have authority to do any act or thing, that can alter or annihilate the constitution of Pennsylvania (both of which will be done by the new constitution) nor are their proceedings in our opinion, at all binding on the people.

The election for members of the convention was held at so early a period and the want of information was so great, that some of us did not know of it until after it was over, and we have reason to believe that great numbers of the people of Pennsylvania have not yet had an opportunity of sufficiently examining the proposed constitution. —We apprehend that no change can take place that will affect the internal government or constitution of this commonwealth, unless a majority of the people should evidence a wish for such a change; but on examining the number of votes given for members of the present state convention, we find that of upwards of *seventy thousand* freemen who are entitled to vote in Pennsylvania, the whole convention has been elected by about *thirteen thousand* voters, and though *two thirds* of the members of the convention have thought proper to ratify the proposed constitution, yet those *two thirds* were elected by the votes of only *six thousand and eight hundred* freemen.

In the city of Philadelphia and some of the eastern counties, the junto that took the lead in the business agreed to vote for none but such as would solemnly promise to adopt the system *in toto*, without exercising their judgment. In many of the counties the people did not attend the elections as they had not an opportunity of judging of the plan. Others did not consider themselves bound by the call of a set of men who assembled at the statehouse in Philadelphia, and assumed the name of the legislature of Pennsylvania; and some were prevented from voting by the violence of the party who were determined at all events to force down the measure. To such lengths did the tools of despotism carry their outrage, that in the night of the election for members of convention, in the city of Philadelphia, several of the subscribers (being then in the city to transact your business) were grossly abused, ill-treated and insulted while they were quiet in their lodgings, though they did not interfere, nor had any thing to do with the said election, but as they apprehend, because they were supposed to be adverse to the proposed constitution, and would not tamely surrender those sacred rights, which you had committed to their charge.

The convention met, and the same disposition was soon manifested in considering the proposed constitution, that had been exhibited in every other stage of the business. We were prohibited by an express vote of the convention, from taking any question on the separate articles of the plan, and reduced to the necessity of adopting or rejecting *in toto*.—'Tis true the majority permitted us to debate on each article, but restrained us from proposing amendments.—They also determined not to permit us to enter on the minutes our reasons of dissent against any of the articles, nor even on the final question our reasons of dissent against the whole. Thus situated we entered on the examination of the proposed system of government, and found it to be such as we could not adopt, without, as we conceived, surrendering up your dearest rights. We offered our objections to the convention, and opposed those parts of the plan, which, in our opinion, would be injurious to you, in the best manner we were able; and closed our arguments by offering the following propositions to the convention.

1. The right of conscience shall be held inviolable; and neither the legislative, executive nor judicial powers of the United States shall have authority to alter, abrogate, or infringe any part of the constitution of the several states, which provide for the preservation of liberty in matters of religion.

2. That in controversies respecting property, and in suits between man and man, trial by jury shall remain as heretofore, as well in the federal courts, as in those of the several states.

3. That in all capital and criminal prosecutions, a man has a right to demand the cause and nature of his accusation, as well in the federal courts, as in those of the several states; to be heard by himself and his counsel; to be confronted with the accusers and witnesses; to call for evidence in his favor, and a speedy trial by an impartial jury of his vicinage, without whose unanimous consent, he cannot be found guilty, nor can he be compelled to give evidence against himself; and that no man be deprived of his liberty, except by the law of the land or the judgment of his peers.

4. That excessive bail ought not to be required, nor excessive fines imposed, nor cruel nor unusual punishments inflicted.

5. That warrants unsupported by evidence, whereby any officer or messenger may be commanded or required to search suspected places, or to seize any person or persons, his or their property, not particularly described, are grievous and oppressive, and shall not be granted either by the magistrates of the federal government or others.

6. That the people have a right to the freedom of speech, of writing and publishing their sentiments, therefore, the freedom of the press shall not be restrained by any law of the United States.

7. That the people have a right to bear arms for the defence of themselves and their own state, or the United States, or for the purpose of killing game; and no law shall be passed for disarming the people or any of them, unless for crimes committed, or real danger of public injury from individuals; and as standing armies in the time of peace are dangerous to liberty, they ought not to be kept up; and that the military shall be kept under strict subordination to and be governed by the civil powers.

8. The inhabitants of the several states shall have liberty to fowl and hunt in seasonable times, on the lands they hold, and on all other lands in the United States not inclosed, and in like manner to fish in all navigable waters, and others not private property, without being restrained therein by any laws to be passed by the legislature of the United States.

9. That no law shall be passed to restrain the legislatures of the several states from enacting laws for imposing taxes, except imposts and duties on goods imported or exported, and that no taxes, except imposts and duties upon goods imported and exported, and postage on letters shall be levied by the authority of Congress.

10. That the house of representatives be properly increased in number; that elections shall remain free; that the several states shall have power to regulate the elections for senators and representatives, without being controuled either directly or indirectly by any interference on the part of the Congress; and that elections of representatives be annual.

11. That the power of organizing, arming and disciplining the militia (the manner of disciplining the militia to be prescribed by Congress) remain with the individual states, and that Congress shall not have authority to call or march any of the militia out of their own state, without the consent of such state, and for such length of time only as such state shall agree.

That the sovereignty, freedom and independency of the several states shall be retained, and every power, jurisdiction and right which is not by this constitution expressly delegated to the United States in Congress assembled.

12. That the legislative, executive, and judicial powers be kept separate; and to this end that a constitutional council be appointed, to advise and assist the president, who shall be responsible for the advice they give, hereby the senators would be relieved from almost constant attendance; and also that the judges be made completely independent.

13. That no treaty which shall be directly opposed to the existing laws of the United States in Congress assembled, shall be valid until such laws shall be repealed, or made conformable to such treaty; neither shall any treaties be valid which are in contradiction to the constitution of the United States, or the constitutions of the several states.

14. That the judiciary power of the United States shall be confined to cases affecting ambassadors, other public ministers and consuls; to cases of admiralty and maritime jurisdiction; to controversies to which the United States shall be a party; to controversies between two or more states—between a state and citizens of different states—between citizens claiming lands under grants of different states; and between a state or the citizen thereof and foreign states, and in criminal cases, to such only as are expressly enumerated in the constitution, and that the United States in Congress assembled, shall not have power to enact laws, which shall alter the laws of descents and distribution of the effects of deceased persons, the titles of lands or goods, or the regulation of contracts in the individual states.

After reading these propositions, we declared our willingness to agree to the plan, provided it was so amended as to meet these propositions, or something similar to them; and finally moved the convention to adjourn, to give the people of Pennsylvania time to consider the subject, and determine for themselves; but these were all rejected, and the final vote was taken, when our duty to you induced us to vote against the proposed plan, and to decline signing the ratification of the same.

During the discussion we met with many insults, and some personal abuse; we were not even treated with decency, during the sitting of the convention, by the persons in the gallery of the house; however, we flatter ourselves that in contending for the preservation of those invaluable rights you have thought proper to commit to our charge, we acted with a spirit becoming freemen, and being desirous that you might know the principles which actuated our conduct, and being prohibited from inserting our reasons of dissent on the minutes of the convention, we have subjoined them for your consideration, as to you alone we are accountable. It remains with you whether you will think those inestimable privileges, which you have so ably contended for, should be sacrificed at the shrine of despotism, or whether you mean to contend for them with the same spirit that has so often baffled the attempts of an aristocratic faction, to rivet the shackles of slavery on you and your unborn posterity.

Our objections are comprised under three general heads of dissent, viz.

We dissent, first, because it is the opinion of the most celebrated writers on government, and confirmed by uniform experience, that a very extensive territory cannot be governed on the principles of freedom, otherwise than by a confederation of republics, possessing all the powers of internal government, but united in the management of their general, and foreign concerns.

If any doubt could have been entertained of the truth of the foregoing principle, it has been fully removed by the concession of *Mr. Wilson*, one of majority on this question; and who was one of the deputies in the late general convention. In justice to him, we will give his own words; they are as follows, viz. "The extent of country for which the new constitution was required, produced another difficulty in the business of the federal convention. It is the opinion of some celebrated writers, that to a small territory, the democratical; to a middling territory (as Montesquieu has termed it) the monarchial; and to an extensive territory, the despotic form of government is best adapted. Regarding then the wide and almost unbounded jurisdiction of the United States, at first view, the hand of despotism seemed necessary to controul, connect, and protect it; and hence the chief embarrassment rose. For, we know that, altho' our constituents would cheerfully submit to the legislative restraints of a free government, they would spurn at every attempt to shackle them with despotic power."—And again in another part of his speech he continues. —"Is it probable that the dissolution of the state governments, and the establishment of one *consolidated empire* would be eligible in its nature, and satisfactory to the people in its administration? I think not, as I have given reasons to shew that so extensive a territory could not be governed, connected, and preserved, but by the *supremacy of despotic power*. All the exertions of the most potent emperors of Rome were not capable of keeping that empire together, which in extent was far inferior to the dominion of America.''

We dissent, secondly, because the powers vested in Congress by this constitution, must necessarily annihilate and absorb the legislative, executive, and judicial powers of the several states, and produce from their ruins one consolidated government, which from the nature of things will be *an iron handed despotism*, as nothing short of the supremacy of despotic sway could connect and govern these United States under one government.

As the truth of this position is of such decisive importance, it ought to be fully investigated, and if it is founded to be clearly ascertained; for, should it be demonstrated, that the powers vested by this constitution in Congress, will have such an effect as necessarily to produce one consolidated government, the question then will be reduced to this short issue, viz., whether satiated with the blessings of liberty; whether repenting of the folly of so recently asserting their unalienable rights, against foreign despots at the expence of so much blood and treasure, and such painful and arduous struggles, the people of America are now willing to resign every privilege of freemen, and submit to the dominion of an absolute government, that will embrace all America in one chain of despotism; or whether they will with virtuous indignation, spurn at the shackles prepared for them, and confirm their liberties by a conduct becoming freemen.

That the new government will not be a confederacy of states, as it ought, but one consolidated government, founded upon the destruction of the several governments of the states, we shall now shew.

The powers of Congress under the new constitution, are complete and unlimited over the *purse* and the *sword*, and are perfectly independent of, and supreme over, the state governments; whose intervention in these great points is entirely destroyed. By virtue of their power of taxation, Congress may command the whole, or any part of the property of the people. They may impose what imposts upon commerce; they may impose what land taxes, poll taxes, excises, duties on all written instruments, and duties on every other article that they may judge proper; in short, every species of taxation, whether of an external or internal nature is comprised in section the 8th, of article the 1st, viz. ''The Congress shall have power to lay and collect taxes, duties, imposts, and excises, to pay the debts, and provide for the common defence and general welfare of the United States.''

As there is no one article of taxation reserved to the state governments, the Congress may monopolise every source of revenue, and thus indirectly demolish the state governments, for without funds they could not exist, the taxes, duties and excises imposed by Congress may be so high as to render it impracticable to levy further sums on the same articles; but whether this should be the case or not, if the state governments should presume to impose taxes, duties, or excises, on the same articles with Congress, the latter may abrogate and repeal the laws whereby they are imposed, upon the allegation that they interfere with the due collection of their taxes, duties or excises, by virtue of the following clause, part of section 8th, article 1st, viz. "To make all laws which shall be necessary and proper for carrying into execution the foregoing powers, and all other powers vested by this constitution in the government of the United States, or in any department or officer thereof."

The Congress might gloss over this conduct by construing every purpose for which the state legislatures now lay taxes, to be for the "*general welfare*," and therefore as of their ju[ris]diction.

And the supremacy of the laws of the United States is established by article 6th, viz. "That this constitution and the laws of the United States, which shall be made in pursuance thereof, and *all treaties* made, or which shall be made, under the authority of the United States, shall be the *supreme law* of the *land*; and *the judges in every state shall be bound thereby; any thing in the constitution or laws of any state to the contrary notwithstanding*." It has been alledged that the words "pursuant to the constitution," are a restriction upon the authority of Congress; but when it is considered that by other sections they are invested with every efficient power of government, and which may be exercised to the absolute destruction of the state governments, without any violation of even the forms of the constitution, this seeming restriction, as well as every other restriction in it, appears to us to be nugatory and delusive; and only introduced as a blind upon the real nature of the government. In our opinion, "pursuant to the constitution," will be co-extensive with the *will* and *pleasure* of Congress, which, indeed, will be the only limitation of their powers.

We apprehend that two co-ordinate sovereignties would be a solecism in politics. That therefore as there is no line of distinction drawn between the general, and state governments; as the sphere of their jurisdiction is undefined, it would be contrary to the nature of things, that both should exist together, one or the other would necessarily triumph in the fullness of dominion. However the contest could not be of long continuance, as the state governments are divested of every means of defence, and will be obliged by "the supreme law of the land" *to yield at discretion*.

It has been objected to this total destruction of the state governments, that the existence of their legislatures is made essential to the organization of Congress; that they must assemble for the appointment of the senators and president general of the United States. True, the state legislatures may be continued for some years, as boards of appointment, merely, after they are divested of every other function, but the framers of the constitution foreseeing that the people will soon be disgusted with this solemn mockery of a government without power and usefulness, have made a provision for relieving them from the imposition, in section 4th, of article 1st, viz. "The times, places, and manner of holding elections for senators and representatives, shall be prescribed in each state by the legislature thereof; *but the Congress may at any time, by law make or alter such regulations; except as to the place of chusing senators.''*

As Congress have the controul over the time of the appointment of the president general, of the senators and of the representatives of the United States, they may prolong their existence in office, for life, by postponing the time of their election and appointment, from period to period, under various pretences, such as an apprehension of invasion, the factious disposition of the people, or any other plausible pretence that the occasion may suggest; and having thus obtained life-estates in the government, they may fill up the vacancies themselves, by their controul over the mode of appointment; with this exception in regard to the senators, that as the place of appointment for them, must, by the constitution, be in the particular state, they may depute some body in the respective states, to fill up the vacancies in the senate, occasioned by death, until they can venture to assume it themselves. In this manner, may the only restriction in this clause be evaded. By virtue of the foregoing section, when the spirit of the people shall be gradually broken; when the general government shall be firmly established, and when a numerous standing army shall render opposition vain, the Congress may compleat the system of despotism, in renouncing all dependance on the people, by continuing themselves, and children in the government.

The celebrated *Montesquieu*, in his Spirit of Laws, vol. I, page 12th, says, "That in a democracy there can be no exercise of sovereignty, but by the suffrages of the people, which are their will; now the sovereigns will is the sovereign himself; the laws therefore, which establish the right of suffrage, are fundamental to this government. In fact, it is as important to regulate in a republic in what manner, by whom, and concerning what suffrages are to be given, as it is in a monarchy to know who is the prince, and after what manner he ought to govern." The *time, mode* and *place* of the election of representatives, senators and president general of the United States, ought not to be under the controul of Congress, but fundamentally ascertained and established.

The new constitution, consistently with the plan of consolidation, contains no reservation of the rights and privileges of the state governments, which was made in the confederation of the year 1778, by article the 2d, viz. "That each state retains its sovereignty, freedom and independence, and every power, jurisdiction and right, which is not by this confederation expressly delegated to the United States in Congress assembled."

The legislative power vested in Congress by the foregoing recited sections, is so unlimited in its nature; may be so comprehensive and boundless [in] its exercise, that this alone would be amply sufficient to annihilate the state governments, and swallow them up in the grand vortex of general empire.

The judicial powers vested in Congress are also so various and extensive, that by legal ingenuity they may be extended to every case, and thus absorb the state judiciaries, and when we consider the decisive influence that a general judiciary would have over the civil polity of the several states, we do not hesitate to pronounce that this power, unaided by the legislative, would effect a consolidation of the states under one government.

The powers of a court of equity, vested by this constitution, in the tribunals of Congress; powers which do not exist in Pennsylvania, unless so far as they can be incorporated with jury trial, would, in this state, greatly contribute to this event. The rich and wealthy suitors would eagerly lay hold of the infinite mazes, perplexities and delays, which a court of chancery, with the appellate powers of the supreme court in fact as well as law would furnish him with, and thus the poor man being plunged in the bottomless pit of legal discussion, would drop his demand in despair.

In short, consolidation pervades the whole constitution. It begins with an annunciation that such was the intention. The main pillars of the fabric correspond with it, and the concluding paragraph is a confirmation of it. The preamble begins with the words, ''We the people of the United States,'' which is the style of a compact between individuals entering into a state of society, and not that of a confederation of states. The other features of consolidation, we have before noticed.

Thus we have fully established the position, that the powers vested by this constitution in Congress, will effect a consolidation of the states under one government, which even the advocates of this constitution admit, could not be done without the sacrifice of all liberty.

We dissent, thirdly, Because if it were practicable to govern so extensive a territory as these United States includes, on the plan of a consolidated government, consistent with the principles of liberty and the happiness of the people, yet the construction of this constitution is not calculated to attain the object, for independent of the nature of the case, it would of itself, necessarily, produce a despotism, and that not by the usual gradations, but with the celerity that has hitherto only attended revolutions effected by the sword.

To establish the truth of this position, a cursory investigation of the principles and form of this constitution will suffice.

The first consideration that this review suggests, is the omission of a BILL OF RIGHTS, ascertaining and fundamentally establishing those unalienable and personal rights of men, without the full, free, and secure enjoyment of which there can be no liberty, and over which it is not necessary for a good government to have the controul. The principal of which are the rights of conscience, personal liberty by the clear and unequivocal establishment of the writ of *habeas corpus*, jury trial in criminal and civil cases, by an impartial jury of the vicinage or county, with the common-law proceedings, for the safety of the accused in criminal prosecutions; and the liberty of the press, that scourge of tyrants, and the grand bulwark of every other liberty and privilege; the stipulations heretofore made in favor of them in the state constitutions, are entirely superceded by this constitution.

The legislature of a free country should be so formed as to have a competent knowledge of its constituents, and enjoy their confidence. To produce these essential requisites, the representation ought to be fair, equal, and sufficiently numerous, to possess the same interests, feelings, opinions, and views, which the people themselves would possess, were they all assembled; and so numerous as to prevent bribery and undue influence, and so responsible to the people, by frequent and fair elections, as to prevent their neglecting or sacrificing the views and interests of their constituents, to their own pursuits.

We will now bring the legislature under this constitution to the test of the foregoing principles, which will demonstrate, that it is deficient in every essential quality of a just and safe representation.

The house of representatives is to consist of 65 members; that is one for about every 50,000 inhabitants, to be chosen every two years. Thirty-three members will form a quorum for doing business; and 17 of these, being the majority, determine the sense of the house.

The senate, the other constituent branch of the legislature, consists of 26 members being *two* from each state, appointed by their legislatures every six years—fourteen senators make a quorum; the majority of whom, eight, determines the sense of that body; except in judging on impeachments, or in making treaties, or in expelling a member, when two thirds of the senators present, must concur.

The president is to have the controul over the enacting of laws, so far as to make the concurrence of *two* thirds of the representatives and senators present necessary, if he should object to the laws.

Thus it appears that the liberties, happiness, interests, and great concerns of the whole United States, may be dependent upon the integrity, virtue, wisdom, and knowledge of 25 or 26 men—How unadequate and unsafe a representation! Inadequate, because the sense and views of 3 or 4 millions of people diffused over so extensive a territory comprising such various climates, products, habits, interests, and opinions, cannot be collected in so small a body; and besides, it is not a fair and equal representation of the people even in proportion to its number, for the smallest state has as much weight in the senate as the largest, and from the smallness of the number to be chosen for both branches of the legislature; and from the mode of election and appointment, which is under the controul of Congress; and from the nature of the thing, men of the most elevated rank in life, will alone be chosen. The other orders in the society, such as farmers, traders, and mechanics, who all ought to have a competent number of their best informed men in the legislature, will be totally unrepresented.

The representation is unsafe, because in the exercise of such great powers and trusts, it is so exposed to corruption and undue influence, by the gift of the numerous places of honor and emoluments at the disposal of the executive; by the arts and address of the great and designing; and by direct bribery.

The representation is moreover inadequate and unsafe, because of the long terms for which it is appointed, and the mode of its appointment, by which Congress may not only controul the choice of the people, but may so manage as to divest the people of this fundamental right, and become self-elected.

The number of members in the house of representatives *may* be encreased to one for every 30,000 inhabitants. But when we consider, that this cannot be done without the consent of the senate, who from their share in the legislative, in the executive, and judicial departments, and permanency of appointment, will be the great efficient body in this government, and whose weight and predominancy would be abridged by an increase of the representatives, we are persuaded that this is a circumstance that cannot be expected. On the contrary, the number of representatives will probably be continued at 65, although the population of the country may swell to treble what it now is; unless a revolution should effect a change.

We have before noticed the judicial power as it would effect a consolidation of the states into one government; we will now examine it, as it would affect the liberties and welfare of the people, supposing such a government were practicable and proper.

The judicial power, under the proposed constitution, is founded on the well-known principles of the *civil law*, by which the judge determines both on law and fact, and appeals are allowed from the inferior tribunals to the superior, upon the whole question; so that *facts* as well as *law*, would be re-examined, and even new facts brought forward in the court of appeals; and to use the words of a very eminent Civilian—"The cause is many times another thing before the court of appeals, than what it was at the time of the first sentence."

That this mode of proceeding is the one which must be adopted under this constitution, is evident from the following circumstances:—1st. That the trial by jury, which is the grand characteristic of the common law, is secured by the constitution, only in criminal cases. —2d. That the appeal from both *law* and *fact* is expressly established, which is utterly inconsistent with the principles of the common law, and trials by jury. The only mode in which an appeal from law and fact can be established, is, by adopting the principles and practice of the civil law; unless the United States should be drawn into the absurdity of calling and swearing juries, merely for the purpose of contradicting their verdicts, which would render juries contemptible and worse than useless. —3d. That the courts to be established would decide on all cases *of law and equity*, which is a well known characteristic of the civil law, and these courts would have conusance not only of the laws of the United States and of treaties, and of cases affecting ambassadors, but of all cases of *admiralty and maritime jurisdiction*, which last are matters belonging exclusively to the civil law, in every nation in Christendom.

Not to enlarge upon the loss of the invaluable right of trial by an unbiased jury, so dear to every friend of liberty, the monstrous expence and inconveniences of the mode of proceedings to be adopted, are such as will prove intolerable to the people of this country. The lengthy proceedings of the civil law courts in the chancery of England, and in the courts of Scotland and France, are such that few men of moderate fortune can endure the expence of; the poor man must therefore submit to the wealthy. Length of purse will too often prevail against right and justice. For instance, we are told by the learned judge *Blackstone*, that a question only on the property of an ox, of the value of *three* guineas, originating under the civil law proceedings in Scotland, after many interlocutory orders and sentences below, was carried at length from the court of sessions, the highest court in that part of Great Britain, by way of *appeal* to the house of lords, *where* the question of law and fact was finally determined. He adds, that no pique or spirit could in the court of king's bench or common pleas at Westminster, have given continuance to such a cause for a tenth part of the time, nor have cost a twentieth part of the expence. Yet the costs in the courts of king's bench and common pleas in England, are infinitely greater than those which the people of this country have ever experienced. We abhor the idea of losing the transcendant privilege of trial by jury, with the loss of which, it is remarked by the same learned author, that in Sweden, the liberties of the commons were extinguished by an aristocratic senate; and that *trial by jury* and the liberty of the people went out together. At the same time we regret the intolerable delay, the enormous expences and infinite vexation to which the people of this country will be exposed from the voluminous proceedings of the courts of civil law, and especially from the appellate jurisdiction, by means of which a man may be drawn from the utmost boundaries of this extensive country to the seat of the supreme court of the nation to contend, perhaps with a wealthy and powerful adversary. The consequence of this establishment will be an absolute confirmation of the power of the aristocratical influence in the courts of justice; for the common people will not be able to contend or struggle against it.

Trial by jury in criminal cases may also be excluded by declaring that the libeller for instance shall be liable to an action of debt for a specified sum; thus evading the common law prosecution by indictment and trial by jury. And the common course of proceeding against a ship for breach of revenue laws by information (which will be classed among civil causes) will at the civil law be within the resort of a court, where no jury intervenes. Besides, the benefit of jury trial, in cases of a criminal nature, which cannot be avoided, will be rendered of little value, by calling the accused to answer far from home; there being no provision that the trial be by a jury of the neighbourhood or county. Thus an inhabitant of Pittsburgh, on a charge of crime committed on the banks of the Ohio, may be obliged to defend himself at the side of the Delaware, and so *vice versa*. To conclude this head; we observe that the judges of the courts of Congress would not be independent, as they are not debarred from holding other offices, during the pleasure of the president and senate, and as they may derive their support in part from fees, alterable by the legislature.

The next consideration that the constitution presents, is the undue and dangerous mixture of the powers of government; the same body possessing legislative, executive, and judicial powers. The senate is a constituent branch of the legislature, it has judicial power in judging on impeachments, and in this case unites in some measure the characters of judge and party, as all the principal officers are

appointed by the president-general, with the concurrence of the senate and therefore they derive their offices in part from the senate. This may bias the judgments
of the senators and tend to screen great delinquents from punishment. And the
senate has, moreover, various and great executive powers, viz. in concurrence
with the president-general, they form treaties with foreign nations, that may
controul and abrogate the constitutions and laws of the several states. Indeed,
there is no power, privilege or liberty of the state governments, or of the people,
but what may be affected by virtue of this power. For all treaties, made by them,
are to be the ''supreme law of the land, any thing in the constitution or laws of any
state, to the contrary notwithstanding.''

And this great power may be exercised by the president and 10 senators (being
two-thirds of 14, which is a quorum of that body). What an inducement would this
offer to the ministers of foreign powers to compass by bribery *such concessions*
as could not otherwise be obtained. It is the unvaried usage of all free states,
whenever treaties interfere with the positive laws of the land, to make the
intervention of the legislature necessary to give them operation. This became
necessary, and was afforded by the parliament of Great-Britain. In consequence
of the late commercial treaty between that kingdom and France—As the senate
judges on impeachments, who is to try the members of the senate for the abuse of
this power! And none of the great appointments to office can be made without the
consent of the senate.

Such various, extensive, and important powers combined in one body of men,
are inconsistent with all freedom; the celebrated Montesquieu tells us, that
''when the legislative and executive powers are united in the same person, or in
the same body of magistrates, there can be no liberty, because apprehensions may
arise, lest the same monarch or *senate* should enact tyrannical laws, to execute
them in a tyrannical manner.''

''Again, there is no liberty, if the power of judging be not separated from the
legislative and executive powers. Were it joined with the legislative, the life and
liberty of the subject would be exposed to arbitrary controul; for the judge would
then be legislator. Were it joined to the executive power, the judge might behave
with all the violence of an oppressor. There would be an end of every thing, were
the same man, or the same body of the nobles, or of the people, to exercise those
three powers; that of enacting laws; that of executing the public resolutions; and
that of judging the crimes or differences of individuals.''

The president general is dangerously connected with the senate; his coinci-
dence with the views of the ruling junto in that body, is made essential to his
weight and importance in the government, which will destroy all independency
and purity in the executive department, and having the power of pardoning
without the concurrence of a council, he may skreen from punishment the most
treasonable attempts that may be made on the liberties of the people, when
instigated by his coadjutors in the senate. Instead of this dangerous and improper
mixture of the executive with the legislative and judicial, the supreme executive
powers ought to have been placed in the president, with a small independent

council, made personally responsible for every appointment to office or other act, by having their opinions recorded; and that without the concurrence of the majority of the quorum of this council, the president should not be capable of taking any step.

We have before considered internal taxation, as it would effect the destruction of the state governments, and produce one consolidated government. We will now consider that subject as it affects the personal concerns of the people.

The power of direct taxation applies to every individual, as congress, under this government, is expressly vested with the authority of laying a capitation or poll tax upon every person to any amount. This is a tax that, however oppressive in its nature, and unequal in its operation, is certain as to its produce and simple in its collection; it cannot be evaded like the objects of imposts or excise, and will be paid, because all that a man hath will he give for his head. This tax is so congenial to the nature of despotism, that it has ever been a favorite under such governments. Some of those who were in the late general convention from this state have long laboured to introduce a poll-tax among us.

The power of direct taxation will further apply to every individual, as congress may tax land, cattle, trades, occupations, etc. in any amount, and every object of internal taxation is of that nature, that however oppressive, the people will have but this alternative, except to pay the tax, or let their property be taken, for all resistance will be in vain. The standing army and select militia would enforce the collection.

For the moderate exercise of this power, there is no controul left in the state governments, whose intervention is destroyed. No relief, or redress of grievances can be extended, as heretofore by them. There is not even a declaration of RIGHTS to which the people may appeal for the vindication of their wrongs in the court of justice. They must therefore, implicitly obey the most arbitrary laws, as the worst of them will be pursuant to the principles and form of the constitution, and that strongest of all checks upon the conduct of administration, *responsibility to the people*, will not exist in this government. The permanency of the appointments of senators and representatives, and the controul the congress have over their election, will place them independent of the sentiments and resentment of the people, and the administration having a greater interest in the government than in the community, there will be no consideration to restrain them from oppression and tyranny. In the government of this state, under the old confederation, the members of the legislature are taken from among the people, and their interests and welfare are so inseparably connected with those of their constituents, that they can derive no advantage from oppressive laws and taxes, for they would suffer in common with their fellow citizens; would participate in the burthens they impose on the community, as they must return to the common level, after a short period; and notwithstanding every ex[er]tion of influence, every means of corruption, a necessary rotation excludes them from permanency in the legislature.

This large state is to have but ten members in that Congress which is to have the liberty, property and dearest concerns of every individual in this vast country at absolute command and even these ten persons, who are to be our only guardians; who are to supercede the legislature of Pennsylvania, will not be of the choice of the people, nor amenable to them. From the mode of their election and appointment they will consist of the lordly and high-minded; of men who will have no congenial feelings with the people, but a perfect indifference for, and contempt of them; they will consist of those harpies of power, that prey upon the very vitals; that riot on the miseries of the community. But we will suppose, although in all probability it may never be realized in fact, that our deputies in Congress have the welfare of their constituents at heart, and will exert themselves in their behalf, what security could even this afford; what relief could they extend to their oppressed constituents? To attain this, the majority of the deputies of the twelve other states in Congress must be alike well disposed; must alike forego the sweets of power, and relinquish the pursuits of ambition, which from the nature of things is not to be expected. If the people part with a responsible representation in the legislature, founded upon fair, certain and frequent elections, they have nothing left they can call their own. Miserable is the lot of that people whose every concern depends on the WILL and PLEASURE of their rulers. Our soldiers will become Janissaries, and our officers of government Bashaws; in short, the system of despotism will soon be compleated.

From the foregoing investigation, it appears that the Congress under this constitution will not possess the confidence of the people, which is an essential requisite in a good government; for unless the laws command the confidence and respect of the great body of the people, so as to induce them to support them, when called on by the civil magistrate, they must be executed by the aid of a numerous standing army, which would be inconsistent with every idea of liberty; for the same force that may be employed to compel obedience to good laws, might and probably would be used to wrest from the people their constitutional liberties. The framers of this constitution appear to have been aware of this great deficiency; to have been sensible that no dependence could be placed on the people for their support; but on the contrary, that the government must be executed by force. They have therefore made a provision for this purpose in a permanent STANDING ARMY, and a MILITIA that may be subjected to as strict discipline and government.

A standing army in the hands of a government placed so independent of the people, may be made a fatal instrument to overturn the public liberties; it may be employed to enforce the collection of the most oppressive taxes, and to carry into execution the most arbitrary measures. An ambitious man who may have the army at his devotion, may step up into the throne, and seize upon absolute power.

The absolute unqualified command that Congress have over the militia may be made instrumental to the destruction of all liberty, both public and private; whether of a personal, civil or religious nature.

First, the personal liberty of every man probably from sixteen to sixty years of age, may be destroyed by the power Congress have in organizing and governing of the militia. As militia they may be subjected to fines to any amount, levied in a military manner; they may be subjected to corporal punishments of the most disgraceful and humiliating kind, and to death itself, by the sentence of a court martial: To this our young men will be more immediately subjected, as a select militia, composed of them, will best answer the purposes of government.

Secondly, The rights of conscience may be violated, as there is no exemption of those persons who are conscientiously scrupulous of bearing arms. These compose a respectable proportion of the community in the state. This is the more remarkable, because even when the distresses of the late war, and the evident disaffection of many citizens of that description, inflamed our passions, and when every person, who was obliged to risque his own life, must have been exasperated against such as on any account kept back from the common danger, yet even then, when outrage and violence might have been expected, the rights of conscience were held sacred.

At this momentous crisis, the framers of our state constitution made the most express and decided declaration and stipulations in favour of the rights of conscience; but now when no necessity exists, those dearest rights of men are left insecure.

Thirdly, The absolute command of Congress over the militia may be destructive of public liberty; for under the guidance of an arbitrary government, they may be made the unwilling instruments of tyranny. The militia of Pennsylvania may be marched to New England or Virginia to quell an insurrection occasioned by the most galling oppression, and aided by the standing army, they will no doubt be successful in subduing their liberty and independency; but in so doing, although the magnanimity of their minds will be extinguished, yet the meaner passions of resentment and revenge will be increased, and these in turn will be the ready and obedient instruments of despotism to enslave the others; and that with an irritated vengeance. Thus may the militia be made the instruments of crushing the last efforts of expiring liberty, of riveting the chains of despotism on their fellow citizens, and on one another. This power can be exercised not only without violating the constitution, but in strict conformity with it; it is calculated for this express purpose, and will doubtless be executed accordingly.

As this government will not enjoy the confidence of the people, but be executed by force, it will be a very expensive and burthensome government. The standing army must be numerous, and as a further support, it will be the policy of this government to multiply officers in every department; judges, collectors, tax-gatherers, excisemen and the whole host of revenue officers will swarm over the land, devouring the hard earnings of the industrious. Like the locusts of old, impoverishing and desolating all before them.

We have not noticed the smaller, nor many of the considerable blemishes, but have confined our objections to the great and essential defects; the main pillars of the constitution; which we have shewn to be inconsistent with the liberty and happiness of the people, as its establishment will annihilate the state governments, and produce one consolidated government that will eventually and speedily issue in the supremacy of the despotism.

In this investigation, we have not confined our views to the interests or welfare of this state, in preference to the others. We have overlooked all local circumstances—we have considered this subject on the broad scale of the general good; we have asserted the cause of the present and future ages; the cause of liberty and mankind.

Nathaniel Breading	Robert Whitehill	Joseph Heister
John Smilie	John Reynolds	Joseph Powell
Richard Baird	Jonathan Hoge	James Martin
Adam Orth	Nicholas Lutz	William Findley
John A. Hanna	John Ludwig	John Baird
John Whitehill	Abraham Lincoln	James Edgar
John Harris	John Bishop	William Todd

The yeas and nays upon the final vote were as follows, viz.

Yeas (46)		Nays (23)
George Latimer	Thomas Campbell	John Whitehill
Benjamin Rush	Thomas Hartley	John Harris
Hilary Baker	David Grier	John Reynolds
Enoch Edwards	John Black	Robert Whitehill
Henry Wynkoop	Benjamin Pedan	Jonathan Hoge
John Barclay	John Arndt	Nicholas Lutz
Thomas Yardley	Stephen Balliott	John Ludwig
Abraham Stout	Joseph Horsefield	Abraham Lincoln
Thomas Bull	David Deshler	John Bishop
Anthony Wayne	John Hunn	Joseph Heister
William Gibbons	George Gray	James Martin
Richard Downing	Samuel Ashmead	Joseph Powell
Thomas Cheyney	William Wilson	William Findley
John Hannum	John Boyd	John Baird
Stephen Chambers	Thomas Scott	William Todd
Robert Coleman	John Nevill	James Marshall
James Wilson	John Allison	James Edgar
Thomas M'Kean	Jonathan Roberts	Nathaniel Breading
William M'Pherson	John Richards	John Smilie
Sebastian Graff	F.A. Muhlenberg	Richard Baird
John Hubley	James Morris	William Brown
Jasper Yates	Timothy Pickering	Adam Orth
Henry Slagle	Benjamin Elliot	John Andre Hannah

Philadelphia, December 12, 1787

Notes

1. The Journals of the conclave are still concealed.

2. The continental convention, in direct violation of the 13th article of the confederation, have declared, "that the ratification of nine states shall be sufficient for the establishment of this constitution, between the states so ratifying the same." —Thus has the plighted faith of the states been sported with! They had solemnly engaged that the confederation now subsisting should be inviolably preserved by each of them, and the union therey formed, should be perpetual, unless the same should be altered by mutual consent.

Richard Henry Lee
Letter from the Federal Farmer

Richard Henry Lee was one of the few aristocrats to be an early and truly democratic advocate of American independence. He worked closely with Sam Adams in the Committees of Correspondence, introduced the first version of the Declaration of Independence in the Congress in June 1776, and served several terms in the Congress before and after the Revolutionary War. He refused to serve as a delegate to the Constitutional Convention, however, and opposed ratification on the double grounds of lack of a bill of rights and inadequate democratic representation and control in the Congress.

December 31, 1787

Dear Sir:

In viewing the various governments instituted by mankind, we see their whole force reducible to two principles—the important springs which alone move the machines, and give them their intended influence and controul, are force and persuasion; by the former men are compelled, by the latter they are drawn. We denominate a government despotic or free, as the one or other principle prevails in it. Perhaps it is not possible for a government to be so despotic, as not to operate persuasively on some of its subjects: nor is it, in the nature of things, I conceive, for a government to be so free, or so supported by voluntary consent, as never to want force to compel obedience to the laws. In despotic governments one man, or a few men, independant of the people, generally make the laws, command obedience, and enforce it by the sword: one-fourth part of the people are armed, and obliged to endure the fatigues of soldiers, to oppress the others and keep them subject to the laws. In free governments the people, or their representatives, make the laws: their execution is principally the effect of voluntary consent and aid; the people respect the magistrate, follow their private pursuits, and enjoy the fruits of their labour with very small deductions for the public use.

The body of the people must evidently prefer the latter species of government; and it can be only those few who may be well paid for the part they take in enforcing despotism, that can, for a moment, prefer the former. Our true object is to give full efficacy to one principle, to arm persuasion on every side, and to render force as little necessary as possible. Persuasion is never dangerous not even in despotic governments; but military force, if often applied internally, can never fail to destroy the love and confidence, and break the spirits, of the people; and to render it totally impracticable and unnatural for him or them who govern, and yield to this force against the people, to hold their places by the peoples' elections.

I repeat my observation, that the plan proposed will have a doubtful operation between the two principles; and whether it will preponderate towards persuasion or force is uncertain.

Government must exist—If the persuasive principle be feeble, force is infallibly the next resort. The moment the laws of congress shall be disregarded they must languish, and the whole system be convulsed—that moment we must have recourse to this next resort, and all freedom vanish.

It being impracticable for the people to assemble to make laws, they must elect legislators, and assign men to the different departments of the government. In the representative branch we must expect chiefly to collect the confidence of the people, and in it to find almost entirely the force of persuasion. In forming this branch, therefore, several important considerations must be attended to. It must possess abilities to discern the situation of the people and of public affairs, a disposition to sympathize with the people, and a capacity and inclination to make laws congenial to their circumstances and condition; it must afford security against interested combinations, corruption and influence; it must possess the confidence, and have the voluntary support of the people.

I think these positions will not be controverted, nor the one I formerly advanced, that a fair and equal representation is that in which the interests, feelings, opinions and views of the people are collected, in such manner as they would be were the people all assembled. Having made these general observations, I shall proceed to consider further my principal position, viz. that there is no substantial representation of the people provided for in a government, in which the most essential powers, even as to the internal police of the country, are proposed to be lodged; and to propose certain amendments to the representative branch: 1st, That there ought to be *an increase of the numbers of representatives*: And, 2dly, That the elections of them ought to be better secured.

The representation is unsubstantial and ought to be increased. In matters where there is much room for opinion, you will not expect me to establish my positions with mathematical certainty; you must only expect my observations to be candid, and such as are well founded in the mind of the writer. I am in a field where doctors disagree; and as to genuine representation, though no feature in government can be more important, perhaps, no one has been less understood, and no one that has received so imperfect a consideration by political writers. The ephori in Sparta, and the tribunes in Rome, were but the shadow; the representation in Great-Britain is unequal and insecure. In America we have done more in establishing this important branch on its true principles, than, perhaps, all the world besides; yet even here, I conceive, that very great improvements in representation may be made. In fixing this branch, the situation of the people must be surveyed, and the number of representatives and forms of election apportioned to that situation. When we find a numerous people settled in a fertile and extensive country, possessing equality, and few or none of them oppressed with riches or wants, it ought to be the anxious care of the constitution and laws, to arrest them from national depravity, and to preserve them in their happy condition. A virtuous people make just laws, and good laws tend to preserve unchanged a virtuous people. A virtuous and happy people by laws uncongenial to their characters, may easily be gradually changed into servile and depraved creatures. Where the people, or their representatives, make the laws, it is probable they will generally be fitted to the national character and circumstances, unless the representation be partial, and the imperfect substitute of the people. However, the people may be electors, if the representation be so formed as to give one or more of the natural classes of men in the society an undue ascendancy over the others, it is imperfect; the former will gradually become masters, and the latter slaves. It is the first of all among the political balances, to preserve in its proper station each of these classes. We talk of balances in the legislature, and among the departments of government; we ought to carry them to the body of the people. Since I advanced the idea of balancing the several orders of men in a community, in forming a genuine representation, and seen that idea considered as chimerical, I have been sensibly struck with a sentence in the marquis Beccaria's treatise; this sentence was quoted by congress in 1774, and is as follows: —"In every society there is an effort continually tending to confer on one part the height of power and happiness, and to reduce the others to the extreme of weakness and misery; the intent of good laws is to oppose this effort, and to diffuse their influence universally and equally." Add to this Montesquieu's opinion, that "in a free state every man, who is supposed to be a free agent, ought to be concerned in his own government: therefore, the legislative should reside in the whole body of the people, or their representatives." It is extremely clear that these writers had in view the several orders of men in society, which we call aristocratical, democratical, merchantile, mechanic, &c. and perceived the efforts they are constantly, from interested and ambitious views, disposed to make to elevate themselves and oppress others. Each order must have a share in the business of legislation actually and efficiently. It is deceiving a people to tell them they are electors, and can chuse their legislators, if they cannot, in the nature of things, chuse men from among themselves, and genuinely like themselves. I wish you to take another idea along with you; we are not only to balance these natural efforts, but we are also to guard against accidental combinations; combinations founded in the connections of offices and private interests, both evils which are increased in proportion as the number of men, among which the elected must be, are decreased. To set this matter in a proper point of view, we must form some general ideas and descriptions of the different classes of men, as they may be divided by occupations and politically: the first class is the aristocratical. There are three kinds of aristocracy spoken of in this country—the first is a constitutional one, which does not exist in the United States in our common acceptation of the word. Montesquieu, it is true, observes, that where a part of the persons in a society, for want of property, age, or moral character, are excluded any share in the government, the others, who alone are the constitutional electors and elected, form this aristocracy; this, according to him, exists in each of the United States, where a considerable number of persons, as all convicted of crimes, under age, or not possessed of certain property, are excluded any share in the government;—the second is an aristocratic faction; a junto of unprincipled men, often distinguished for their wealth or abilities, who combine together and make their object their private interests and aggrandizement; the existence of this description is merely accidental, but particularly to be guarded against. The third is the natural aristocracy; this term we use to designate a respectable order of men, the line between whom and the natural democracy is in some degree arbitrary; we may place men on one side of this line, which others may place on the other, and in all disputes between the few and the many, a considerable number are wavering and uncertain themselves on which side they are, or ought to be. In my idea of our natural aristocracy in the United States, I include about four or five thousand men; and among these I reckon those who have been placed in the offices of governors, or members of Congress, and state senators generally, in the principal offices of Congress, of the army and militia, the superior judges, the most eminent professional men, &c. and men of large property—the other persons and orders in the community form the natural democracy; this includes in general the yeomanry, the subordinate officers, civil and military, the fishermen, mechanics and traders, many of the merchants and professional men. It is easy to perceive that men of these two classes, the aristocratical, and democratical, with views equally honest, have sentiments widely different, especially respecting public and private expences, salaries, taxes, &c. Men of the first class associate more extensively, have a high sense of honor, possess abilities, ambition, and general knowledge; men of the second class are not so much used to combining great objects; they possess less ambition, and a larger share of honesty; their dependence is principally on middling and small estates, industrious pursuits, and hard labour, while that of the former is principally on the emoluments of large estates, and of the chief offices of government. Not only the efforts of these two great parties are to be balanced, but other interests and parties also, which do not always oppress each other merely for want of power, and for fear of the consequences; though they, in fact, mutually depend on each other; yet such are their general views, that the merchants alone would never fail to make laws favourable to themselves and oppressive to the farmers, &c. the farmers alone would act on like principles; the former would tax the land, the latter the trade. The manufacturers are often disposed to contend for monopolies, buyers make every exertion to lower prices, and sellers to raise them; men who live by fees and salaries endeavour to raise them, and the part of the people who pay them, endeavour to lower them; the public creditors to augment the taxes, and the people at large to lessen them. Thus, in every period of society, and in all the transactions of men, we see parties verifying the observation made by the Marquis; and those classes which have not their centinels in the government, in proportion to what they have to gain or lose, must infallibly be ruined.

Efforts among parties are not merely confined to property; they contend for rank and distinctions; all their passions in turn are enlisted in political controversies.—Men, elevated in society, are often disgusted with the changeableness of the democracy, and the latter are often agitated with the passions of jealousy and envy; the yeomanry possess a large share of property and strength, are nervous and firm in their opinions and habits; the mechanics of towns are ardent and changeable, honest and credulous, they are inconsiderable for numbers, weight and strength, not always sufficiently stable for the supporting free governments; the fishing interest partakes partly of the strength and stability of the landed, and partly of the changeableness of the mechanic interest. As to merchants and traders, they are our agents in almost all money transactions; give activity to government, and possess a considerable share of influence in it. It has been observed by an able writer, that frugal industrious merchants are generally advocates for liberty. It is an observation, I believe, well founded, that the schools produce but few advocates for republican forms of government; gentlemen of the law, divinity, physic, &c. probably form about a fourth part of the people; yet their political influence, perhaps, is equal to that of all the other descriptions of men; if we may judge from the appointments to Congress, the legal characters will often, in a small representation, be the majority; but the more the representatives are encreased, the more of the farmers, merchants, &c. will be found to be brought into the government.

These general observations will enable you to discern what I intend by different classes, and the general scope of my ideas, when I contend for uniting and balancing their interests, feelings, opinions, and views in the legislature; we may not only so unite and balance these as to prevent a change in the government by the gradual exaltation of one part to the depression of others, but we may derive many other advantages from the combination and full representation; a small representation can never be well informed as to the circumstances of the people, the members of it must be too far removed from the people, in general, to sympathize with them, and too few to communicate with them; a representation must be extremely imperfect where the representatives are not circumstanced to make the proper communications to their constituents, and where the constituents in turn cannot, with tolerable convenience, make known their wants, circumstances, and opinions, to their representatives; where there is but one representative to 30,000 or 40,000 inhabitants, it appears to me, he can only mix, and be acquainted with a few respectable characters among his constituents, even double the federal representation, and then there must be a very great distance between the representatives and the people in general represented. On the proposed plan, the state of Delaware, the city of Philadelphia, the state of Rhode Island, the province of Maine, the county of Suffolk in Massachusetts will have one representative each; there can be but little personal knowledge, or but few communications, between him and the people at large of either of those districts. It has been observed, that mixing only the respectable men, he will get the best information and ideas from them; he will also receive impressions favourable to their purposes particularly. Many plausible shifts have been made to divert the mind from dwelling on this defective representation, these I shall consider in another place.

Could we get over all our difficulties respecting a balance of interests and party efforts, to raise some and oppress others, the want of sympathy, information and intercourse between the representatives and the people, an insuperable difficulty will still remain. I mean the constant liability of a small number of representatives to private combinations; the tyranny of the one, or the licentiousness of the multitude, are, in my mind, but small evils, compared with the factions of the few. It is a consideration well worth pursuing, how far this house of representatives will be liable to be formed into private juntos, how far influenced by expectations of appointments and offices, how far liable to be managed by the president and senate, and how far the people will have confidence in them. . . .

The Federal Farmer

3. The Contemporary Critique
Democracy Revived?

John F. Manley
Class and Pluralism in America
The Constitution Reconsidered

John F. Manley, Professor of Political Science at Stanford University, discusses the Constitution in the context of two theories that purport to explain political power in America: pluralism, which sees society as comprised of diverse groups and puts little emphasis on class, and class analysis, which sees classes as the basic fact of social life and treats groups as fractions of classes. Manley contends that the Founding Fathers understood society in class terms, and that the Constitution is best understood as a case of class conflict in American history.

The conflict between modern pluralism and Marxist class analysis permeates law, history, and the social sciences.

At times, modern pluralists are so impressed with the absence of class conflict that they speak of the *"fact* that the fundamental political problems of the industrial revolution have been solved: the workers have achieved industrial and political citizenship; the conservatives have accepted the welfare state; and the democratic left has recognized that an increase in over-all state power carries with it more dangers to freedom than solutions for economic problems" (Lipset 1963, pp. 442–43; italics added).

In less extreme versions, the prism of class is declared "too crude to follow the swift play of diverse political groups" (Bell 1961, p. 66). Modern pluralists sometimes describe democracy in America as a system of group conflicts in which "minorities rule" (Dahl 1963, p. 133). As Polsby summarizes the essential propositions:

> Pluralists, who see American society as fractured into a congeries of hundreds of small special interest groups, with incompletely overlapping memberships, widely differing power bases, and a multitude of techniques for exercising influence on decisions salient to them, are not surprised at the low priority

101

Americans give to their class memberships as bases of social action. In the decision making of fragmented government . . . it is the claims of small intense minorities that are usually attended to. Hence it is not only inefficient but usually unnecessary for entire classes to mobilize when the preferences of class members are pressed and often satisfied in piecemeal fashion. The empirical evidence supporting this pluralist doctrine is overwhelming . . . (Polsby 1980, p. 118).

This article raises questions about modern pluralism by examining the case for a class analysis of the U.S. Constitution. Evidence is presented showing that the Founding Fathers saw society in terms of class, perceived dangers from class conflict, wrestled with the contradiction between political equality and economic inequality, and devised the Constitution informed by a class analysis of the society in which they lived.

The argument begins with a look at the classic that stands at the intersection of all these issues, Charles A. Beard's *An Economic Interpretation of the Constitution*. There the Framers in general and the Father of the Constitution, James Madison, are shown to be acute students of class and class conflict. A close look at Madison's theory distinguishes his pluralism, rooted in class, from modern pluralism which denies or discounts class. Madisonian pluralism and Marxist class analysis, it is argued, give a better explanation of the Constitution than modern pluralism. Modern pluralism not only fails to explain the Constitution; it may be shown, by extension, to be inferior to and subsumed by class analysis as a general theory of American politics.

The Legacy of Charles Beard

"The thing to do is to lay a mine," Beard once told his student Raymond Moley, "store it with nitro, and then let it off in such a fashion that it rips the bowels out of something important, making it impossible for the fools to travel that way any more" (Nore 1983, p. 56).

To one so inclined, controversy was not likely to remain a stranger.

Before the appearance of J. Allen Smith's (1907) and Beard's (1913) critiques of the Constitution, the dominant historical perspective on the Founding Fathers was Bancroft's. His almost lyrical view saw the Constitution as the "sublime achievement" of a people "led by statesmen of earnestness, perseverance, and public spirit . . . warmed by the mutual love which proceeds from ancient connection, harmonious efforts in perils, and common aspirations" (Bancroft 1882, v. 1, p. 3). Generations of Americans had been taught to rank the Constitution next to the Bible. The shrill response to Beard sounded the depths of Constitution-worship in the United States. William Howard Taft led a national chorus of denunciation of Beard's book. Nicholas Murray Butler, the conservative President of Beard's home university, when asked if he had read the Columbia Professor's last book replied, "I hope so!" (Nore 1983, p. 63).

Beard's demystification of the Framers showed that they had more on their minds in Philadelphia than democracy. His argument that many also had financial stakes in the adoption of the Constitution resonated well with progressive and populist critiques of American society then in vogue (Hofstadter 1968; Smith 1907).

But Beard went further. He had been influenced by Marx, and this raised the issue of class. In 1913, improper suggestions about the Framers in a Marxist context were doubly anathema.

They still are, and that is why Beard's questions recur.

After the initial furor over Beard's book died down, the economic interpretation was widely accepted among historians for nearly fifty years (Kenyon 1966, p. xxxv). Beard continued to draw spirited criticism from constitutional scholars who felt he slighted such things as the "patriotic sincerity of the motives of the Framers" (Warren 1937, p. 5). But the most serious criticism came in the 1950s when a series of attacks appeared.

After a painstaking chapter-by-chapter attack on Beard, one critic concluded that the "Constitution was adopted in a society which was fundamentally democratic, not undemocratic," and warned future historians against beginning "with the illusion that the Beard thesis of the Constitution is valid" (Brown 1956, p. 200). Beard was faulted for violating the strictures of "scientific," value-free history. Brown argued that there were no propertyless masses excluded from voting in 1787, that practically everybody had an interest in protecting property, that the Framers believed they were writing a Constitution for a democratic society, and that Beard's analysis of the economic interests of the Framers was simply wrong (Brown 1956, pp. 194–200).

Forrest McDonald, in an even more exhaustive critique, outlined what he called a "pluralistic" study of the Constitution. Granting the economic factor some importance, he treated Beard as a value-laden economic determinist who, with unerring consistency, got almost everything about the Constitution wrong (McDonald 1958, pp. 400–17).

Political scientists Martin Diamond and John P. Roche joined the case against Beard by viewing the Framers as democrats, not class-inclined partisans. Diamond rejected the common claim that the Constitution embodied a reaction against the democratic principles of the Declaration of Independence on the grounds that the Framers believed that political authority derived from the great body of citizens (Diamond 1959, p. 54). Roche says of the Framers "not only were they revolutionaries, but also they were democrats. Indeed, . . . they were first and foremost superb democratic politicians" (Roche 1961, p. 799).

The Constitutional Convention, in his view, is best seen as a democratic reform caucus in action.

Contrary to the impression sometimes left by his critics, Beard did not present the Framers merely as venal politicians out to secure their property interests; nor did he claim that the economic factor was the only one involved in the Constitution. But in talking of "economic determinism," in tracking down the Framers' personal financial interests, in pitting finance capital, manufacturing, and commercial interests against small farmers and debtors, and in speaking of the exclusion of a large propertyless mass from influence at the Convention, he gave his critics much to attack. Parts of Beard's thesis have been confirmed by historians (Main 1961; Benson 1960), but although the thesis has not been demolished its former supremacy has been seriously impaired (Kenyon 1963, p. 327).

From the Marxist perspective, the problem with Beard's analysis goes even deeper.[1] Although Beard was influenced by Marx, the influence was slight. Ironically, had Beard been better acquainted with Marx's theory he would have avoided many of the traps that mar his analysis. He would have been more concerned, for example, with the class and structural issues of the Convention, and less concerned with the elusive financial holdings of the Framers. As Max Lerner notes:

> What was relevant was not the property *holdings* of the members of the Convention but their property *attitudes*. To be sure, their attitudes might be inferred from their holdings, but it was a roundabout procedure and one that laid Beard open to the charge of stressing the crass aspects of men's motivation. . . . Here a more Marxian approach, rather than a straight Madisonian one, would have been helpful (Lerner 1940, p. 162).

Class analysis sees society as made up of conflicting classes, groups, and individuals. At the broadest level, society is divided into those with property and those without, the haves and have-nots. Although conflict is objectively rooted in these relationships, it is prosecuted at the class level only during special, revolutionary moments. Groups and individuals operating at subclass levels are crucial to controlling the outbreak and outcome of class conflict. This view does not pit groups against class but rather sees groups as fractions of classes. Groups and classes may be more or less united or hostile. In this light, it is no surprise to see important class and group conflicts surface at Philadelphia. Nor is it surprising that the Framers see society in terms of conflicting classes and groups, a perception that underpins the Constitution. If one asks the modern pluralist question, did the Framers see society as so fractured into competitive groups that class was not a problem, the answer is no. This is precisely what the Constitution was intended to help achieve, an observation that locates the origins of the Constitution correctly in group *and* class conflict, not just the former.

The Framers' View of Society

A common historical view sees the United States of 1787 as a relatively egalitarian and homogeneous society of small farmers. There was no large industrial working class. Most white men were independent producers who worked for themselves. Land was readily available, the frontier was vast, and the democratic ethos had recently received classic expression in the Declaration of Independence.

As the Framers looked at this society, however, they did not see equality. They saw inequality, heard popular demands to change it, and acted to block these demands. Their basic model of society was conflict, not consensus; accordingly, they approached their work with resolving conflict uppermost in mind.

At least most of them did. One of the delegates, Charles Pinckney, argued the case for a consensus model, but his analysis was overwhelmingly rejected by James Madison, Alexander Hamilton, and other leaders of the Convention.

As Pinckney saw it, the United States was singular because "there are fewer distinctions of fortune and less of rank, than among the inhabitants of any other nation" (Farrand 1937, v. 1, p. 400). There were different classes in America, he acknowledged, and he even named them (landed, professional, and commercial). But because their interests were not in conflict, he concluded, a strong national government was not needed to protect the property interests of members of the upper class (Farrand 1937, v. 1, pp. 397–404, 410–412).

The day after Pinckney presented his consensus theory of American society Madison took the floor to refute it. Madison and others wanted to strengthen government to stabilize a society they saw as turbulent. They could hardly let Pinckney's argument stand unchallenged. At issue was social equality.

Madison admitted that the United States did not have hereditary distinctions of rank, nor the extremes of wealth and poverty found in Europe. But he rejected consensus as dangerously misleading. "In all civilized countries," he told the delegates, "the people fall into different classes having a real or supposed difference of interests." There are creditors and debtors, farmers, merchants, and manufacturers. "There will be particularly the distinction of rich and poor," he added. We cannot be regarded even now, he continued, as "one homogeneous mass." In the future, importantly, there will be even greater inequality. This posed a problem:

> An increase of population will of necessity increase the proportion of those who will labour under all the hardships of life, and secretly sigh for a more equal distribution of its blessings. These may in time outnumber those who are placed above the feelings of indigence. According to the equal laws of suffrage, the power will slide into the hands of the former. No agrarian attempts have yet been

made in this country, but symptoms of a levelling spirit, as we have understood, have sufficiently appeared in a certain quarters [sic] to give notice of the future danger (Farrand 1937, v. 1, pp. 422–23).

The Father of the Constitution thought the issue of class important enough to return to it later in the Convention.

Madison admitted that "the United States have not reached the stage of society in which conflicting feelings of the class with, and the class without property, have the operation natural to them in countries fully peopled." But, looking ahead, in "future times a great majority of the people will not only be without landed, but any other sort of, property." This posed a twofold danger: one, interests will either combine under the influence of their common situation, in which case the rights of property and the public liberty will be put at risk; or, two, the people will become the "tools of opulence and ambition, in which case there will be equal danger on another side" (Farrand 1937, v. 2, pp. 203–04). Madison's message was clear: inequality and property were at risk, and had to be protected, Pinckney's rosy views to the contrary notwithstanding.

No one agreed more heartily than Hamilton. Although Hamilton is usually regarded as having little influence at the Convention, his four-to-five hour speech on June 18 probably had a profound effect on his listeners. In this speech, which Gouverneur Morris declared one of the ablest he had ever heard, Hamilton drew the class lines sharply. In "every community where industry is encouraged," he said, "there will be division of it into the few and the many." Separate interests, especially that between creditors and debtors, will inevitably arise. "Give all power to the many," he warned, "they will oppress the few. Give all power to the few they will oppress the many." Which was to be feared most? He left no doubt on this question as he talked of the "violence and turbulence of the democratic spirit," and of "popular passions" that "spread like wild fire, and become irresistible [sic]" (Farrand 1937, v. 1, pp. 288–89).

As for the consensus view, Hamilton argued that nothing like equality of property existed. Indeed, he contended, as long as liberty existed, inequality would exist, for inequality "would unavoidably result from that very liberty itself." Efforts to level society were useless. He, like Madison, believed that inequality in the United States would not only exist but inevitably increase. "The difference of property is already great amongst us. Commerce and industry will still increase the disparity. Your government must meet this state of things, or combinations will . . . undermine your system" (Farrand 1937, v. 1, pp. 424, 432).

When Hamilton warned that government must deal with rising social inequality, or combinations would arise that would undermine the system, he stated the fundamental task of the Convention. He and his colleagues came to this view after years of experience with threats to property from the "people" and democratic state legislatures. The driving force behind the Convention was the widespread perception that a stronger national government was needed to bolster the ability of government to protect property from real threats.

It is true, as Beard's critics contend, that the Framers were interested in promoting national control of commerce and protecting the union from dissolution. But these objectives were not in competition with the concern for property. Indeed, national control of commerce was a way of preventing threats to property at the state and local levels, and the fear of dismemberment was related to the economic anarchy that prevailed in many states.

A sense of urgency was created by Shays's Rebellion, the latest in a long line of threats to property. This Massachusetts debtor uprising in the fall of 1786 generated fear among creditors and property owners all over the country. Madison, Washington, and others received alarming reports from such observers as Henry Lee. Lee warned Madison not to be deceived by reports of moderate aims among Shays and his followers, for they intended "the abolition of debts public and private, a division of property and a new government founded on principles of fraud and inequity, or re-connexion with G.B." (Rutland 1975, v. 9, p. 144).

Madison took the warning seriously. In November he wrote his father about the "great commotions" in Massachusetts. He said he feared an "appeal to the sword" because the discontented were said to be as numerous as the friends of government, and he relayed Lee's judgment that the rebellion sought to abolish debts and divide property (Rutland 1975, v. 9, p. 154).

Madison was not alone. On November 5, 1786, George Washington wrote him about the "impending storm." Washington quoted a letter he had received from General Knox which described Shays as believing that since the property of the United States had been secured from the British by the joint exertion of *all*, it "therefore ought to be the *common property* of all." As Washington saw it, the rebels meant to have "agrarian laws" and paper money, which were just ways of redistributing property (Rutland 1975, v. 9, pp. 161–62. Italics his).

Washington drew an important political lesson from Shays's Rebellion: want of "energy" in government was a grave threat. He warned Madison that "thirteen sovereignties pulling against each other, and all tugging at the federal head will soon bring ruin on the whole. . . ." A new liberal and energetic Constitution, he said, was needed to restore respectability (Rutland 1975, v. 9, pp. 161–62).

"Energy" in government was a favorite theme of the Federalists. It was, in fact, code for the protection of property. Madison replied to Washington that based on reports he had received the situation outside Congress was "desperate," but, on a hopeful note, the legislature had agreed to the Annapolis call for a convention and had also unanimously rejected petitions for depreciating military certificates (Rutland 1975, v. 9, p. 166). In January 1787 Madison, still alarmed by Shays, feared that "civil blood" would be shed, and cited these events as furnishing "new proofs of the necessity of such a vigour in the General Government as will be able to restore health to any diseased part of the federal body"

(Rutland 1975, v. 9, p. 231). The Convention was set for May.

Viewed from Paris, and through the special lens of Thomas Jefferson, the "late troubles in the Eastern states" did not appear too serious. It was on this occasion that Jefferson commented to Madison "that a little rebellion now and then is a good thing, and as necessary in the political world as storms in the physical" (Rutland 1975, v. 9, p. 248).

But viewed from Congress, the "spirit of insurrection," as Madison called it, was a threat to nothing less than the survival of republican government in the United States. Madison also felt that if the Convention failed to agree on some remedy the union would dissolve: "The late turbulent scenes in Massachusetts and infamous ones in Rhode Island, have done inexpressible injury to the republican character in that part of the United States. . . ." He noted a propensity toward monarchy in certain quarters but predicted that the bulk of the people "will probably prefer the lesser evil of a partition of the union into three more practicable and energetic Governments" (Rutland 1975, v. 9, p. 295). Madison opposed separation, and set out to prevent it.

Madison's allusion to Rhode Island revealed his fear of the "people." In 1786 the country or paper money party won control of the governorship and legislature in Rhode Island. It tried to force merchants and creditors to accept depreciated currency. The lower house even refused to help Massachusetts apprehend insurgents from Shays's Rebellion. Madison's fears were reinforced by reports from Virginia where, in the face of a scarcity of hard money, Virginians were cooperating against buying property sold by execution, supporting debt payments in property or on installment, and even talking about following Massachusetts's lead in preventing the courts from enforcing property laws (Rutland 1975, v. 9, p. 381). A month before the Convention Madison defined the central constitutional issue as follows:

> In republican Government the majority however composed, ultimately give the law. Whenever therefore an apparent interest or common passion unites a majority what is to restrain them from unjust violations of the rights and interests of the minority, or of individuals? (Rutland 1975, v. 9, p. 355).

The above evidence shows that the Framers did not see their society as so dominated by small group conflicts that class conflict was not a consideration. The inability of government to deal with class conflict in fact threatened the entire system. Two leaders not at the Convention, but who may nonetheless be called Founding Fathers, may also be cited here. Thomas Jefferson, one of the most democratic leaders of the day, and John Adams, one of the most elitist, for all their differences, saw society in remarkably similar, class, terms.

As Jefferson put it:

> Men by their constitution are naturally divided into two parties. First, those who fear and distrust the people, and wish to draw all powers from them into the

hands of the higher classes. Secondly, those who identify themselves with the people. . . . Call them therefore liberals and serviles, Jacobins and Ultras, whigs and tories, republicans and federalists, aristocrats and democrats . . . they are the same parties still and pursue the same object. The last appellation of aristocrats and democrats is the basic one expressing the essence of all (Foner 1944, p. 800).

Adams was even more explicit. He had a deep fear of the people (Dauer 1953, p. 39). "The moment the idea is admitted into society," he wrote, "that property is not as sacred as the laws of God, and that there is not a force of law and public justice to protect, anarchy and tyranny commence" (Adams 1971, v. 6, p. 9).

Adams noted that in every nation the great majority is usually destitute of property, and asked incredulously whether ". . . if all were to be decided by a vote of the majority, the eight or nine millions who have no property, would not think of usurping over the rights of the one or two millions who have?" (Adams 1971, v. 6, p. 8). As he saw it, "the populace, the rabble, the *canaille* move as naturally in the circle of domination, whenever they dare, as the nobles or a king; nay, although it may give pain, truth and experience force us to add, that even the middling people, when uncontrolled, have moved in the same circle; and have not only tyrannized over all above and all below, but the majority among themselves has tyrannized over the minority" (Adams 1971, v. 6, p. 10).

Adams' views are important because he spoke for one of the leading factions in America, the "Adams Federalists." But his views are also important because he articulated a view of human nature congruent with his view of society, and both were widely shared among the Founding Fathers.

The Fathers granted to all people a certain moral equality, but Adams and others scorned those who argued for egalitarian democracy. Inequality of property was rooted in inequality of ability. Take a hundred people, Adams wrote John Taylor, and make them a "democratical" republic. After a few sessions, the superior few will emerge and democracy will give way to an aristocracy of the able few. "Aristocracy was, from the beginning, now is, and ever will be, world without end, independent of all these artificial regulations. . ." (Adams 1971, v. 6, p. 457). Even if wealth were broken up and distributed equally, it would inevitably become unequal. Inequalities, he concluded, are a part of the natural history of man (Adams 1971, v. 6, p. 458).

Jefferson, the egalitarian, agreed. In a famous 1813 letter to Adams, Jefferson concurred that there was a natural aristocracy among men. Jefferson was careful to distinguish the natural aristocracy based on talent and virtue from that of the "pseudo-aristoi" of wealth and birth (Foner 1944, p. 715), but Adams had no quarrel with this distinction. The two leaders differed over such important questions as how much reliance to place on the people in distinguishing the natural from the false aristocrats, not on the basic question of inequality.

The evidence that the Framers were primarily concerned with protecting property is overwhelming, but this does not mean the voice of the ''people'' was absent from the Convention. A few delegates defended the people when they felt their colleagues veered too far in the aristocratic direction, but the single greatest restraint on aristocracy was probably fear of what the people might do if aroused.

As a delegate from conflict-torn Massachusetts, Elbridge Gerry spoke to this point with special authority. Gerry, an aristocrat who had earlier warned the Convention that the people in the east supported the ''wildest ideas of Government,'' such as abolishing the Massachusetts Senate and giving all power to the other branch, resisted pressure from Benjamin Franklin and others to sign the Constitution because he feared that it went so far in protecting property that it might provoke civil war. As Madison summed up Gerry's remarks: ''In Massachusetts, particularly he saw the danger of this calamitous event. In that State there are two parties, one devoted to Democracy, the worst he thought of all political evils, the other as violent in the opposite extreme'' (Farrand 1937, v. 2, p. 647). Gerry's fears of immediate civil war proved excessive, but his analysis of the situation clearly shows the importance of class in the thinking of the Framers.

Madison's Theory of Class

A remarkable fact about Madisonian or classical pluralism, which separates it radically from modern pluralism, is that far from being opposed to class analysis it was deeply embedded in it.

When Madison spoke to the Convention about the ''class with and the class without property,'' warning that the latter would naturally and dangerously increase in number, class considerations were obviously very much on his mind. This raises the possibility that instead of being hostile to Marxian class analysis, Madisonian pluralism may have interesting parallels in Marx. If Madison and Marx both see society as comprised of classes and fractions of classes (groups), then on this crucial point Madison may be seen as a forerunner of Marx, not an antagonist. The essential difference between them may be, as Lerner notes, more the difference between Madison's brilliant *aperçus* and Marx's more systematic theory of political economy than anything fundamental (Lerner 1940, p. 165).

Before presenting the evidence on this, it is important to note a point on which Madison and Marx obviously disagree. Madison saw the existence of groups in society as the key to preventing class conflict. Marx saw groups as something that had to be overcome to foment it. Again, however, one sees important agreement: political values aside, groups are central to understanding class, and class is central to understanding groups.

It is possible, of course, that Marx and Madison defined ''class'' so differently that any agreement between them is illusory. But this is not the case.

Both use the term to refer to how people in society define and establish their social relations in the course of producing what they absolutely have to have, first to live, and then to live well.[2] The material necessities and niceties of life come first for Marx and Madison.

Listen to Madison writing in 1829:

> It is a law of nature, now well understood, that the earth under a civilized cultivation is capable of yielding subsistence for a large surplus of consumers, beyond those having an immediate interest in the soil; a surplus which must increase with the increasing improvements in agriculture and the labor-saving arts applied to it.
>
> And it is a lot of humanity that of this surplus a large proportion is necessarily reduced by a competition for employment to wages which afford them the bare necessaries of life.
>
> That proportion being without property, or the hope of acquiring it, can not be expected to sympathize sufficiently with its rights, to be safe depositories of power over them.

Listen to a younger but equally mature Madison in *Federalist 10*:

> . . . the most common and durable source of factions has been the various and unequal distribution of property. Those who hold and those who are without property have ever formed distinct interests in society. Those who are creditors, and those who are debtors, fall under a like discrimination. A landed interest, a manufacturing interest, a mercantile interest, a moneyed interest, with many lesser interests, grow up of necessity in civilized nations, and divide them into different classes, actuated by different sentiments and views (Hamilton, Madison and Jay 1961, p. 79).

As the simple agrarian society of his day was replaced by "wealthy capitalists and indigent labourers" Madison believed that inequality would grow worse. He predicted that capital accumulation would not be inhibited by inheritance laws, so great wealth in the hands of the few would not be "unfrequent." The question recurs:

> . . . whenever the majority shall be without landed or other equivalent property and without the means or hope of acquiring it, what is to secure the rights of property against the danger from an equality and universality of suffrage, vesting complete power over property in hands without a share in it: not to speak of a danger in the mean time from a dependence of an increasing number on the wealth of a few? (Meyers 1973, pp. 504–05).

Madison realized that not all groups were equal. There was a most common and durable source of faction, "property." On this point, he and Marx are one.

Madison was not only aware of class, he was one of its most profound students. This was not a paradox for Madison because he did not recognize the modern division between pluralism and class. His integrated conception emerges clearly when, as constitution-makers must, he looks to the future. "In framing a system which we wish to last for ages, we should not lose sight of the changes which ages will produce," he drolly told the Convention in the same breath that he told them an increase in population would of necessity increase the proportion of those who will secretly sigh for a more equal distribution of life's blessings (Farrand 1937, v. 1, p. 422).

The paradox for Madison was that property, the raison d'être of society, was simultaneously society's greatest threat. His answer to this threat was hyperpluralism: class conflict could be avoided by maximizing group conflicts. In what was to be one of the most brilliant invocations of divide and conquer ever made, Madison devised a pluralist solution to class conflict.

Madison's Solution

Hyperpluralism was Madison's solution to class conflict because it made it hard for the majority to find a common interest or, if found, to act successfully on it.

"Extend the sphere," Madison writes in *Federalist 10*, "and you take in a greater variety of parties and interests; you make it less probable that a majority of the whole will have a common motive to invade the rights of other citizens. . . ." The advantage of such a system? "A rage for paper money, for an abolition of debts, for an equal division of property, or for any other improper or wicked project, will be less apt to pervade the whole body of the Union than a particular member of it . . ." (Hamilton, Madison, and Jay 1961, pp. 83–84).

Madison said the same thing behind the Convention's closed doors. The rich could oppress the poor, but the chief threat was to property, not from it:

> The only remedy is to enlarge the sphere, and thereby divide the community into so great a number of interest and parties, that in the first place a majority will not be likely at the same moment to have a common interest separate from that of the whole or of the minority; and in the second place, that in case they should have such an interest, they may not be apt to unite in the pursuit of it (Farrand 1937, v. 1, pp. 135–36).

There was, of course, another solution to the problem of inequality, the "socialist" solution. Government could be used to promote social equality thereby removing what Madison saw as the chief *cause* of faction. Madison faced this question squarely and made the *first* object of government precisely the opposite: the protection of the differences in natural faculties from which inequality in property necessarily flows. He, like Adams, believed that men were by nature unequal. Madison, writing about the "diversity in the faculties of men, from which the rights of property originate," said:

The protection of these faculties is the first object of government. From the protection of different and unequal faculties of acquiring property, the possession of different degrees and kinds of property immediately results, and from the influence of these on the sentiment and views of the respective proprietors, ensues a division of the society into different interests and parties (Hamilton, Madison, and Jay 1961, p. 78).

The causes of faction, in Madison's famous phrase, are sown in the nature of man. They cannot be cured by the repression of liberty, even though liberty yields inequality, for this is worse than the disease. Nor can they be cured by promoting consensus on the common good. Ideology and beliefs have limits. The only solution to the problem of faction is to deal with its effects. For this, Madison proposed a large pluralistic society matched by a stronger and more pluralistic government operating under a Constitution rooted in respect for private property.

Class and Constitutional Balance

Class considerations openly dominated the Framers' consideration of how the national government should be structured, lending strong evidence to Gordon Wood's contention that the pivotal battle at Philadelphia was that between aristocracy and democracy (Wood 1969, p. 485).

Elbridge Gerry expressed the dominant view when he said the "evils we experience flow from the excess of democracy." Claiming he still supported "republican" government, he confessed he "had been taught by experience the danger of the levelling spirit" (Farrand 1937, v. 1, p. 48).

The question, of course, was how to structure the system to protect against the levelling spirit; the answer was checks and balances.

The system of checks and balances is often linked to the Framers' fear of concentrated political power, but in fact the system had a sharp political-economic point: through checks and balances ordinary people could be given some representation in government while being kept from dominating it. John Adams understood the general principle well:

In every society where property exists, there will ever be a struggle between rich and poor. Mixed in one assembly, equal laws can never be expected. They will either be made by numbers, to plunder the few who are rich, or by influence to fleece the many who are poor. Both rich and poor, then, must be made independent, that equal justice may be done, and equal liberty enjoyed by all (Adams, 1971, v. 6, pp. 68–69).

Following the example of the states, most of which had bicameral legislatures, the House of Representatives was to be the repository of the democratic principle in the new government. Several delegates worried about even this much "democracy.'' John Dickinson proposed property qualifications on voters for the House, explaining that such a restraint was ''a necessary defense against the dangerous influence of those multitudes without property and without principle, with which our country, like all others, will in time abound'' (Farrand 1937, v. 2, p. 202).

Roger Sherman opposed popular election of the House because the people lack information and are easily misled. Gouverneur Morris expressed similar views, predicting that ''the time is not distant when this country will abound with mechanics and manufacturers who will receive their bread from their employers'' (Farrand 1937, v. 2, p. 202).

In the end, property restrictions were not adopted. But a bow to democracy in the House was made easier by the knowledge that Congress would consist of two houses, the second of which would ''filter'' predictable democratic excesses from the people's chamber. As Edmund Randolph put it: ''The object of this second branch is to control the democratic branch of the National Legislature'' (Farrand 1937, v. 1, p. 218). Such a need, he felt, had been amply demonstrated by the ''democratic licentiousness'' of state legislatures.

Madison concurred. According to Yates's summary of Madison's comments on the Senate, ''Landholders ought to have a share in the Government. . . . They ought to be so constituted as to protect the minority of the opulent against the majority'' (Farrand 1937, v. 1, p. 431).

Gouverneur Morris summed up the prevailing view when he said they had all witnessed excesses against personal liberty and private property from the democratic branches of state legislatures. He feared the rich as well, he said, for they would seek to enslave the rest. The only solution was to balance these classes in Congress. The first branch would be democratic, the second aristocratic—and, he felt, it should be chosen for life. ''Such an aristocratic body will keep down the turbulency of democracy,'' he concluded (Farrand 1937, v. 1, p. 517). He did not add that the House would also keep down the turbulency of the aristocracy, but this fear was not as pronounced as fear of the people.

The above evidence shows that the Framers were highly conscious of the dangers to property from democracy. By no stretch of the evidence can this meeting be considered a democratic reform caucus in action. If more proof is needed it was supplied when the Framers got into a discussion of the most general question of all: the purpose of society.

On this question, they showed themselves to be in full agreement with John Locke: men create government for the protection of property. Gouverneur Morris touched the discussion off by observing that ''property was the main object of Society.'' He conceded that the savage state of nature was more favorable to liberty than the civilized state. This state was preferred, he said, by all men who had not acquired a taste for property, and ''was only renounced for the sake of property which could only be secured by the restraints of regular Government . . .'' (Farrand 1937, v. 1, p. 533).

Morris's views received strong support. Rutledge and Butler of South Carolina agreed, and so did King of Massachusetts. As King summarized Morris's speech, "Men don't unite for liberty or life, they possess both in the savage state in the highest perfection, they unite for the *protection of property*" (Farrand, 1937, v. 1, p. 536).

Not everyone agreed with this view. Wilson did not believe that property was the sole or even the primary object of government and society: cultivation and improvement of the mind were (Farrand 1937, v. 1, p. 605). The records of the Convention report no one agreeing with him.

Conclusion: Pluralism, Class, and the Constitution

The Framers saw society in terms of class, government in terms of protecting property, and the people as a threat. As "republicans" most of them opposed monarchy and accepted the necessity of some role for the "people" in government. But Randolph of Virginia was not alone in identifying the chief danger as the democratic parts of the state constitutions, none of which provided sufficient checks against democracy (Farrand 1937, v. 1, p. 27). The Framers established a mixed or republican system in which the majority without property (or much of it) would be satisfied to coexist with the propertied minority. They recognized that conditions were propitious: most of the white male population held land. But they also recognized that this had not prevented serious threats to property (Shays) and they expected society to grow more unequal in the future. The Constitution was designed as a balance between democracy and aristocracy which could protect justly acquired property from democratic disturbance. From this view of class, the Framers proposed the Constitution as a potential solution to the riddle of economic inequality and political democracy. It is fitting that Madison, who had most to do with the design, stated it best in 1833:

> Those who framed and ratified the Constitution believed that as power was less likely to be abused by majorities in representative Government than in democracies, where the people assembled in mass, and less likely in the larger than in the small communities under a representative Government, inferred also that by dividing the power of Government and thereby enlarging the practicable sphere of Government, unjust majorities would be formed with still more difficulty . . ." (Meyers 1973, p. 524).

If groups and class were joined in Madison, why were they split? The question also arises as to whether the separation renders society and constitutions easier or harder to understand.

Groups and class were split after Marx published his critique of capitalism. To dispel any doubt over whether these two events are linked, the father of modern pluralism, Arthur F. Bentley, offers his theory explicitly as an answer to Marx.

Pluralists since Bentley have followed his lead, and the two theories remain opposed today (Manley 1983).

Bentley likens American society to a spherical mass through which pass an unlimited number of planes, each representing a different principle of group organization: race, ethnicity, region, religion, language, etc. The result is a great confusion of groups, and a denial of class. "When the groups are adequately stated," Bentley says, "everything is stated." For emphasis, he adds, "When I say everything I mean everything" (Bentley 1908, p. 208).

According to Bentley, Marx raised the group to the level of class and spun a theory of history around the fictitious aggregate. The failure of the so-called proletariat to unite behind a common interest proved Marx's theory wrong, in Bentley's view. Indeed, Bentley declares that a "proletariat class, such as Marx and Engels conceived it, simply did not exist" (Bentley 1908, p. 467). The central social reality is neither the individual nor class, but groups.

Bentley recognized that not all groups are equal. "Wealth groups" had special advantages, but were by no means the entire story. Groups could join forces and for such alliances he used the term "class." But classes form rarely, which is just as well, for Bentley links them with despotic government. "The economic basis of political life must, of course, be fully recognized," Bentley writes, "though it does not necessarily follow that the economic basis in the usual limited use of the word is the exclusive, or even in every detail the dominant basis of political activity" (Bentley 1908, p. 209).

Since it would be hard to find anyone who ever treated the economic as the exclusive or in every detail the dominant basis of politics, a bit of straw enters Bentley's argument here. But with only slight variation, Bentley's charge of economic determinism, his assertion of the primacy of social and political variables over class variables, and the "failure" of Marx's prediction regarding proletarian revolution have become core items in pluralism's rejection of Marx.[3] John Dewey, who proposed scientific method and organized intelligence as substitutes for Marx's class struggle, and who, with Bentley, laid the philosophical foundations of modern pluralism, summed up the modern pluralist case as follows:

> In spite of the existence of class conflicts amounting at times to veiled civil war, any one habituated to the use of the method of science will view with considerable suspicion the erection of actual human beings into fixed entities called classes, having no overlapping interests and so internally unified and externally separated that they are made the protagonists of history—itself hypothetical (Dewey 1935, p. 80).

Madisonian pluralism avoids the anticlass pitfalls of modern pluralism. Madison and his colleagues had a profound appreciation for the dangers and reality of class conflict; and they proposed the encouragement of pluralism as a way to prevent it.[4]

The Framers needed a theory that could explain the conflict among groups and classes that continually occurred in the world as they knew it. The best minds among them developed such a theory. This theory rejected classical democracy, justified social inequality, and defended property. Rather than choose between human rights and property rights they saw property as *the* human right. It was only proper therefore for other rights to bow to it.

Beard's interpretation of the Constitution went off in a number of easily criticized directions, but on the basic point he was right. The Constitution cannot be understood apart from property and class.

Bentley's response to Marx erected a false choice between pluralism and class. His formulation of pluralism has been a popular answer to Marx, or at least to one version of Marx. But modern pluralism's insistence on denying or minimizing class weakens it compared to a theory that sees both as essential components of society. A theory of class that subsumes groups is more powerful than a theory of groups that denies class.

Notes

1. Beard appears to have little understanding of the dialectics of class conflict or the complex ways in which economic and other factors in combination produce a result. He is therefore vulnerable to Kenyon's argument that many factors other than the economic (especially the Framers' ideology) played an important role (Kenyon 1966, p. xxxvi). By asserting the "primordial" importance of the economic, Beard made the mistake of treating economic, social, and political variables as if they were separate. Arid disputes followed over the relative weight to give the economic compared to the political or social, in a situation where no one had agreed-upon measures of any of the variables. To call into doubt the entire economic interpretation, therefore, Beard's critics had only to find and assert plausibly the primacy of some (putatively) noneconomic influence. Beard replied that he never reduced everything to the economic, and this was true. But in treating the variables as separate instead of dialectically joined, he could only claim the primacy of the economic, he could not show it (Beard 1962, p. xii).

2. As is well known, the chapter on classes in volume three of *Capital* breaks off after a page and a half, thus depriving scholars of Marx's mature theory of class (*Capital* 1967, v. 3, p. 885). Still, it is possible to piece together a coherent view of Marx's position from a number of his writings, especially *Capital*, *The Communist Manifesto*, *The 18th Brumaire of Louis Bonaparte*, and *Wage Labour and Capital*. For a convenient source on these see Tucker 1978).

3. It would take us too far afield to refute in detail modern pluralism's reduction of Marx to economic determinism, its claim that noneconomic variables are superior to class, and its reading of the "failure" of Marx's predictions. But on all three points, it may be noted, modern pluralism is seriously flawed. To see Marx as a crude economic determinist misconstrues the dialectic, the essence of which is the interaction of variables, their mutual determination, and complex interdependence. As Sidney Hook wrote long ago, "One could fill pages with quotations to show how unjust such a characterization is" (Hook 1933, p. 93). To present Marxism as a simplistic bipolar social theory ignores the fact that

Marx was well aware of the middle class and of diverse "fractions" within classes. To rebut Marx's prediction of proletarian revolution is to ignore his later work which explains how a sufficiently large economic surplus may support a middle class and prevent capitalist society from splitting into two (Nicolaus 1970; Ehrlich 1982, p. 144).

4. In terms of classical democratic theory, it was well understood in eighteenth-century America that classical democracy could only be practiced in a small territory with a relatively homogeneous population. On this point, the Framers' opponents, who argued that an extensive territory cannot be governed on the principles of freedom, were more democratic than the nationally minded Federalists (Storing 1985, p. 201; Kenyon 1966, pp. xlix-lxi).

References

Adams, J. *Works*. New York: AMS Press, 1971. Vol. 6.

Bancroft, G. *History of the Formation of the Constitution of the United States of America*. New York: D. Appleton, 1882.

Beard, C.A. *An Economic Interpretation of the Constitution*. New York: Macmillan, 1962.

Bell, D. *The End of Ideology*. New York: Collier, 1961.

Benson, L. *Turner and Beard*. Glencoe, Ill.: Free Press, 1960.

Bentley, A.F. *The Process of Government*. Chicago: University of Chicago Press, 1908.

Brown, R. *Charles Beard and the Constitution*. Princeton: Princeton University Press, 1956.

Dahl, R.A. *A Preface to Democratic Theory*. Chicago: University of Chicago, 1963.

Dauer, M. *The Adams Federalists*. Baltimore: Johns Hopkins, 1953.

Dewey, J. *Liberalism and Social Action*. New York: G.P. Putnam, 1935.

Diamond, M. "Democracy and the Federalist: A Reconsideration of the Framers' Intent." *American Political Science Review*, 53, 1959, 52-68.

Ehrlich, S. *Pluralism On and Off Course*. Oxford: Pergamon, 1982.

Farrand, M. (ed.). *The Records of the Federal Convention of 1787*. New Haven: Yale University Press, 1937. Vols. 1-3.

Foner, P.S. (ed.). *Basic Writings of Thomas Jefferson*. New York: Willy Book Co., 1944.

Hamilton, A., Madison, J., Jay, J. *The Federalist Papers*. New York: New American Library, 1961.

Hofstadter, R. *The Progressive Historians*. New York: Knopf, 1968.

Hook, S. *Toward the Understanding of Karl Marx*. New York: John Day, 1933.

Kenyon, C. (ed.). *The Antifederalists*. Indianapolis: Bobbs Merrill, 1966.

Kenyon, C. "An Economic Interpretation of the Constitution After Fifty Years," *The Centennial Review*, 7, 1963, 327-52.

Lerner, M. *Ideas Are Weapons*. New York: Viking, 1940.

Lipset, S.M. *Political Man*. Garden City, N.Y.: Anchor Books, 1963.

Main, J.T. *The Antifederalists*. Chapel Hill: University of North Carolina, 1961.

Main, J.T. "Charles Beard and the Constitution." *William and Mary Quarterly*, 17, 1960, 86-110.

Manley, John F. "Neo-Pluralism: A Class Analysis of Pluralism I and Pluralism II," *American Political Science Review*, 1983, pp. 368-83.

Marx, K. *Capital*. New York: International Publishers, 1967. Vols. 1,3.

McDonald, F. *We the People*. Chicago: University of Chicago, 1958.

Meyers, M. (ed.). *The Mind of the Founder*. Indianapolis: Bobbs Merrill, 1973.

Nicolaus, Martin. "Proletariat and Middle Class in Marx: Hegelian Choreography and the Capitalist Dialectic," in James Weinstein and David W. Eakins (eds.), *For a New America*. New York: Random House, 1970, pp. 253-83.

Nore, E. *Charles A. Beard*. Carbondale: Southern Illinois University Press, 1983.

Polsby, N.W. *Community Power and Political Theory*. New Haven, Conn.: Yale University Press, 1980.

Roche, J.P. "The Founding Fathers: A Reform Caucus in Action." *American Political Science Review*. 55, 1961, 799–816.

Rutland, R.A. (ed.). *The Papers of James Madison*. Chicago: University of Chicago, 1962–1977. Vols. 9–10.

Smith, A. *The Wealth of Nations*. London: Dent, 1971. Vol. 2.

Smith, J. Allen. *The Spirit of American Government*. New York: Macmillan, 1907.

Storing, H. (ed.). *The Anti-Federalist*. Chicago: University of Chicago, 1985.

Tocqueville, A. *Democracy in America*. New York: Vintage, 1960. Vol. 1.

Tucker, R. (ed.). *The Marx-Engels Reader*. 2d ed.; New York: Norton, 1978.

Warren, C. *The Making of the Constitution*. Boston: Little, Brown, 1937.

Wood, G. *The Creation of the American Republic*. Chapel Hill: University of North Carolina Press, 1969.

Kenneth M. Dolbeare and Linda Medcalf
The Dark Side of the Constitution

Kenneth M. Dolbeare teaches political economy at The Evergreen State College. He and Linda Medcalf, also a political scientist, argue that the Framers' Constitution clearly reflects Alexander Hamilton's elitist political-economic vision for the new republic. As such, it must take some share of the blame for current problems of governance in the United States. The authors call for more realistic discussion of desirable first principles of government for America's third century, and less rhetoric of the type that has been characteristic of the bicentennial celebration.

The golden glow of the Constitution's bicentennial celebration—already well launched—threatens to blind us all at a time when Americans most need to see clearly. We do not refer to the harmless factual errors and the merely misleading exaggerations that accompany this latest patriotic spectacular. Our national myopia is far more serious. In the midst of institutional paralysis, an urgent but unaddressed policy agenda, and the protracted withdrawal of the American public from "public" affairs, we continue to celebrate the Constitution as an unrivaled political achievement. When we most need to critically examine our fundamental structures, we embark on a laudatory extravaganza—and do so with full scholarly support.

But, from its inception, there has been a dark side to the United States Constitution that accounts in part for many of the acknowledged ills of contemporary American politics. Low voter turnout, lack of confidence in government, the decline of the political parties, institutional deadlock and indecisiveness, the pervasiveness of protest, frustration, and resentment—all these can be traced to the deliberate antidemocratic design of our founding document and the way it was completed by Alexander Hamilton's nation-building program.

In effect, the Framers, and Alexander Hamilton in particular, wrought too well. Their chief ambition—a strong and stable political economy insulated from

120

popular control—is now threatened by the consequences of the very methods chosen to achieve that goal 200 years ago.

There is no news in the point that the men of 1787 sought to protect property and contain democracy. They have more than amply testified to this themselves. It is only later celebrants who have sought to make the Framers into "realistic" architects of a neutral political system; the Framers, and their opponents, knew better. But the celebrants have written history, and held office, in a country where democracy became a vital symbol. It became increasingly necessary to change the definition of democracy, in order to fit the reality of the limitations on popular impact that the Framers so artfully designed. Just as the proponents of the Constitution preempted the label "Federalist," turning it into its opposite, the celebrants of the Constitution worked similar magic with the word "democracy."

Alexander Hamilton's vital contributions to the development of a strong central government have been noted often, although by a minority of commentators. The crucial contract clause, several key Federalist essays, ratification in New York, and the various programs on credit, funding, the bank, and manufacturing are all recognized as major contributions to the development of the new nation. However, these are usually seen episodically, as independent events or specific isolated achievements in a context evolving in response to many other initiatives. Few have adequately appreciated Hamilton's grand design in its entirety, understood it as an agenda partially completed by the convention and partially by Hamilton later, or recognized its full realization in our twentieth-century history and contemporary situation. Instead, the utterly unrealized Jeffersonian image, more consistent with our attachment to "democracy," has dominated our national self-conception and our national rhetoric.

Inherent in Hamilton's grand design is a set of political implications with profound importance. He created an intricate central government machine that encouraged and rewarded behavior appropriate to his vision of a national commercial-financial-industrial economy—the entrepreneurial, productive, growth-oriented behavior that was to define our economic, political, and cultural life and identity for centuries. It was our first "industrial policy," incubating capitalism as a crucial by-product.

Hamilton also insulated the machine against the possibility that popular majorities or political chicanery might alter the outcomes he deemed essential to the creation of a great nation. In the process, by building upon the dark side of the Constitution, the Framers' property-protecting provisions and fear of democracy, Hamilton succeeded in almost completely removing the *substance* of public policy from popular hands. We live amidst the consequences today.

In this paper, we first review briefly the Framers' intentions and actions regarding the protection of property, both absolutely and from the interference of popular majorities. We shall see, as have many historians and political scientists before us, that the Framers were both class-conscious and thorough in their efforts.

Then we explore Hamilton's grand design, its political implications, and the protection he added to assure that his system would be insulated in multiple ways against popular impact. Hamilton wove a web that deliberately deflected popular preferences away from the most sensitive and crucial areas of public policy—financial affairs, and the nature and distribution of wealth in the country. More specifically, he developed major expansive constitutional doctrines and set up the power of judicial review. One of the most important and intended results was the ensuing heavy reliance upon the law and the courts as decisionmakers, and a governing role for the legal profession. This erected an ostensibly neutral and objective shield that first obscured what was happening and then made it seem natural and inevitable.

Finally, we show how this system, in its twentieth-century maturity, has come to threaten the very political stability and productive national economy that were the Framers' and Hamilton's goals. What the more knowingly purposeful defenders of this system did when faced with the inescapable prospect of popular participation was *first*, to build a maze of multiple limits on the effects of that participation, and *second*, to remove the substance of key policies into another, more remote, decisionmaking system. What its subsequent defenders have done is to triumphantly label the result "democracy."

Ironically, the great republican experiment has been converted into something like what the Framers feared almost as much as democracy—an absolutist monarchy complete with ongoing baronial struggles for court power and privilege, subject only to the occasional disturbance of crowds running in the streets. In the discouraging character and prospects of our contemporary politics, therefore, we have not experienced the *perversion* of the Framers' intent so much as we have seen the *fulfillment* of the dark side of the Constitution.

I. The Framers' Constitution

The Framers' Attitudes

As is well known, only a few of the delegates to the convention of 1787 were distinguished by concern for the rights and goals of popular majorities. Most of these dropped out or ended up among the Antifederalists in opposition to ratification. The general attitude of the main body of Framers can be summarized in the phrase "too much democracy."[1] As James Madison put it in *Federalist No. 10*:

> Complaints are everywhere heard from our most considerate and virtuous citizens, equally the friends of public and private faith and of public and personal liberty, that our governments are too unstable, that the public good is disregarded in the conflicts of rival parties, and that measures are too often decided, not according to the rules of justice and the rights of the minor party, but by the superior force of an interested and overbearing majority.[2]

Or, as Hamilton wrote in *Federalist No. 15*: "There are material imperfections in our national system and . . . something is necessary to be done to rescue us from impending anarchy."

Concerns focused on "a rage for paper money, for an abolition of debts, for an equal division of property, or for any other improper or wicked project."[3] All these improper projects and unjust legislation, of course, sprang from the state legislatures, where "men of more humble, more rural origins, less educated, and with more parochial interests" held sway.[4] Even Jefferson could not support such an excess: "173 despots would surely be as oppressive as one," he wrote. "An *elective despotism* was not the government we fought for."[5] Shays's Rebellion was much on the delegates' minds, and for many, provided the final straw. As Gordon Wood points out:

> Finally, when even Massachusetts with its supposedly model constitution [one of the less democratic of the states] experienced popular excesses, including Shays' Rebellion and the subsequent legislative "tyranny" of Shaysite sympathizers, many leaders were ready to shift the arena of constitutional change from the states to the nation.[6]

The Framers' contemporaries were well aware of the backgrounds and biases of those who drafted our founding document. The Antifederalist writings of the period are full of accusations on this count. According to Jackson Turner Main, "the criticism that the Constitution favored the few at the expense of the many was almost universal."[7] In the words of one prominent Antifederalist: "It changes, totally changes, the form of your present government. From a well-digested, well-formed democratic, you are at once rushing into an aristocratic government." The late Herbert Storing, who collected and edited the Antifederalist writings, called this "the underlying theme of a vast quantity of the specific criticism by the Anti-Federalists of the proposed Constitution."[8]

"The Federal Farmer," a prominent opponent of the Constitution, argued that the state conventions should revise and amend the proposed Constitution as needed, before ratification. Otherwise, the liberty of free men will be lost to those who "avariciously grasp at all power and property." An aristocratic group had

> taken the political field, and with its fashionable dependents, and the tongue and the pen, is endeavouring to establish in great haste, a politer kind of government. . . . The fact is, these aristocrats support and hasten the adoption of the proposed constitution, merely because they think it is a stepping stone to their favorite object. I think I am well founded in this idea; I think the general politics of these men support it, as well as the common observation among them.[9]

In addition, the Federal Farmer asserted,

This system promises a large field of employment to military gentlemen, and gentlemen of the law; and . . . it will afford security to creditors, to the clergy, salary-men and others depending on money payments.[10]

[Once] power is transferred from the many to the few, all changes become extremely difficult; the government, in this case, being beneficial to the few, they will be exceedingly artful and adroit in preventing any measures which may lead to a change.[11]

"Centinel," in his letters in opposition, was even more forceful, terming the effort to foist the Constitution on unsuspecting citizens "a most daring attempt to establish a despotic aristocracy among freemen, that the world has ever witnessed."[12] He added:

From this investigation into the organization of this government, it appears that it is devoid of all responsibility or accountability to the great body of the people, and that so far from being a regular balanced government, it would be in practice a *permanent ARISTOCRACY.*[13]

Nor have historians been unaware of these basic attitudes. The Progressive Era brought forth a significant reaction against the celebratory school of constitutional historiography. By no means was this limited to Charles Beard, whose work many now consider "crude"; J. Allen Smith's *The Spirit of American Government*, published in 1907, preceded Beard. In that widely read volume, according to his editor:

Smith looked beyond the government and fixed the responsibility for the nation's ills on the Constitution, which he felt, with Beard, represented wealth and the upper classes. As a product of social conflict and conservative reaction, the Constitution represented for Smith the chief obstacle to both democracy and political and economic reform.[14]

In Smith's own words: "[I]t was the almost unanimous sentiment of the Convention that the less the people had to do with the government the better."[15]

V.L. Parrington, in his Introduction to the 1930 edition of *Growth and Decadence of Constitutional Government*, declared that "the chief contribution of the Progressive movement to American political thought [was] its discovery of the essentially undemocratic nature of the federal constitution."[16]

Subsequent historians such as Merrill Jensen, Jackson Turner Main, Staughton Lynd, or William A. Williams have kept these themes alive. For example, Merrill Jensen, in quoting a John Adams letter of 1801, wrote:

[T]he Federalist Party was organized to destroy a constitution embodying ideals of self-government and economic practice that were naturally abhorrent to those elements in American society of which that party was the political expression. The Federalist Party . . . was the party of "the education, the talents, the virtues, and the property of the country." As such it had no faith in the democracy made possible by the Articles of Confederation.[17]

Even the consensus historians have recognized the pro-property biases, anti-majoritarianism, and class attitudes of the Framers. For example, one leading American history text notes:

Fifty-five delegates representing twelve states attended the Philadelphia Convention in the summer of 1787. . . . Although many of the delegates were young men . . . most were well educated and experienced members of America's political elite. . . . Nearly all were gentlemen, "natural aristocrats," who took their political superiority for granted as an inevitable consequence of their social and economic position.[18]

A major American political science textbook gives this judgment:

[T]he men who dominated the convention shared common economic interests, which were jeopardized by state debtor legislation and the weaknesses of the Confederation. . . . Yet although the delegates clearly sought to protect property interests and curb the excesses of democracy, they were also committed to the experiment in self-government.[19]

Hamilton also had little faith in the "people." Many authors make it a point to quote Hamilton's famous statement "The people, sir, are a great beast." In 1775 he observed:

The same state of the passions which fits the multitude, who have not a sufficient stock of reason and knowledge to guide them, for opposition to tyranny and oppression, very naturally leads them to a contempt and disregard of all authority.[20]

However, Hamilton was strangely silent during most of the Constitutional Convention, having enough faith in the founding fathers to leave the rulemaking to them. He had come "to understand that procedures determine actions, that rules of conduct govern what can and will be done."[21] "No one way of organizing power was *intrinsically* better than another."[22] The important thing was to first create the energy, the power, in the national government. Hamilton knew, with reasonable expectation, that he would have an opportunity to fill in the substance once the Constitution was ratified.

The Lure of the New Economy

As early as 1785, Hamilton and others had more in mind than merely the containment of democracy. They began to envision a new kind of commercial economy that would replace production for one's own use with production for sale elsewhere. Trade, transportation, and accompanying financial opportunities would be vastly expanded on a national scale. Eventually, such a national market and exchange system would penetrate parochial communities and replace the almost subsistence-level agricultural economies characteristic of all but the seacoast towns and cosmopolitan centers of the time.

But there would be no national commercial economy unless the Articles of Confederation could be replaced by some more powerful central government. That central government would not only put the brakes on the pernicious projects of the local majorities, but would protect the "property"—the contracts, bonds, paper, credit, etc.—essential to a commercial economy. Such a government would defend the hard money that made for a sound economy, promote the national market through uniform laws and otherwise overcome state protectionism, use import regulations both for taxes and to protect American goods against British competition, and establish sound credit in the international commercial community.

There were two prospective opponents whose interests would be directly damaged by such a new government. One was the mass of heavily indebted backcountry farmers still stirred by the Revolutionary dream of equality and individual rights. The other was the state legislatures whose support the farmers sought in their struggle against their creditors and others of the "better people," and which would have had ample institutional reasons to be opposed to any strengthening of the center. An adequate new government would have to control both these threats.

The public campaign for the new government began with the call to the Annapolis Convention in 1786, though its origins are visible much earlier in the correspondence and speeches of advocates. A rather full reform proposal came from Hamilton as early as September 3, 1780, in his letter to James Duane, in which he stated that "The first step must be to give Congress powers competent to the public exigencies."[23] In its call for the Annapolis Convention, the Virginia Legislature was more specific:

> To take into consideration the *trade* and *commerce* of the United States; to consider how far an uniform system, in their commercial intercourse and regulations, might be necessary to their common interest and permanent harmony, and to report to the several States such an act relative to this great object, as when unanimously ratified by them, would enable the United States, in Congress assembled, effectually to provide for the same.

As is well known, the Annapolis Convention was attended by only 12 delegates from five states. Among them was Alexander Hamilton, who seized the opportunity to issue the call for the constitutional convention, as follows:

> Your Commissioners cannot forbear to indulge an expression of their earnest and unanimous wish, that speedy measures may be taken, to effect a general meeting of the States, in a future Convention, for the same and such other purposes, as the situation of public affairs, may be found to require. . . .
>
> In this persuasion your Commissioners submit an opinion, that the Idea of extending the powers of their Deputies, to other objects, than those of Commerce . . . will deserve to be incorporated into that of a future Convention. . . .
>
> That there are important defects in the system of the Federal Government is acknowledged by the Acts of all those States, which have concurred in the present Meeting; That the defects, upon a closer examination, may be found greater and more numerous, than even these acts imply, is at least so far probable . . . as may reasonably be supposed to merit a deliberate and candid discussion. . . .
>
> Your Commissioners . . . beg leave to suggest their unanimous conviction, that it may essentially tend to advance the interests of the union, if the States, by whom they have been respectively delegated, would themselves concur, and use their endeavours to procure the concurrence of the other States, in the appointment of Commissioners, to meet at Philadelphia on the second Monday in May next, to take into consideration the situation of the United States, to devise such further provisions as shall appear to them necessary to render the constitution of the Federal Government adequate to the exigencies of the Union. . . .[24]

Shays's Rebellion, that heroic and desperate act by a handful of farmers, is surely the dominant symbol of the period and in many ways the real source of the Constitution. It was the frightening, triggering event that caused a particular selection of delegates to be appointed by their legislatures, induced them to spend a hot summer at an uncertain task in Philadelphia, and provided the context for their work and its later reception. For Hamilton and his cause, it was a godsend. For the convention, it was the ever-present threat that led to acceptance of several of the preventive provisions of the Constitution.

For us, Shays's Rebellion may serve to synthesize and express the two streams of thinking that led to the Constitution. The need to protect property and contain democracy could hardly be made more compelling. The need for a powerful central government that could protect commercial interests against citizens, if necessary, is indelibly clear. The basic principles that would have to be enforced in order to prevent such incidents were precisely those that would help to build the new national commercial economy.

The Framers' Constitution responds to both of these concerns, but leaves a substantial part of the second less explicit, and thus subject to Hamilton's later completion in the first administration. While there was little or no disagreement about the need to protect property and contain democracy, some delegates (particularly from the South) certainly would have had reservations about the new national economy and its implications for central government power if they had fully realized what was happening. The convention avoided potential conflict by leaving some provisions incomplete or undefined, in effect passing the responsibility to the first Congress.

In effect, several Framers (Hamilton central among them) were calling for the country—or at least its decisive elites—to make a crucial choice. The choice they advocated was to move from the current mostly agricultural economy (large plantations in the South, and small farms throughout the country) to a national commercial economy in which trade and finance would be dominant. They did not make this call openly, of course, and perhaps some of them did not grasp its totality or significance. Small wonder that their opponents did not see and oppose their design in explicit ways.

The Constitution as Synthesis

The Constitution's many provisions limiting the potential impact of popular majorities are too well known to require extensive comment. They range broadly from the design of basic structures, to methods of constituting the government, to limits on its powers. Examples in each category are separation of powers and checks and balances, the various forms of insulating elections, and prohibitions against specific acts that might impinge upon property rights.

More interesting and perhaps less familiar—at least in their totality as a means of instituting a new economy—are the several provisions that create and defend the new national commercial economy through central government power. Many of these provisions were unselfconsciously promoted under the rubric of "protection of property." They were meant to insure that "the rules of justice and the rights of the minor party," as Madison said, would be maintained, even in the face of the "superior force of an interested and overbearing majority." Many do double duty as limits on popular majorities, *but that is exactly the point*. The new economy *necessitated* a national political system in which commercial and financial interests were assured that new and potentially unpopular rules and practices would nevertheless be enforced reliably and consistently—and, it was hoped, be accepted under the more widespread acceptance of the necessity of protection for property rights.

The powers granted to the Congress in Article I, Section 8 and denied to the states in Section 10 amount to the framework for a new fiscal and commercial public policy. Congress gains the power to declare what shall constitute money and to control its value, while the states are forbidden to coin money, emit bills of credit, or allow anything but gold and silver coin in payment of debts. As a result, the states (and their "too democratic" legislatures) were prevented from issuing paper money or defining what might serve as legal tender for the payment of debts, and the gold and silver preferred by bankers and creditors would continue as the basis of the economy.

The Congress also acquired effective taxing powers, and with them the potential to become a creditworthy engine of economic development. Paying existing debts would make it possible to borrow more, to stabilize the currency, and to encourage investment and expansion in various ways. Vital among these tax powers was the power to impose duties and imposts. These are not only the easiest way to collect taxes, but also a means to manage access to the American market—whether to protect infant American industries or to open up other nations' markets. By contrast with the new powers of Congress and the past practice of the states alike, the states were firmly and completely excluded from all such powers (except for the strictly limited purposes of inspections).

The centrality of the famous "commerce clause" to the creation of the new national economy can hardly be debated, even if the question of exclusivity remains at issue today. Hamilton and some of the Framers would undoubtedly have preferred that the mere presence of this provision be understood to preclude the states from acting in the field of interstate commerce at all. But it is not a serious obstacle to their ends that the states be allowed to employ their police or regulatory powers in this area when the Congress has not fully occupied the field or acted in ways that conflict with such state legislation. More important to the creation of the new economy were the requirements for uniformity on the part of national laws pertaining to commerce.

Finally, the contract clause must be appreciated as something more than a prohibition that would assure creditors against any future Shays-type rebellions. Article I, Section 10 includes the prohibition against state laws impairing the obligations of contract as one of a long series of limitations starting with "No state shall . . . ." Clearly, this would render unconstitutional and void any state law that changed the terms of repayment of any existing private contract. By making such contracts into fixed "givens" of economic life, it also tended to discourage popular majorities from seeking redress of economic grievances from their state legislatures.

In Hamilton's hands, the clause applied equally to *public* contracts, so that state legislatures would lose the long-standing sovereign privilege of changing or withdrawing prior grants or franchises. Stability and predictability would be assured, but at the cost of legislative responsiveness to shifting popular preferences.

As Forrest McDonald has shown, this clause may also be distinguished as having been inserted in the Constitution through something like a Hamiltonian coup.[25] At least we know that the convention had twice rejected the principle, and that it was re-inserted by the five-member Committee of Style at the last moment and (apparently) accepted without argument by a weary convention. McDonald makes the case that Hamilton was the only one of the five to grasp the potential in such a clause and therefore must have brought about its last-minute inclusion almost single-handedly.

These primarily economic provisions only sketch the outline of the Framers' intent. They do not by any means constitute the Constitution's entire commitment to the support of the new commercial economy. There are many other provisions that, when taken together, add up to some extensive buttressing of that economy. These include the privileges and immunities of state citizens (to do business in other states), full faith and credit requirements (so that contracts could be enforced and debtors pursued), authorization for a federal court system (for some of the same purposes), and the guarantee and supremacy clauses.

In the United States of the 1780s, it would have been politically difficult, if not impossible, to devise a government that was not, at the least, republican. The Framers had to devise a document with at least the appearance of some democracy, and which could be defended as "republican." Thus, the Constitution does have "democratical" features. However, between the fear of the majority and the desire to protect the newly developing property of the commercial classes, the Framers found it necessary to create a document with a darker side, as we have outlined.

The spare and often ambiguous language of the Constitution was ideally suited to Hamilton's interpretation and expansion. It is Hamilton's interpretations, such as that involving the necessary and proper clause and the creation of the bank, and his expansions, such as in the development of the power of judicial review, that really brought the new national commercial economy into life in the Constitution.

The Framers sketched an outline, but Hamilton made it real. Commercial property and its developing economic relations were protected, and, by the completion of Hamilton's program, removed from the public policy agenda. The ability to change the economy, to deal with substantive public policy issues such as the distribution of wealth and fiscal and monetary measures, was effectively removed from popular control. The "majority" was now contained.

II. Hamilton's Grand Design and Legislative Programs

As a constitutional architect of vision and purpose, no American compares with Alexander Hamilton. From his earliest critiques of the Articles to the legal cases he argued after leaving the Cabinet, Hamilton pursued a single comprehensive image of a future economy and a government that would promote and defend it. If one person can be singled out, surely Hamilton—not Madison—was the primary driving force behind the origin, character, and ultimate meaning of the American Constitution.

Hamilton's Federalist essays are widely known for their emphasis on the weakness of the Articles and the contrasting need for energy in government, taxing powers to maintain that government's creditworthiness, a strong executive, direct application of national laws to individuals, and the like. All of these reflect characteristic Hamiltonian principles, and together they indicate a direction for the new system.

But the Hamiltonian design comes into its clearest focus from two other major sources which represent the main thrust of his efforts to complete the work of the convention. The first of these is the set of Reports and accompanying legislation and opinions that Hamilton authored as Secretary of the Treasury.[26] The other is *Federalist No. 78* and its argument for the power of judicial review, a bold and in many respects original expansion of central government power which helped to raise the courts, the law, and the legal profession to a governing role unprecedented then and unequaled elsewhere today.

Hamilton's first *Report on Credit* proposed a complex plan for imposing substantial new import duties and excise taxes, funding the unpaid national debt incurred by the Congress in order to fight the Revolutionary War, assuming the debts of the states, floating new loans overseas, creating a national bank, and initiating a repayment plan that would favor current holders of government securities rather than their original purchasers. As we unpack the internal relationships and implications of these various components, we shall see that in every case Hamilton had in mind creating and encouraging practices appropriate to a modern commercial economy and tying the fortunes of the wealthy to the new nation.

To begin, Hamilton had to find the revenue necessary to convince the nation's creditors that it *could* pay its debts, and then demonstrate such determination that they would also believe that it *would* do so. The new taxes were vital, but so was the funding program's dedication of sufficient revenues therefrom to pay debts as they became due. Hamilton was soon able to borrow new money, both to pay debts and to establish the solvency of the national government.

By assuming the debts of the states, Hamilton increased the total national obligations and drew new numbers of wealthy investors and banks into a kind of dependency on the success of the new government. In one of his more creative moves, Hamilton deliberately sought greater debt, in order to make it into a form of circulating currency that would help to energize the economy. In effect, he monetized the debt by prescribing it as one of the bases for stockholding in the national bank and gaining rights to purchase western lands owned by the national government. The new national bank also would aid in managing the value of government securities and indirectly affecting the value of other forms of currency.

But funding the national debt and assumption of the state debts entailed a basic political-economic conflict with important implications for the character of the future economic system. Hamilton proposed to fulfill the government's obligations (either repaying or granting rights to purchase stock or land) to the current holders of these previously almost worthless bonds, rather than to those citizens who, often for patriotic reasons, had been the original purchasers during the Revolutionary War.

Madison argued that justice required some compensation for the original purchasers, because the current holders (often speculators, banks, or other wealthy investors) had bought many bonds at sharply depreciated prices in the years prior to the Constitutional Convention. Pennsylvania had worked out a sharing formula of this kind in the repayment of some of its outstanding bonds.

Hamilton, however, argued forcefully against any compensation for original purchasers—and eventually won, even in Madison's Congress. His purpose was to establish negotiability for all indicia of indebtedness without regard to the possibility of any future challenge to the holder's right to full value on the date due. A commercial economy could not allow any questions about the validity of the paper that was the lifeblood of its transactions; all bills and notes had to be enforceable in the hands of a good faith holder. Older notions of a "just price," or of the right to challenge the fairness of any of the transactions leading up to the current holder's demand for payment, had to be discarded if the modern economy were to work smoothly.

In his opinion on the constitutionality of the bank, Hamilton was not only arguing for an expansive interpretation of the necessary and proper clause of Article I, Section 8, but also for the inherent powers of the national government to exercise the attributes of sovereignty. Given the convention's rejection of Congressional power to create corporations *or* banks, Jefferson and Randolph were probably correct in lawyers' terms. But Hamilton was not one to be confined by such niceties when important issues were at stake. It was his opinion that carried the day with Washington, and later found expression in constitutional doctrines enunciated by his dedicated follower John Marshall.

In later Reports, particularly the initially unfulfilled one on Manufactures, Hamilton offered a bold lesson in industrial policy. By urging national commitment to such internal improvements as turnpikes and canals, he started a process—and a constitutional argument—that is still expanding. By proposing import duties on selected manufactured goods and/or bounties to American manufacturers of the same goods, he started the national government on the path to purposeful shaping of the winners and losers in the nation's economy and the assumption of responsibility for its overall success.

What Hamilton demonstrated in these Reports was a clear conception of the national government's capacity to serve as the manipulator of an array of carrots and sticks that would move the economy in desirable directions. Hamilton was also clear about who should determine what those desirable directions might be, and who should benefit from such purposeful action. Men of commercial foresight and experience, and probably of property, should hold such powers, and use them for mutual—and hence national—benefit. Most of all, no such system could tolerate significant popular involvement or impact.

Hamilton's design, let us acknowledge, was intended to build national strength and grandeur, on the model of the British Empire he so much admired. In practical terms, it added up to a new set of legal concepts, new financial principles and methods at the national level, and a new overall developmental role for the national government. His incipient commercial-financial economy (soon to emerge, with industrialization, as capitalism) required changing a number of key legal principles long established in the pre-commercial common law. It required creative use of the national debt, deliberate management of the currency, purposeful industrial policy, and conscious inducements in the form of grants of rights to the vast lands inexpensively acquired by the national government through treaties and conquest.

Most of all, Hamilton's design required insulation against reactions from all sides, and particularly against popular efforts to change the patterns of wealth distribution that this design would accomplish. Hamilton's answer to this compelling need was twofold.

First, as we have just seen, he placed the reins of power as far from the people as he could—in a centrally guided financial and development system that would be as hard to identify as it would be to reach and change. Hamilton's system had an early demonstration while he was Secretary of the Treasury, and was legitimated by Jefferson's failure to demolish it while in office. But it was visible only in isolated pieces—growing, merging, self-validating pieces like the restoration and refinement of the Bank, the development of the tariff and internal improvements and the income tax, the vigorous use of judicial review, the triumph of the legal profession—until its full flowering in the Progressive–New Deal Era.

Hamilton stood for an economy that would be dynamic, responsive to opportunities, and oriented to long-term growth. That economy required far-sighted elites to assure that the government would offer incentives for development, stabilize its context, and control its excesses. Government could also serve by providing a means of deflecting or absorbing popular complaints. For all of these goals, the government had to be big, powerful, highly centralized, and removed from the people—but apparently highly responsive to them. Herbert Croly aptly named the twentieth-century version of Hamilton's design "a Hamiltonian government for Jeffersonian ends." Thus the two ever-contending strands of American political thought—our two major images of the desirable American political economy—came to an ultimate merger. Together, they gave credence to labeling Hamilton's national government with the venerable Jeffersonian symbol of "democracy."

The *second* means by which Hamilton sought insulation from popular impact was through transferring as much policymaking as possible into the far less visible and apparently neutral and mechanical hands of courts and lawyers. This strategy encompassed not only the usual and often discretionary law-enforcing role of courts, but more significantly a deliberate law-changing function and—most important of all—a major policymaking role for the Supreme Court at least equal to that of the other branches.

We noted earlier that Hamilton gave special emphasis to the principle of having national laws apply directly to individuals without the intermediation of the states or other governments. In this way, assuming as Hamilton did that a federal judiciary would be promptly created (as it was), the national government would have all the legitimacy and effective enforcement potential of the law and the courts behind its enactments. Individuals would be isolated and vulnerable to a variety of court-imposed sanctions.

Hamilton assumed that the federal courts would have common law powers, making them even more effective supplements to the lawmaking and order-maintaining capabilities of the national government, but Jefferson managed to frustrate this goal for some time. The state courts and their uncontested common law powers, however, soon proved more than adequate to the necessity of changing the law, as first Perry Miller and then Morton Horwitz have so well documented.[27]

Let us summarize these developments briefly. At the same time as lawyers were laying exclusive claim to the right to serve as judges, the early nineteenth-century courts were pushing jurors back from their accustomed law-making as well as fact-finding roles. Many of the Antifederalist objections to the ratification arose from what they correctly perceived to be a reduction in the role of juries.[28] Popular participation as judges and jurors, long the established practice, was sharply reduced. Lawyers and judges asserted their expertise as "scientists" to discover the (new, American, common) law governing property and economic transactions generally.

What they discovered in this manner was a new version of the law, complete with new definitions of property and new rules for doing business that were appropriate to the rising capitalist economy. For example, not only did the law of bills and notes and commercial practices have to be changed, but so did established land and water rights have to give way to the need for railroad entrepreneurs and mill owners to be free of liabilities for the (growth-producing) way they used *their* property. Property in the form of real estate had to be converted into a commodity and made subject to ready sale and/or use as security for the credit or loans needed for development. Other kinds of property rights to intangibles had to be created and made enforceable.

Why the law was used in this manner is made very clear by Morton Horwitz:

> Change brought about through technical legal doctrine can more easily disguise underlying political choices.
>
> .   .   .
>
> For the paramount social condition that is necessary for legal formalism to flourish in a society is for the powerful groups in that society to have a great interest in disguising and suppressing the inevitably political and redistributive functions of law.[29]

At the close of his extensive analysis of the extent to which the legal system was used to put the burden of paying for economic development on people other than the entrepreneurs and financiers who were its beneficiaries, he says:

> . . . it does seem fairly clear that the tendency of subsidy through legal change during this period was dramatically to throw the burden of economic development on the weakest and least active elements in the population.[30]

From Horwitz's analysis, it is clear that the purpose of using the increasingly self-conscious and willing legal system and changing the concept of property and the substance of commercial law turn out to be the same.

The key to this governing role for the legal profession, a hallmark of the American system at least since De Tocqueville's famous observations, was Alexander Hamilton. First he created the public image that the Constitution was "law" and therefore properly the province of lawyers, rather than being "values" or "policy" and properly the province of the people or their elected representatives. Then he helped to raise the visibility and potential of the Supreme Court to unprecedented heights, and provided the rationale for Marshall's eventual success in establishing the Court as a co-equal policymaker. Finally, in his private practice after leaving the Cabinet, he made himself a model of what a lawyer could do with a clear sense of policy objectives.

In *Federalist No. 78* and his later opinions, Hamilton seized upon the supremacy clause's declaration that the Constitution is "the supreme *law* of the land" (emphasis added) to argue that the interpretation of the Constitution's words and phrases was peculiarly the responsibility of lawyers and judges. The issue, of course, turns on the nature of the choice involved in determining what any given provision means.

If (as Hamilton argued) it is a choice of a purely "ministerial" kind involving no discretion—a choice wholly determined by past precedent or rule admitting of a single answer and available to be discovered by appropriate experts—then it might as well belong to lawyers as any other skill group. But if (as Jefferson argued) it is a choice involving values and preferences which might be contested—a choice in which reasonable alternatives are available—it would seem that the people should be involved in some direct way. Needless to say, Hamilton's argument won, and the Constitution is "law," and therefore belongs in an especially proprietary manner to the legal profession.

Federalist No. 78 is also justly famous for its next argument, to the effect that the Supreme Court should have the power to declare when the Congress or the President have exceeded the authority granted them in the Constitution. The boldness involved in staking this claim so openly in 1788 is not often recognized: not only did this make plain that the Federalists obviously expected the Court to exercise judicial review as well over the acts and decisions of the states, but it also might have jeopardized ratification in the key remaining states. Although the argument was not finally won until *Marbury* and *Dred Scott* were re-validated in the 1890s, the Court reviewed the constitutionality of an act of the Congress as early as 1796 in *Hylton v. U.S*; Hamilton argued the case for the government.

Hamilton insisted that the Constitution was law, and peculiarly the province of courts and lawyers. The Supreme Court had the power of judicial review, he said, but that was a purely neutral and objective decision—"an act of judgment, not of will." Could Alexander Hamilton have been so naive as to believe that the choices judges would make in interpreting the meaning of the Constitution would not involve values and preferences? Or did he know quite well what would be involved, and build a powerful argument for conferring that choice upon the most trustworthy and available skill group he could find? Surely Hamilton was a conscious builder of the legal mystique, and not merely an early victim of the slot-machine theory of law so often articulated at celebratory moments.

In any event, Hamilton's argument applied equally to courts and judges at all levels of the federal and state legal systems. The temptation was far too strong for most judges to resist the opportunity, and lawyers were quick to offer it again and again. In every state, the notion of judicial review by state supreme courts (and therefore by lower courts) became increasingly accepted and its exercise routine. The legal profession had acquired its dominant position as the means of transacting the nation's economic and political affairs by about the 1840s.

The Supreme Court exercised the power of judicial review over acts of the states and state court decisions several times in the early nineteenth century, but did not receive a volume of cases until the Fourteenth Amendment provided what came to be recognized as a broad new channel for reaching the Court. By the 1890s, its frequent use of the power over both states and Congress was widely approved by the business community and thus thoroughly established. In addition, the lower federal courts began to exercise, and the Supreme Court to endorse, just the kind of common law powers that Hamilton had hoped for— particularly in such areas as injunctions on behalf of employers in labor disputes.

But Hamilton's impact was not limited to the power of his *Federalist No. 78* or his later opinions. It owes a great deal to the example he set as a practicing attorney, and to the fervor with which the authors of the two leading Commentaries on American law—James Kent and Joseph Story—endorsed his views of the law.[31] Because for many years there were few ways that an American lawyer could identify authoritative adaptations of the English common law, or locate applicable precedents from the American state or federal legal systems, the Commentaries were widely used and carried enormous prestige. Both Kent and Story were completely captured by Hamilton as a constitutional thinker and as a courtroom attorney, and they made his view of the law central to their interpretations of the nature of American law on a wide range of subjects.

The effect of Hamilton's various efforts in this area was to raise courts, the law, and the legal profession into a covert policy-making system representing his best hope of protecting the national economy from popular interference. He was apparently willing to pay the price of the law's rigidities and tendency toward backward-looking in order to insulate the economy and its distribution patterns in this way. But the price paid by the people—and ultimately by the constitutional system itself—has yet to be calculated.

III. The Consequences of the Dark Side

Any list of the basic problems of current American politics would surely include institutional deadlock, the decline of the political parties, domination by special interests, the multiplicity and complexity of issues, television's role in diverting attention away from public policy, and the deplorable levels of knowledge and interest on the part of most citizens. For each problem, there are one or more standard explanations.

Most of the explanations (and prescriptions for improvement when the situation is not deemed totally hopeless) take one of two forms. The first involves a focus on specific causal factors, i.e., the effects of incumbency, patterns of campaign contributions, the candidate focus of the media, and so forth. The second is more or less an inventory of the incurable failures of the American people: low and declining turnout at elections, ignorance and self-interestedness, an enduring spectator orientation, apparent manipulability by money and media, and an inability to grasp and act on issues.

These standard explanations amount to a massive exercise in blaming the victim. More important, the situation is actually *worse*, and much more fundamental, than generally suggested. We have no quarrel with the list of problems. If anything, we would lengthen and deepen any such list, and would predict that many others will soon be doing so. The United States is already beginning to emerge from the self-congratulatory stupor of the early 1980s. Realism will be in vogue again by the next recession.

Many of the problems of our politics have their origins in the deliberate design of the Constitution, particularly as it was developed by Hamilton. The problems are *real*. The people's response to them is *rational*. What is missing is recognition that the *roots* of the problem lie in Hamilton's very success.

Today's national government is highly centralized, a huge and distant bureaucracy related in a merely episodic manner to gridlocked and unresponsive policymaking institutions. The web of special interests is a pragmatic answer, albeit one that represents only the most powerful few. Media and money call the tune for parties and candidates. People may quite rationally decide not to study issues or to participate in such a system.

What has brought about this set of problems and popular response? One absolutely fundamental cause is Hamilton's successful removal of the substance of policy from popular reach. The major pieces of Hamilton's design—the financial system and the legal system—were put in place in the late 1700s and early 1800s by Hamilton and his followers. They became fully integrated and coherently employed in the Progressive Era, from which the rise of the truly centralized

Hamiltonian state can be dated.

These two major pieces of Hamilton's design, however, had more than proved their value in the nineteenth century. Each served effectively to obscure unpopular basic national policies from visibility, displace and eventually absorb popular complaints within apparently neutral and objective machines, and frustrate even quite determined popular movements. As Morton Horwitz has shown, the legal system took on its economic role as covert redistributor and allocator of financial burdens as early as the 1820s and 1830s.[32] As opponents of the Bank alleged from the start, and as Goodwyn, Sharkey and others have shown with respect to the financing of the Civil War, the financial system effectively enriched the wealthy while putting the burden on the working and later the middle classes.[33]

When the high point of judicial review was reached in the early 1890s and successfully defended in the election of 1896, the full Hamiltonian legal system was in place. The Supreme Court's power was confirmed; the multitude of state courts were encouraged; and the governing role of an increasingly elite and corporate-oriented Bar was further legitimated.[34] Passage of the Federal Reserve Act offered a final financial link and means of leverage for the same corporate-banking-legal community.[35]

Once this system was consolidated in the First World War, participation could actually be encouraged because there was little chance that popular majorities could do much damage. If the basic defenses erected by the Framers did not work, then surely Hamilton's system would divert and absorb popular efforts until they were harmless. Nevertheless, the "better people" were still fearful, not just because of the near-success of labor and the Populists in the 1890s, but also because of the growing ranks of immigrants. Thus, deliberate repression sought to discourage lower class opposition and electoral participation for a decade or more, just as Hamilton's system was crystallizing. A newly refurbished ("democratic") rationalizing ideology was soon bolstered by powerful new means of communication and indoctrination.

The net result of all these efforts was dramatic decline in electoral turnout in the twentieth century.

Women were added to the eligible electorate in 1920, and blacks and many immigrants had been effectively subtracted in the previous decades, so that turnout percentages are not strictly comparable. However, it is still a shock to realize that elections in the 1880s and 1890s generally had turnout levels over 70 percent and often exceeding 80 percent. Today, when women have had 60 years of experience with the franchise and a whole new generation of black voters has entered the active electorate, we count ourselves lucky to attract more than half of the eligible electorate to the polls.

Where have all the voters gone? They have caught on that the system is rigged. Popular majorities' efforts to change either the distribution of wealth and power or the basic policies that seem necessary to maintain that structure of wealth and power simply don't seem possible. To be sure, decades of accomplishment by the ideological defenders and celebrants of this system have encouraged Americans to accept it as "democracy." Americans learn to want or, more likely, consider inevitable whatever is produced, to settle for various diversionary satisfactions, and/or to fear change and even suspect that those who do seek change must have self-interested and unpatriotic motives. These are ideological rationalizations for the central fact that the Hamiltonian Constitution excludes people from directly affecting important public policy outcomes.

This is not to say that there is no history of popular impact on government, or that the Supreme Court is merely a tool of the corporations. Either such caricature of our argument would be silly. What is important is that popular impact, such as it is, can be made effective only in very limited ways through the electoral process. For the most part, it must come through disruption—riots, massive strikes, demonstrations involving the threat of violence, and other attacks on the social order itself. What does it mean for a popular government that its people are politically effective only when they threaten to destroy it?

The Supreme Court has made many decisions, particularly in the middle years of this century, that advanced basic democratic rights. But that was a result of judicial appointments, not an attribute of the institution. The Supreme Court has, and can, and may well again, make precisely the opposite kinds of decisions. What does it mean for a popular government that its basic policies can be set by a transitory majority drawn from a body of nine life-appointed lawyers?

What we are saying is that the Framers' two major goals are threatened today by the success with which Hamilton and his followers implemented those goals. We do not have a stable political economic system, and we do not have the capacity to make the choices necessary to assure a strong and successful American political economy.

Our political system works by fits and starts. It is neither responsive nor accountable and it lacks solid grounding in the body of its people. It sits and waits for the next crisis. Unfortunately, to solve that crisis, it may have to transform itself into something that will be *very* difficult to rationalize as "democracy."

We have not addressed the great issues of nuclear war, planetary survival, or even American economic viability in a drastically changing world economy—not because the people don't care, but because there is no linkage between the people's felt needs and their policymakers. No such basic policies can be implemented, even if policymakers were to concur, without the sustained support of some major portion of the people.

To solve our problems, or merely to fulfill the Framers' goals in the wholly different conditions of our times, we will have to come to terms with Hamilton's Constitution in a realistic manner. Perhaps the best way to honor the Framers' work is not to join in obfuscating celebrations, but to act as they did under like circumstances.

We might start by critically exploring the ways in which today's analogue of the Articles of Confederation is defective in achieving goals that are necessary and desirable for the *future*. Obviously, like the Framers, we would have to address basic principles of social order and purpose—if we have not completely forgotten how to do so. (That we *have* forgotten is strongly suggested by the nature of the proposals currently offered for constitutional "reform."[36])

Curing the defects of Hamilton's Constitution may not be possible, for many reasons. It may be that patterns of material advantage, or the depth of the problems we face, or the sheer size of the country, make it practically impossible. Or our situation may be even worse: perhaps generations of structural deflection—of elites as well as of the general public—from considering the Constitution in a realistic manner has made it impossible for us to do so now. Decades of cultural lowering of the criteria of democracy may have made it impossible for us to recapture its fuller definition and potential.

If there is a route out of our crisis, it lies in deliberately reversing Hamilton's strategy. That is, we must seek to re-engage the people in their government, and particularly in ways that enable them to have direct impact on the substance of important public policies. Without regard to what might be "realistic" or "practical" in the light of today's power distribution, or to questions of strategy, the kinds of measures to which consideration might be given are of the following order:

(a) Radical decentralization, perhaps to some regional system, reserving only a few global functions for the national government, to put government within reach of the people;

(b) Removing the incumbent character of the national government by putting limits on the number of terms that Representatives and Senators can serve;

(c) Reducing the role of money by requiring free television time for public affairs issues, party deliberations and arguments, and candidates' presentations;

(d) Sharply contracting the policymaking role of courts and lawyers by transferring jurisdiction of constitutional and major policy issues to openly political forums;

(e) Instituting mechanisms for direct action—the old initiative and referendum in modern form, with encouragement and provision of educational opportunities and some screen for levels of information;

(f) Making registration immediate and eligibility for voting open to all, if necessary by decentralized computer access;

(g) Reviving the parties by starting at the local and state levels and providing a series of thresholds through which, by showing increasing levels of popular participation, parties might increasingly acquire control over campaign funding and nominations;

(h) Overhauling the public education system to make public affairs a vital and exciting part of the curriculum, welcome controversy, and set future-oriented public service once again at the center of the aspirations of all citizens.

These suggestions are only a start, intended to illustrate the combined fundamental-and-electoral level at which rethinking must begin. They are easily caricatured, and of course they are not "realistic." The point is that institutional tinkering will not suffice.

When problems such as we have described are real, remedies must be radical;

that is the lesson the Framers taught in 1787. Only when the people are re-engaged in a government within their reach will Hamilton's damage be undone. At that point, we can proceed to build upon his successes, and seek to truly achieve the stable political system and productive economy that were his vision for the new nation. Only the bright hope of a new twenty-first–century vision can finally transcend the dark side of our much-celebrated eighteenth-century Constitution.

Notes

1. Gordon S. Wood, "Democracy and the Constitution," *How Democratic Is the Constitution?* Robert A. Goldwin and William A. Schambra, eds. (Washington, D.C.: American Enterprise Institute for Public Policy Research, 1980), p. 8.

2. All quotes from the collection known as the *Federalist Essays* are taken from the edited collection called *The Federalist Papers*, introduction by Clinton Rossiter (New York: New American Library, 1961) and will simply be identified by number.

3. Madison, *Federalist No. 10.*

4. Wood, *supra*, p. 12.

5. Quoted in Wood, *supra*, p. 8.

6. Wood, *supra*, p. 9.

7. Jackson Turner Main, *The Antifederalists: Critics of the Constitution 1781–1788* (New York: W.W. Norton & Company, 1961), p. 132.

8. Herbert J. Storing, ed., *The Complete Anti-Federalist*, Volume 1, *What the Anti-Federalists Were For* (Chicago: University of Chicago Press, 1981).

9. Storing, *supra*, Volume 2, *Objections of Non-Signers of the Constitution and Major Series of Essays at the Outset*, "Letters from the Federal Farmer," pp. 214–357, p. 253.

10. Storing, *supra*, p. 252.

11. Storing, *supra*, p. 251.

12. Storing, *supra*, "Letters of Centinel," pp. 130–213, p. 139.

13. Storing, *supra*, p. 142.

14. Dennis L. Thompson, in his Introduction to the 1972 Edition of J. Allen Smith, *The Growth and Decadence of Constitutional Government* (Seattle, Washington: University of Washington Press, 1972), p. xviii.

15. J. Allen Smith, *The Spirit of American Government* (Cambridge, Mass.: The Belknap Press, 1965), p. 37.

16. V.L. Parrington in the "Introduction to the 1930 Edition," Smith, *supra*, p. xi.

17. Merrill Jensen, *The Articles of Confederation: An Interpretation of the Social-Constitutional History of the American Revolution 1774–1781* (Madison, Wisconsin: University of Wisconsin Press, 1963), p. 3.

18. Bernard Bailyn, et al., *The Great Republic: A History of the American People*, 2nd edition (Lexington, Massachusetts: D.C. Heath and Company, 1981), p. 253.

19. Kenneth Prewitt and Sidney Verba, *An Introduction to American Government*, 4th Edition (New York: Harper & Row, 1983), p. 31.

20. Mary Jo Kline, ed. *Alexander Hamilton: A Biography in His Own Words* (New York: Harper & Row, 1973), p. 45.

21. Forrest McDonald, *Alexander Hamilton: A Biography* (New York: W.W. Norton & Company, 1979), p. 28.

22. McDonald, *supra*, p. 103.

23. Kline, ed., *supra*, p. 85.

24. Kline, ed., *supra*, pp. 156–157.

25. Forrest McDonald, "The Constitution and Hamiltonian Capitalism," in Robert A. Goldwin and William A. Schambra, eds. *How Capitalistic Is the Constitution?* (Washington, D.C.: American Enterprise Institute for Public Policy Research, 1982), pp. 59–62.

26. These papers can be found in Alexander Hamilton, *Papers on Public Credit, Commerce, and Finance* (New York: Bobbs-Merrill Company, Inc., 1957).

27. Perry Miller, *The Life of the Mind in America From the Revolution to the Civil War*, Book Two, "The Legal Mentality" (New York: Harcourt, Brace & World, Inc., 1965) and Morton J. Horwitz, *The Transformation of American Law: 1780–1860* (Cambridge, Mass.: Harvard University Press, 1977).

28. For example, see Storing, *supra*, Volume 2, pp. 12, 30, 136.

29. Horwitz, *supra*, pp. 101 and 266, respectively.

30. Horwitz, *supra*, p. 101.

31. As quoted in Perry Miller, *supra*: "In 1836, when Jackson was President and Kent had delivered another of his panegyrics on Hamilton, Story wrote, 'I always believed that his title to renown was as great as you have portrayed it.'" (p. 111). See also James Kent, *Commentaries on American Law* (1st Ed., 4 vols., 1826–1830) and Joseph Story, *Commentaries on Equity Jurisprudence* (1836) and *Commentaries on the Law of Promissory Notes* (1845).

32. See Horwitz, *supra*.

33. Lawrence Goodwyn, *The Populist Moment in America* (New York: Oxford University Press, 1978); Robert Sharkey, *Money, Class, and Party* (Chapel Hill, N. C.: University of North Carolina Press, 1961).

34. Two works that summarize this process very well are Arnold Paul, *Conservative Crisis and the Rule of Law* (New York: Harper & Row, 1960) and Jerrold Auerbach, *Unequal Justice* (New York: Oxford University Press, 1976).

35. Two major works summarize this process also: Gabriel Kolko, *The Triumph of Conservatism, 1900–1916* (Chicago: Quadrangle Books, 1963) and James Weinstein, *The Corporate Ideal in the Liberal State* (Boston: Beacon Press, 1968).

36. Donald Robinson, ed., *Reforming American Government: The Bicentennial Papers of the Committee on the Constitutional System* (Boulder, Col.: Westview Press, 1985) and James L. Sundquist, *Constitutional Reform and Effective Government* (Washington, D.C.: The Brookings Institution, 1986).

Jeanne Hahn
NeoHamiltonianism
A Democratic Critique

Jeanne Hahn teaches history and political economy at The Evergreen State College. She likens the proposals of today's Committee on the Constitutional System to Hamilton's Constitutional arguments and later practice. Her critique of the Committee's proposals is cast within the democratic Antifederalist tradition and concludes with a call for applying a revived version of that tradition to today's constitutional dialogue.

In the midst of the carefully orchestrated, highly celebratory bicentennial commemoration of the framing of the Constitution,[1] a group of American citizens has advanced a unique and profoundly Hamiltonian critique of our basic governing document. The Committee on the Constitutional System (CCS) argues, always with proper deference to the framers, that certain structural features of the Constitution are inadequate to the pressures of the late twentieth century. It recommends a series of reforms designed to "improve the performance of government by modifying its basic structure and process."[2]

The Committee is correct in identifying what, over two hundred years, have become serious structural problems in the separation-of-powers and checks-and-balances provisions of the Constitution. Many of these now work to produce "gridlock" on critical issues and a standoff between the executive and legislative branches. But its proposals for reform are, at best, narrow, technocratic, and legalistic, and at worst, profoundly elitist. The CCS is frequently disdainful of the public attention necessary to implement the sort of structural changes it urges. It seems that it is moved by many of the same impulses that led the 1787 framers to devise the very structures these modern reformers now seek to refine.

The Committee's "Statement of the Problem"[3] echoes in tone and temper the attack on the governability of the nation under the Articles of Confederation that is set forth in *The Federalist*. Its solutions are taken from the same mold that Alexander Hamilton constructed two hundred years ago and from which the new nation was firmly launched on its political-economic course. In this respect the Committee can be understood as neoFederalist, a group of nationally minded men (and women) who view the present governmental structure as inadequate to the demands of late-twentieth–early-twenty-first-century capitalism.

Their vision, while not as clearly or forthrightly articulated as that of the prescient Alexander Hamilton, is of a more powerful and centralized state. Such a state would be able to act with energy and dispatch, unencumbered by demands and inefficiencies stemming from those to whom the Committee refers, in pejorative shorthand, as "special interests." Much like the Federalist plan realized in the 1787 Constitution, the Committee's proposals would remove the government further from the reach of its citizens, while centralizing power even more firmly in the hands of a tightly interwoven governing elite. The largely Madisonian solution of structurally breaking, checking, and fractionalizing the power of the people at the national level, through the elaborate and cumbersome system of checks and balances and separation of powers, is understood by the Committee as largely antiquated. They see a substantially restructured electoral system and significantly strengthened political parties as adequate to the task of disciplining "special interests" (Madison's "factions") and subordinating the latter's substantive claims to the more compelling ends of efficiency and effectiveness.

This neoHamiltonianism would not be the first major adjustment of the Federalist scheme. The Federalist system has needed periodic adjustment, particularly as the country moved from its early commercial-financial-agricultural base into heavy industrialization and mature capitalism. Fundamental reforms bracketing the turn of the century—the "system of '96" and the Progressive movement—attempted to rationalize the changing political-economic system, manage its transforming features, and ease the move to corporate capitalism. At the same time, they avoided addressing the systemic problems of boom and bust or the needs of a burgeoning working class now divorced from the land and/or without skills and the means necessary to produce on a small scale for its own livelihood. The programs and their underlying rationale came predominantly from the Hamiltonian mold and can be understood as the second phase of the Hamiltonian system.

We are now, in the work of the Committee on the Constitutional System, facing phase three of the Hamiltonian rationalization. As in the first and second phases, there will be easily distinguishable winners and losers. And once again it is critical that an alternative vision of what the future might be—a new Antifederalism—should be placed on the public agenda.

Also much like these past reform proposals, those of the Committee do not address the underlying critical issues or spell out the long-term implications for the daily lives of most Americans. The Committee apparently does not recognize, or does not care to acknowledge, the breakdown of liberal capitalism and the post–World War II growth coalition.[4] Until the late 1960s, this coalition enabled the two parties to preside over the political direction of the country, albeit with increasing stress, division, and alienation among the public. It allowed the United States and its multinational corporations to dominate the world political economy, albeit with growing hostility, instability, and challenge from those dominated.

The Committee is advancing its proposals in the midst of a major political-economic crisis in which both political parties are stalemated. The Republicans are unable to build a stable majority capable of governing, and the Democratic party seems hopelessly shattered by the collapse of its New Deal coalition and the inability, and in some cases unwillingness, of organized labor to act as the guarantor of its working class constituency. As a result, neither party is willing or able to ask hard questions and provide programmatic answers to the political-economic problems facing the nation. The result is increasing deadlock and stalemate at the national level.

Yet an animating assumption behind the proposals is that, once in place, the structural reforms will somehow strengthen and reenergize the two-party system and insure its ability to govern and lead. By attributing the problems to structural defects in the Constitution—meanwhile ignoring the larger and more fundamental structural transformations in the postwar political economy—the Committee avoids the necessity of drawing the overriding conclusions. The matter is that the Constitution no longer reliably protects capitalist interests, and structural reform that further centralizes power and control is unlikely to overcome the long-term contradictions in the larger political economy.

Moreover, behind the Committee's limited criticism and informing its proposals for "structural reform" is a particular set of assumptions. Most often these are only implicit. But it is clear that the members of the Committee distrust the common sense and political will of the citizenry and value a strengthened party system as a mechanism for disciplining the act of voting (which they consider the citizen's fundamental and only significant political act). They would enable the state, through party discipline of elected officials as well as their constituencies, to act as a collective capitalist, harmonizing and coordinating various fractions of the capitalist class to their larger advantage. These informing assumptions point to the worst possible results of such reform, results that would further trivialize and discourage political participation and constrain democracy, further centralize and commingle economic and political power, and redound to the interests of corporate power in consolidating its control of the state.

In this essay, I first describe the Committee's proposals and their underlying assumptions to expose the historical amnesia and shallow analysis upon which the proposals are based. Then I argue that the proposed reforms actually have two contrasting implications. They represent a danger in their search for the stability necessary for further rationalization of the political economy of corporate capitalism. But they also offer an opportunity for development of a reenergized electorate willing and able to act democratically and programmatically to limit the domination and power of corporate capital and to create and implement substantive public policy that promotes the general welfare of all Americans.

It is time for a newly conceptualized, broad-based, and forward-looking version of the Antifederalist impulse that can provide a coherent and programmatic counterargument to the latest version of the Hamiltonian solution. Rather than celebrate the 1787 Constitution or consider proposals to further solidify its antidemocratic tendencies, the bicentennial year would be better used to reexamine the debate of 1787 and to place the issue of a vibrant, substantive democracy back on the national agenda.

The Committee on the Constitutional System (The Framers at Age 200)

The Committee on the Constitutional System was formed in 1982 as a group of two hundred "prominent citizens" whose "basic concerns have been the effectiveness and accountability of government."[5] That portion of its work and its thinking widely available to the public is found in two recent books, *Reforming American Government: The Bicentennial Papers of the Committee on the Constitutional System*, edited by Donald L. Robinson, and James Sundquist's *Constitutional Reform and Effective Government.*[6] Sundquist, a senior fellow at the Brookings Institution, is also a member of the Committee's Board of Directors.[7] The material in these two books will serve as the basis for the discussion and critique presented in this section.

The Committee came together primarily out of a recognition of the twin dangers of the "imperial presidency" as demonstrated in the Johnson and Nixon years and the stalemate and deadlock experienced in the Ford and Carter administrations. Their simultaneous emergence in the Reagan presidency in the form of Grenada and Iran (imperial presidency) and the deficit (deadlock) further convinced the Committee that these dangers were "structural"; that is, that they were primarily political and institutional and could be largely overcome by proper adjustments to the basic structures that define our system of governance.

It was out of these concerns and this understanding of the parameters of the problem that the Committee came into being. One co-chair is Washington superlawyer, trilateralist, and former White House counsel to President Carter, Lloyd Cutler. The other is investment banker and former Secretary of the Treasury, C. Douglas Dillon. In 1984 Republican Senator Nancy Landon Kassebaum of Kansas was added as a third co-chair.

As the Committee's discussions took form, its concerns came to focus on what they identified as "the two essential measures of democratic constitutionalism, competence and accountability."[8] Their questions were summarized by Donald Robinson:

> Is the government capable of framing and implementing a coherent policy, or does it tend to fall into stalemate and deadlock and then resort to extra-constitu-

tional means to cope with emergencies? Are the mechanisms of popular accountability adequate? Is the electorate capable of rendering an effective verdict on the
performance of the government, and is it possible to replace a failed government?[9]

Their answers added up to a series of proposed changes in the Constitution, in
statutory law, and in party rules and procedures. It is evident, however, from
reading the Committee's papers that these "questions" were simply framing
assumptions to lead quickly to its proposals. The questions themselves are not
carefully explored nor are the implications of their answers probed.

The Committee cautions that its proposals are still in their formative stages,
and a number of variants on each is still under discussion.* But basic proposals
designed to reduce the risk of divided government, facilitate the breaking of
deadlocks between executive and legislative branches, and strengthen political
parties and the electoral system appear widely agreed upon by members of the
Committee. According to Robinson, these proposals, listed below, "constitute
one of the Committee's most important contributions."[10]

The Committee's Proposals (The Hamiltonian System, Phase III)

I. Constitutional amendments

A. *To solve primarily the problem of divided government:*

1. Coordinated terms of office for elected members of the executive and legislative
   branches would be established;
2. Presidential and congressional candidates would run as a team on a political party
   slate;
3. The party electing the President would receive bonus seats in the Senate and House;
4. Members of the Senate and House would be eligible to fill offices in the executive
   branch;
5. The President would have the power to appoint cabinet secretaries to the Senate and
   House;
6. The two-term limit on the presidency (twenty-second amendment) would be repealed.

B. *To solve primarily the problem of deadlock:*

1. The President and Congress would have the power to issue a proclamation or
   resolution of no confidence which would result in special elections for President and
   all members of Congress;
2. Provisions would be made for a national referendum;
3. The one-house override would be available to House and Senate;
4. The President would be empowered with the item veto;

---

*Indeed, in its final report, *A Bicentennial Analysis of the American Political Struc-
ture: Report and Recommendations of the Committee on the Constitutional System*,
published after this essay was written, the Committee omits a number of the proposals advanced in the Robinson and Sundquist volumes.

5. Congress would be empowered with the legislative veto;
6. Treaty ratification would occur by a reduced majority.

II. Federal statutes to reform the electoral system

1. Two-phase federal elections would be established in which the President would be elected four weeks prior to Congress;
2. Candidates for federal office would have an option to run on party slates;
3. Public financing of campaign broadcasts would be provided.

III. Party rules to reform the electoral system

1. Restrictions would be placed on campaign expenditures;
2. Bicameral nominating conventions would divide delegates to national conventions into a popular and a congressional chamber.

Many of these proposals, and much of the analysis on which they depend, may be found in previous books by major academics now associated with CCS.[11] The problem they see is that a post–World War II constitutional dilemma has developed in which the structural features of the national government, specifically, separation of powers and checks and balances, have worked increasingly to (1) create situations of deadlock between President and Congress in which responsibility cannot be fixed; (2) deny the country the ''energy'' to speak and act with ''one clear voice'' in foreign affairs and ''to act promptly and energetically in the face of a crisis''; and (3) hinder the ability of either political party to ''form a government'' able to carry out a coherent overall program.[12] The dilemma, as the Committee sees it, is that a ''governmental structure crafted to frustrate would-be tyrants must also, inevitably, frustrate democratic leaders exercising these powers for worthy ends.''[13]

Much like the framers of the Constitution whom they so admire, and particularly like Alexander Hamilton whose analysis they most closely follow, the Committee is intent on modernizing our basic governing document to make it adequate to the pace of the times. Like the Federalists in their move away from the Articles of Confederation, the Committee professes much concern with ''effectiveness and accountability'' of government, while underneath its proposed structural alterations lurk distrust of the people's ability to make considered political choices and a desire to further centralize political-economic power in the hands of a government that would come to look even more like the parliamentary systems that Hamilton so admired.[14]

In its discussion of the dilemma of the American constitutional system, the Committee echoes Hamilton's ''dark catalogue of our public misfortunes'' in *The Federalist*, No. 15. The Committee is concerned with disunity and deadlock verging, in its analysis, on crisis and paralysis brought on by ''weaknesses'' in the national structure. Hamilton was concerned with the disunity and deadlock verging, in his opinion, on anarchy resulting from ''thirteen distinct sovereign wills'' held together by a league of friendship. But the underlying analysis and the political vision are strikingly similar. The Committee certainly would agree with Hamilton that ''there are material imperfections in our national system and that something is necessary to be done to rescue us from impending anarchy."[15] And so it is not surprising that the Committee views its task as one "as exacting—but also as compelling—as the one undertaken in Philadelphia in the summer of 1787."[16]

Much like the membership of the Philadelphia Convention, the Committee is composed of a narrow band of economic, political, and professional elites who see themselves as more farsighted and capable than most members of the general public. Of course, in the late twentieth century, one must be a bit more circumspect on these matters than were our founding fathers, and one also must show some awareness of the need for gender and other representation.

The Committee is also worried about growing voter apathy, which it understands to result from a loss of faith and respect in the government and its ability to carry through with its promises.[17] Implicit in its discussions is an understanding of the legitimizing function of voter participation and a concern that the continued erosion of procedural democracy will further hasten the looming crisis it sees threatening under an unreformed Constitution. The Committee clearly recognizes that well-functioning political parties have served to legitimize the capitalist political economy by providing the illusion of democratic participation in its direction. Thus, restructured and greatly strengthened political parties are seen as a vital by-product of Constitutional reform.

In his day, Hamilton sought to detach citizens' loyalties from their state and local governments and reattach them to the national government. The Committee's implicit goal is to dilute the political influence of grassroots efforts, minor parties, insurgent movements, and their spokespeople and candidates. The Committee seeks to refocus people's political vision on good foot-soldier behavior in hierarchically organized, highly structured, nationally focused and disciplined political parties.In closing off many of the existing avenues for grassroots access to the ongoing political process and in blocking entry points for citizen-initiated policy, the Committee's proposals strike at the heart of the basic requisites for a vital and democratically healthy body politic.

Given these guiding assumptions, a closer look at the Committee's proposals and overall argument should enable us to better fathom its agenda. While every proposal could be implemented independently and could stand on its own as a minor reform, each proposal is best understood as one piece of an overall package. It is their cumulative impact that we must consider. Only when viewed *in toto* do the antidemocratic and sweeping substantive implications of these reforms become fully evident.

Rather than the overall impact, the Committee's authors emphasize the modesty and neutrality of their proposals. For example, Sundquist calls them "*incremental* steps that might bring more unity to the American government,"[18] and Robinson talks about the need to "improve the performance of our government by *adjusting* its basic structure and processes."[19]

All of the authors are careful to assert that the changes proposed are "structural,'' not substantive, that only the institutional structure would be altered in such a way as to enable the government to be more efficient, more effective, and more decisive. More efficient, effective, and decisive toward what substantive end? None of the authors say; there is total silence on this question. The proposals are seen as issues of adjustment of the mechanism, not matters of substance. Hence, questions of value and ultimate ends need not be raised. Furthermore, these technical issues can be treated exclusively by experts, unhampered by the views of the larger, presumably uninterested, body politic.

The Committee's unconcern and even disdain for public decision making, and its contrasting confidence in experts of various kinds, is regularly evidenced in its papers.[20] There is very little attention paid to the people except as ratifiers and reactors. Hamilton has indeed found a new voice. But to see the real (and cumulative) impact of these proposed changes, we must take them up in the sequence in which they are proposed.

The Proposals (Munching at the Grassroots)

The Divided Government Amendments

The Committee puts forward twelve constitutional amendments directed specifically at overcoming the problems of divided government. The first set (amendments A.1 through 6 above) is aimed at modifying the separation-of-powers principle so as to allow the executive and legislative branches to act more often in concert and accord.

The first amendment, *coordinated terms of office*, has been put forward a number of times previously and in several different combinations.[21] The version favored by the Committee extends the term of members of the House of Representatives from two to four years to run concurrently with that of the President. In addition, the term of senators would be extended from six to eight years, and the Senate would be divided into two classes with one class to be elected every four years.[22]

Sundquist argues that presidents enjoy a "window of opportunity" for at best the first year of their presidency. This enables them to put forward and pass a legislative program before the immediacy of mid-term elections, and their resulting outcomes (often the loss of a presidential majority in Congress) work to destroy whatever unity may have existed between legislature and executive at the outset of the presidential term.[23]

Sundquist sees extended terms for Congress and the elimination of mid-term elections as a major, but only partial, step toward greater party cohesion and harmonious cooperation between Congress and the White House. Such cooperation is necessary for enactment of the ruling party's legislative program and achieving the effectiveness and accountability that are the express goals of the Committee. The Committee has no doubt that two-year terms are "unquestionably'' too short for legislators, tie them too closely to their districts, and cause them to take positions independent of the President, and often of their party.[24]

The Committee believes longer terms will promote greater engagement of voters with their government. As one author argues:

> Coterminous elections of President and Congress would go far to strengthen the voter's *feelings*, now systematically diminished by the separation of power and the methods of nominating and electing federal officials, that they are sharing in the creation of the government and the opposition. The voters should thereby have a *sense of participation* in the awesome and necessary task of governing the nation. Voters would be linked to the government or to the opposition by bonds of partisan *feeling*.[25] (Emphasis added)

Presumably, the next two amendments—the presidential-congressional team ticket and bonus seats in Congress for the President's party—would also give the citizen a greater "sense" of selecting a government. Contrary to the analysis advanced by their authors, the amendments are unlikely to lead to greater (and certainly not more substantive) involvement in the formation of a government. They are designed as powerful agents that would work to overcome the manifestations of all three of the structural defects of our current system identified by their proposers—divided government, deadlock, and weak parties. In so doing, they would exacerbate further the lack of citizen access to national policymaking.

The *team ticket amendment* would require candidates for the presidency (or for presidential elector), the Senate, and the House to run on a political party slate, with state candidates having the option to join the team ballot. (Presumably there would be strong pressure on nonnational candidates to join.) Split-ticket voting, at the national level at least, would be prohibited; and if a voter were to cast separate votes for individual candidates, they would not be counted. The intent is to significantly strengthen party cohesion and to make it more likely that one party will dominate both elected branches of government.[26]

Sundquist recommends an end to split-ticket voting in order to provide a critical path back to united party control of government. He does not address the fundamental transformation in the American (and world) political economy that gave rise to the postwar dissolution of party discipline in the first place, nor, as we shall see later, does he address any of the long-term political-economic tendencies which have wrought change in the twentieth century and of which the Progressive movement and the Committee itself are only manifestations. As attention is focused so intently on institutional problems and their technical solutions, the underlying questions drop from sight. The problem can be thus defined as purely political and then even more narrowly focused on the aggrandizement of power of a small group of political actors. This is clearly seen in the treatment of the relationship of third-party movements to the proposed changes.

The result of a constitutionally mandated team ticket, particularly when combined with lengthened terms of office and bonus seats in Congress, would be to further diminish the already problematic possibility of any viable third-party movement. None of the proposals would alter the single-member, winner-take-all scheme of representation that so handicaps third-party efforts. A vibrant multi-party system and substantive grassroots activity that would require a plan for proportional representation is anathema to the Committee and its goals of unity and stability under party discipline. A rather disingenuous Sundquist tells us that:

> If a John Anderson were serious, under the team-ticket scheme, he would be forced to organize a full-fledged party, one capable of governing—and that would be all to the good. Any presidential candidacy would have to reflect, as it should, more than the individual ambition of a maverick politician. It would have to grow out of broad political forces—as, for example, the Populists in the 1890s or the Dixiecrats and American Independent Party (AIP) in the postwar South. And such solidly based parties would have probably as favorable a prospect in a team-ticket electoral system as they do now. . . .[27]

The point is that even under the current system they do not have a favorable prospect: winner-take-all elections, single-member districts, a campaign financing law whose restrictive formula channels public funding primarily to the Republican and Democratic parties, and equal time laws for television that are easily and systematically violated all make it extraordinarily difficult for third parties to seriously contest for power. The proposals put forward would make it virtually impossible.

But Sundquist unabashedly tells us more:

> [T]he experience of the Populists suggests that any party with a depth of popular support can field a winning team. In carrying five states for its presidential candidate in 1892, the People's party elected three senators and eleven representatives.[28]

This is simply bad history, and a more careful look at our past leads to a very different conclusion. The fragile success of the People's Party in 1892 was smashed as the party was gutted, its independence lost, and its "shadow" issue—free silver—was taken by William Jennings Bryan into the Democratic Party in the election of 1896.[29] In the four-year interim between the 1892 success Sundquist points to and the election of 1896, a vital and programmatic challenge to the power of monopoly capital was broken, southern blacks and poor whites were disenfranchised, and the politics of sectionalism and Republican hegemony in the East and Midwest effectively eliminated the possibility of the emergence of a class-based third party as America moved solidly into its period of heavy industrialization. The resulting "system of '96"[30] defined the parameters of the two-party system well into the twentieth century. From that time forward, the Democratic and Republican parties advanced alternative strategies for furthering capitalist interests. A restructuring of the political-economic system along lines other than those compelled by monopoly capitalism was no longer to be addressed.

After the Populist loss in the crucial election of 1896, key issues regarding the distribution of wealth and power and the building of a Jeffersonian society of independent producers were removed from the political agenda. The voting population was sharply reduced; corporate power firmly established itself in both Republican and Democratic parties; and, as Lawrence Goodwyn argues, the "reform tradition of the twentieth century unconsciously defined itself within the framework of inherited power relationships."[31]

The Committee on the Constitutional System stands fully within this tradition. Its proposals would resolidify a now somewhat shaky system of '96, enabling the two parties to consolidate their power internally and exert discipline and control over their members in public office. Insurgency within the established parties or viable third-party movements would be nowhere on the scene.

Charles Hardin, in the proposals set forth in his *Presidential Power and Accountability*, would go even further in destroying the base for grassroots politics by allowing, through statute, committees composed of the leading candidates of their respective parties to "reject local nominees on the ground that they have refused to accept party discipline."[32] He further states:

> Enabling the national parties to veto the nominations of persistent mavericks in Congress would both strengthen parties and also educate the voters to the governing function of parties—that the winning party is elected to govern and the individual congressman is supposed to share in concerting policies necessary to govern rather than to make a career of independence.[33]

One begins to see how, under these proposals, "the people's choice" would be narrowly circumscribed.

The third and closely related proposed amendment, *providing bonus seats in Congress to the party winning the election*, would further enhance elite manipulation of the people's choice. This amendment would allow the party winning the presidency to appoint "bonus" (but voting) members to the House and Senate. One person would be appointed to the House for every five congressional districts, and one to the Senate for each state. These House and Senate appointees would have all the rights, privileges, and duties of elected members. If enacted, this amendment would add to Congress a total of 137 nonelected, fully empowered lawmakers with very close ties to the national leadership of the party holding the presidency.

The requirement for regional representation only partially veils the centralizing thrust of this amendment. Regionally grounded as they may be, the Committee is eager to point out that:

. . . distinguished and experienced citizens, such as former legislators, cabinet members and governors, would probably accept party designations to serve as additional members even though they would not run for individual constituency seats. Their presence in Congress could contribute greatly to its deliberations and its emphasis on national over local and pressure group interests.[34]

In the discussion following the proposal, it is blandly asserted that the "proposed amendment is designed to prevent divided government and to enhance cooperation between the executive and legislative branches, and thereby to reduce the danger of governmental deadlocks."[35] Moreover:

[The] proposed amendment would also make it easier to fix responsibility for the success or failure of governmental programs. Armed with the bonus seats, which generally would enable the President to enact his party's programs, a President and his party would be unable to blame the shortcomings of their administration on the other party's opposition in Congress.[36]

This is neoHamiltonianism with a vengeance, and an excellent example of the sort of "effectiveness and accountability" that the Committee would bring to the national government. Obviously, this amendment would also strengthen the internal workings of dominant political parties, as the Committee approvingly asserts. "The loyalty of these additional members to the party's programs should be much stronger than that of the constituency members less dependent on the party to retain their seats."[37] And further, "persons chosen by the political parties would generally reflect the national concerns of a party and its presidential nominee, rather than the concerns of a single state."[38] Be that as it may, as we have seen from an analysis of the first two amendments, even "constituency" members of Congress would be subject to much tighter party control than is currently the case. The cumulative impact of these three very closely articulated proposals is staggering.

Aware of the criticism the bonus seats proposal is likely to raise, the Committee has included two additional sections in the amendment. Under the first, each party would be required, no less than thirty days before the election, to compile and publish lists of those who would be appointed to Congress if the party's presidential candidate were elected. And second, in order to insure the oversight and investigatory roles of the minority party, at least one-third of the seats of every committee and subcommittee would be filled by members of the minority party and one-third of the committee and subcommittee membership would be able to initiate investigations and issue subpoenas.[39] These latter two provisions are presumably intended to blunt criticism of the overreaching power granted by the first two sections of the amendment and to insure some operational power to the minority party.

Nonetheless, in its "analysis" of the bonus seats amendment, the Committee enumerates a half-dozen anticipated objections but, with only one exception, makes no response to them. As to the expected objection that the amendment would unduly increase the authority of political parties, enabling them to engage in decision making immune from adequate popular scrutiny and approval, the Committee responds with a statement that speaks volumes about its understanding of democracy: ". . . publication of the list of potential designees to congressional office *satisfies the demands for public scrutiny and control* and would prevent the appointment of unreflective party members."[40] This should not surprise us, as the Committee views the strengthening of political parties (implicitly the existing two-party system) through hierarchial organization and top-down discipline to be an important and valued consequence of many of its proposals.

The fourth and fifth proposed constitutional amendments would modify the separation-of-powers principle to permit *legislators in the executive branch* and *cabinet secretaries in Congress*. The proposals put forward in the Robinson book would (a) empower Congress to designate not more than fifty offices in the executive branch to which members of both houses would be eligible for appointment, *en bloc*, by the President[41]; and (b) authorize the President to appoint a limited number of principal executive department officers to Congress. These individuals, in whose appointment Congress must concur, would have all the rights and privileges accorded to the members of the house to which they have been appointed, except the right to vote on bills.[42]

These two amendments are designed, in the eyes of the Committee, to facilitate a closer and harmonious working relationship between the legislative and executive branches. Their most problematic aspect is seen to be a fear on the part of legislators that executive branch officials in Congress would enhance executive power, while former cabinet officers have expressed fear that Congress would gain power under such arrangements.[43] No discussion is provided as to the possible effects that such amendments, in their potential consolidation of national power, would have on the body politic and its ability to force, much less participate in, a substantive hearing on issues of public policy.

The final proposed amendment in this set of six aimed at "modification" of separation of powers would *repeal the two-term limit on the presidency*. It should follow from the discussion of the previous five proposals that the Committee would find the twenty-second amendment a serious impediment to a strong, effective President able to form a government, execute a program, and lead a party. The list of reasons urging repeal ends with the limp and unexplained statement that "the amendment [repealing the twenty-second] returns to the electorate the choice of chief executive."[44]

These six amendments are designed to restructure the Constitution to encourage "effectiveness and accountability" between legislative and executive branches. The arguments advanced in the 1787 convention and *The Federalist* in support of separation of powers and checks and balances appear now as antiquated curiosities that have clearly outlived their usefulness. With the rise of political parties, and increasingly in the post–World War II period, a unified government able to execute a coherent program and act with the "energy and dispatch" so desired by Hamilton and other Federalists has become increasingly problematic.

The authors of the various papers make it clear that the modern political party is not a "faction" in the Madisonian sense, nor is it in any position to impose the tyranny the framers so feared.[45] Thus, it should not be handicapped by structural barriers to concerted and programmatic action. This set of proposed amendments would in fact dismantle many of the Madisonian "safeguards" against factions in order to give freer reign to the Hamiltonian vision of a powerful and energetic state able to devise and execute policy unencumbered by such bothersome impediments. A House carefully controlled and run through party discipline apparently does not present itself as the "inconveniency"[46] that Madison sought to mitigate through elaborate divisions and separations of power.

The Committee regards "special interest groups" as major sources of the current deadlock. These are the new factions that keep government from its business, and they would be tamed or eliminated if they were disciplined and subsumed by a strengthened party system that provided limited access to national policy-making arenas. Perhaps we could say that in the Committee's proposals, Hamiltonian practice has swallowed Madisonian theory.

The Deadlocked Government Amendments

Following the presentation and discussion of its first set of amendments, the Committee turns to its second set, clustering its amendments under the heading "Breaking Deadlocks."[47] The Committee declares that "the popular will is the ultimate arbiter in a constitutional democracy."[48] But it appears that the means for expressing such popular will are quite limited. A quick glance at these proposals reveals that only two of the set—dissolution followed by special elections and referendum—call on the public to express its will. The remaining four deal exclusively with breaking deadlock between the executive and legislative branches and do not involve any consultation with members of the public. As in the first set, the major thrust here is to encourage Congress and the White House to cooperate and work together in the "public interest." Once again, the proposals, taken together, would further insulate nationally elected officials from their electoral constituencies and facilitate their identification of common interests among themselves.

The first proposal in this set, *dissolution and special elections*, allows the President, any time during the first three years of a term, to proclaim "no confidence" in the Congress; and the Congress, by majority vote, may adopt a resolution of no confidence in the President, not subject to executive veto. The special election then required would fill the offices of President and Vice President as well as all House and Senate seats for new terms of four years.

This proposal appears to boil down to placing the proverbial shotgun behind the door, in order to remind elected national officials of the desirability of cooperation and cohesion as an alternative to the possibility of a nationwide plebiscite. The Committee feels confident that:

> [The] mutual risk of dissolution and removal should encourage both Congress and the President to cooperate in fulfilling their governmental responsibilities, while the longer presidential and congressional terms could allow such cooperation the time needed to produce results.[49]

In the meantime, there is drought at the grassroots. The operation of the amendment would, of course, allow for the expression of the "popular will," although only in the narrow sense of having the "opportunity to break an impasse by electing a President and majorities of both houses pledged to break the deadlock one way or another."[50]

A national plebiscite is, however, a major risk most incumbent politicians would be unwilling to take, particularly keeping in mind that, as part of the larger package, the President's party would also control Congress. Moreover, the major thrust of the reforms is to encourage the executive and legislative branches to cooperate and work closely together, thus obviating the need for such an extraordinary measure as an appeal to the public. There would not be much of an opening for citizen influence on such a government.

The second proposed amendment in this set, *the national referendum*, fulfills a similar function. Although ostensibly it is a mechanism to involve the public in the resolution of a major policy issue on which the government is stalemated, the very existence of the amendment would work against its use. The amendment would enable the President to submit to popular vote in a national referendum any bill passed by one house of Congress but not the other during the same session. A majority vote of the people would determine the fate of the bill. The amendment would limit the President's power to evoke its provisions to two bills in any four-year term.[51]

As with the provision for dissolution and special elections, the Committee is here of the opinion that in most cases the amendment itself would create "the incentive . . . for presidents and legislators to avoid the risks of the referendum process by working things out themselves."[52] Once again, the shadow of democratic control and accountability is further dimmed. And if a referendum were to occur, the electorate would be asked simply to vote up or down on the proposed legislation. This is not the sort of participatory democracy that allows for substantive debate, differing points of view, and compromise that reconciles conflicting interest. Neither special elections nor the referendum would enhance the substantive dimension of political democracy or voter efficacy.

The remaining four proposals in this set—the one-house override, item veto, legislative veto, and reduced majority for treaty ratification—are all internal structural mechanisms for blunting checks and balances. The "popular will" is nowhere involved in these adjustments; rather, the adjustments further insulate the initiation and making of public policy from intrusion by the public.

The *one-house override* would provide another mechanism for breaking deadlocks by enabling two-thirds of either house to present a bill passed by that house but not by the other to the President for signature.[53] The *item veto* would empower the President to veto individual items pertaining to appropriations contained in bills passed by Congress. Congress would have the power to override by a two-thirds vote in each house.[54] The *legislative veto*, which had been in widespread use until declared unconstitutional in 1983,[55] would provide Congress a direct means of exerting control over administrative action taken under its authorization. This proposed amendment would establish a constitutional means for a two-house veto of action taken under legislation containing such a provision. This would enable Congress to continue a practice, begun in 1932 and interrupted in 1983, of delegating power to the executive branch but of reviewing actions under the delegation before they take place.[56]

Finally, the *reduced majority for treaty ratification* would amend the Constitution to empower the President to make treaties with three-fifths concurrence of the Senate or, as an alternate proposal, with a majority of each house.[57] The executive would be able to move more quickly and decisively than is currently the case under the two-thirds requirement of Article I, Section 2. In the Committee's view, the inertia resulting from the two-thirds requirement is extremely costly. It is also pointed out that:

> [O]ne principal evil resulting from the two-thirds rule is that it permits a small number of senators—motivated perhaps by wholly parochial considerations arising from the composition of certain constituencies, or even by personal animosity—to block treaties backed with overwhelming national support. . . .[58]

Again it becomes clear that the Committee's concern with insuring energy and dispatch will be gained at the cost of considered public debate.

These twelve constitutional amendments comprise the list of the Committee's most frequently proposed structural amendments to "adjust its basic structure and processes." In addition, partly in recognition of the difficulties involved in the amending process but perhaps more important to complete the package, the Committee has put forward three federal statutes and two changes in political party rules. After a brief discussion of these remaining proposals, we can evaluate the potential impact of the entire package.

Reforming the Electoral System: Federal Statutes and Party Rules

The five remaining proposals are directed at reforming the electoral system, specifically, at strengthening the two-party system through federal statutes and changes in party rules. The Committee begins from the premise that voting in elections constitutes the citizen's fundamental political act. The emphasis is on procedure and process rather than substance and continuing involvement:

> Elections are fundamental to a constitutional democracy. They are the process by which "government of the people, by the people, and for the people" renews itself. They draw the nation into a debate about its purposes and policies, and they confer legitimacy on those who win.
>
> Thus, the conduct of elections is crucial to the health of a democracy. It is not enough just to invite the people to cast ballots. Dictatorships do that. Democracies must be sure that elections are competitive, and that the competition is free and fair. Citizens must have ample opportunity to participate in the campaign. Winners must be put in position to deliver on their campaign promises. Unless these conditions are met, the appearance of popular sovereignty is fraudulent.[59]

From this premise the Committee moves to the problem of voter apathy and—considering its limited and strictly political framework—points quickly to necessary reforms:

> All of these problems—the need for individual candidates to raise vast sums of money, the tendency for candidates to approach campaigns as individual entrepreneurs, the inability of winners to carry out their promises, the cynicism of voters—reflect the weakness of political parties in our electoral process. If parties had clear and relatively distinct platforms, if they were able to recruit candidates committed to these programs, if they had sufficient resources to conduct appealing campaigns, and if they could induce their candidates, once in office, to work together for the achievement of the promises the party had made during the campaign, then elections might more closely realize the promise of popular sovereignty.[60]

This is fine rhetoric, but the proposals belie the rhetoric and suggest that the Committee is working from a very narrow view of popular sovereignty.

These proposals could be enacted without constitutional amendment, but the sort of "party government" the Committee envisions is not possible without most of the major constitutional reforms it also proposes. The distinction between the amendment route and statutory change comes only when the Committee soberly assesses the obstacles to such fundamental constitutional alteration. Its primary concern is with the "party-in-government"—that is, with "the political level of the administration, headed by the President, and the majorities of the House and Senate, fewer than five hundred persons in all."[61] The Committee sees moves that would strengthen the party-outside-government as important adjuncts in the furtherance of governmental unity.[62] From this perspective, its desire to overcome voter apathy is merely instrumental. Greater participation would more substantially legitimize the party-in-government. A look at the remaining proposals will make this clear.

Federal Statutes

The first statute would require *two-phase federal elections* in presidential election years, in which members of the House and Senate would be elected in November, four weeks after the October election of the President and Vice-President. The primary intent of delayed congressional elections would be to allow voters who wish to avert governmental deadlock to support congressional candidates belonging to the incoming President's party.[63] Like the constitutional amendments designed to forestall deadlock, two-phase elections would go a great distance toward insuring one-party control of the governmental apparatus.

At the same time, the voter's role is, in effect, reduced in the second election to ratifying the decision made a month previously or to registering mild dissent. Citizen-candidate involvement in the crafting of issues and positions would not be encouraged, nor would third parties, but this is not acknowledged by a single one of the various writers. Third parties and local concerns would almost certainly be lost in the rush to vote for the new President's team or to lend some support to the other major party, now doomed to minority status for at least four years (barring a dissolution and special election).

Anticipating the argument that such an electoral system would likely result in a significant falloff in voter turnout in the November congressional elections, the Committee joins this proposal with its proposed constitutional amendment calling for coordinated terms of office, thus eliminating the mid-term elections.[64] Clearly, two-phase federal elections would be incompatible with the team ticket proposal; yet they are designed to serve similar ends and either one, accompanied by coordinated terms of office, would work toward the desired result.

The second proposed statute would provide an *option for candidates for federal office to run on political party slates*. This statute is presented as an alternative to the proposed constitutional amendment which would make the team ticket mandatory, presumably because it is thought that its noncompulsory nature would make passage easier. The statute is clearly seen as a weaker, and hence less desirable, alternative. Its weakness, to the Committee's way of thinking, is that locally popular and/or independently minded candidates might refuse to join a team ticket, and that consequently, party control would probably not be increased significantly by this route.[65]

The final statutory proposal would provide *public financing of campaign broadcasts*. This would be done through the creation of a Congressional Campaign Broadcast Fund modeled on the existing Presidential Campaign Fund.[66] Like the law after which it is patterned, this proposal would create a fund made up of money designated on income tax returns and then supplemented by federal matching funds.

Like the Presidential Campaign Fund, the broadcast fund would in several respects be deleterious to the development of vital third parties and grassroots political activity. While intended to lessen the impact of private funding in federal elections, the fund would make monies available only to "major" political parties, defined as "parties that received 25 percent of the national popular votes cast in the preceding elections for senators and representatives."[67] A major result of such a statute would be to further reinforce the dominance of the two parties existing at the time of enactment, and to further handicap a third party's ability to develop a vital opposition to the status quo.

In addition, under this proposed law, committees within the major parties would have the full discretion to distribute the funds to candidates of their choice. This would strengthen the party leadership's ability to discourage responsiveness to local needs or the development of a programmatic opposition within the party. A far more equitable solution might be to treat all campaign broadcasts as public service announcements, available to all parties, regardless of size, but with an equally distributed ceiling, so as not to flood the air waves.

Party Rules

Finally, the Committee advances two changes in party rules. The first suggests reforming party rules along the lines of the Federal Campaign Act.[68] It would place *restrictions on the total campaign expenditures* a candidate could make from contributions and personal funds, as well as on the size of campaign contributions a candidate could receive. All contributions received by individual candidates would go to the treasurer of that person's party, to be held in the candidate's account.[69]

While the Committee voices as a primary objective in advancing this reform "the reduction of the importance of financial resources in the American electoral process and the combating of existing campaign financing abuses,"[70] it also looks with favor on the enhanced party unity that would result. The proposers do not mention the fact that the limitations are on *individual* candidates; the parties themselves are omitted from the rule. This omission would enable a party's treasurer to channel "excess" contributions to those candidates whose contributions or expenditures had not reached the rule's limit. Like the proposed public financing statute, the benefits of this rule would redound to the established two parties, upon which no limitations would be placed.

The second change in party rules, *bicameral nomination conventions*, would divide the national convention into a popular chamber and a congressional chamber (composed of the party's House and Senate candidates and its continuing Senators), each of which would separately and simultaneously select a presidential candidate by majority ballot. If the chambers selected different candidates, a runoff election between the two candidates would be held, the winner receiving the party's nomination. The party platform also would require approval of both chambers; differences would be worked out by conferees from each chamber.[71]

The expressed intent of this rule is to increase substantially the role of each party's congressional wing in nominating its presidential and vice-presidential candidates. The hope is that this would enhance unity between party members in the congressional and executive branches. Also implicit in the Committee's discussion of this proposal is the hope that it would minimize the possibility that "outsiders" might capture the presidential nomination (e.g., a Reagan, a Carter, an Eisenhower, or, looking ahead, a Lee Iacocca or a Pat Robertson).

The Committee points out that in the twenty chances to nominate a presidential candidate since World War II, the two major parties have nominated only three who were incumbent members of Congress at the time (Kennedy, Goldwater, and McGovern) and that the nominee had congressional experience in only eleven of the twenty cases.[72] The operation of this rule would make it much more likely that the presidential candidate and the congressional candidates of a party would be in accord on the elements of a coordinated and comprehensive legislative program. But it would also further constrict the ability of the broad base of each party's membership to determine the presidential and vice-presidential candidates and to shape the policy proposals contained in the platform.

The proposal is also intended to bring the nominating process back under control of the party professionals where (it may be presumed from the tone in the Committee's work) it belongs. It would strike at the post-1968 attempts to open up the public's role in selecting the presidential candidate and to weaken the control of party "bosses" over the process. The rules developed in the Democratic Party through the work of the McGovern Commission[73] were intended to allow traditionally excluded groups—women, young people, and racial minorities—access to the party's presidential selection process and at the same time to lessen the control of the traditional party bosses on the nominating process.

The resulting explosion of direct primaries as a method of delegate selection dramatically changed the complexion of the Democratic national conventions. Sundquist tells us with some nostalgia that:

> A candidate who dominates the primaries can no longer be jettisoned at the convention as was Roosevelt in 1912, Dewey in 1940, or Kefauver in 1952. The party elders no longer have the votes.
>
> This has grave implications for the unity of the party-in-government. The party elite that includes the party's senators and representatives has lost the means to defend itself against the election of an outsider to the White House.[74]

And Lloyd Cutler complains that

> Presidential candidates are no longer selected, as Adlai Stevenson was selected, by the leaders or bosses of their party. Who are the party leaders today? There are no such people. The party is no longer the instrument that selects the candidate.[75]

Although the 1969 McGovern reforms have been modified several times in order to reestablish some of the party officials' former convention and nominating power, these modifications have not been sufficient for the Committee. This proposal, in particular, is aimed at further restoring the *status quo ante*.[76]

The Republican Party has suffered a similar, but not as extreme, fate. The Committee looks warily at the process that brought Ronald Reagan the 1980 nomination over more party-oriented contenders, at the increasing tension between party professionals and activists, and particularly at the growing influence of the Christian right. When taken in conjunction with other of the Committee's proposals that would more hierarchically structure the party system and more clearly concentrate power at the top (i.e., national) level, this rule change can be seen as another step in distancing the public from the locus of decisionmaking.

A NeoFederalism for the Twenty-first Century

This concludes the discussion of the most prominently featured of the Committee's proposals. If we now consider the entire package—twelve amendments, three federal statutes, and two changes in party rules[77]—there is no mistaking their cumulative impact. What the Committee puts forward as "adjustment" and "incremental steps" would, if translated into practice, bring major change to the political-economic system, and ultimately to the larger culture in which it is embedded. Yet in disarming language, co-chair Lloyd Cutler assures us that the Committee "is proceeding on the theory that a constructive way to commemorate the bicentenary of our constitutional system is to analyze its few weaknesses along with its many strengths, and to consider how those weaknesses might be corrected."[78]

As for the Committee's professed twin goals of efficiency and accountability, the first would be achieved with a vengeance. Once in place, the package would work to purify parties, to make them more internally homogeneous and like-minded, and to muffle the voice of those groups that had begun to be heard for the first time, while the elected branches of government would lose whatever meager separate bases of support, diversified constituencies, and distinctiveness they now have. The judiciary would also fall quickly into line. Even more than is now the case, federal judges and Supreme Court justices could be expected to be proven party loyalists ideologically in tune with the national leadership, and unlikely to demonstrate independence once on the bench.

It would be a very efficient government indeed. But accountable to whom? Certainly not the people, from whom it would be largely insulated. The people are excluded from the proposed process except in their one role as atomized voters—disciplined, or required by constitutional directive, to vote a party slate. Elections under this system would become a mass spectacle, with all elected federal officials (except one-half of the Senate) changing every four years, and no elections in the interim except in the extraordinary case of no confidence, an unlikely occurrence given all the other changes. Mass voting as a legitimation mechanism would become critical to the party-in-government, and some popular interest in the elections would have to be stimulated in order to generate the requisite turnout. Is this the accountability the Committee has in mind?

When it does speak of this side of its dual goal (overwhelming emphasis being placed on the efficiency side rather than accountability), it is an accountability that comes from drastically reducing the current division of authority between legislative and executive branches, so that responsibility for events can be placed on one party or person.[79] There is certainly nothing wrong with accountability, but the Committee's version is a strange kind of top-level accountability that applies among a small circle of like-minded elites across the two governmental branches and through the top party echelons. The team ticket, the control that parties would have in selecting desirable and weeding out undesirable candidates, the eighty-seven House and fifty Senate bonus seats awarded to the party winning the presidency, and the coordinated terms of office would mean that a party, once elected, would be in a position to implement the program outlined in its campaign rhetoric.

If it did not, presumably the (very weak) losing party would be able to propose a resolution of no confidence in the President and call new elections—*if*, according to the provisions of the proposed amendment, the losing party could garner an absolute majority of the members of each house in the no-confidence vote. This seems highly improbable. The cohesiveness of the party-in-government and its overwhelming majority in Congress, which should enable it to act with energy and dispatch, must be what the Committee has in mind when it speaks of "accountability."

The people have no role in this accountability process except as dutiful voters. Their influence as citizens on the shape and direction of "their" government would be encapsulated, trivialized, and extinguished in a single act every fourth year. The minority party would have to count on some congressional dissenters from the well-disciplined majority in order to pass its no-confidence resolution. And so the question begins to emerge as to what would keep the party-in-government from running away with the government? Although lip service is paid to the need for an opposition,[80] scant provision is made for one. (The only guarantee in the package is in the team-ticket and bonus seats amendments, which insure the minority's ability to initiate investigations and subpoenas within committees and subcommittees.) Furthermore, under such a system it would be even less likely than at present that the two parties would take distinctly different positions on major issues. They would continue to provide alternative policies in the service of corporate capitalism or of various competing fractions of the capitalist class, but would not distinguish themselves through substantially different programs. While the Committee claims to want to encourage distinct, competitive parties, it gives no hint as to what might be the major defining distinctions between them. But it is quite evident that what the Committee does not have in mind is distinct class-based parties. The "revitalized" party system would provide the parties the institutional and structural backbone to act as stern gatekeepers to public access to policymaking. It is a scheme to depoliticize the public and further privatize the economic sphere. As we will see, this new plan takes the

Hamiltonian scheme and its modernization through the system of '96 one step further along the road to imperious government. It raises the strong possibility that if popular action is to take place, if substantive changes are to occur, or if a class-based politics is to develop, they will have to find space outside the ever-more-completely circumscribed political arena.

While the authors of the various papers are concerned that rivalries between the two branches will be a major obstacle to the acceptance of their proposals (another example of the deleterious workings of separation of powers and checks and balances), scant attention is paid to the possible reaction of the public. In fact we are told, repeatedly, that the public is not interested in such "technical" adjustments, that it is satisfied with things as they are and cannot be expected to take an active role in this sort of "adjustment."

The emphasis is on urgency and dispatch. A basic premise underlying all the proposals is that "indecisive, stalemated government can place the nation in peril—and that these risks outweigh the danger that decisive government will make unwise decisions."[81] There is a massive means/ends confusion here, or, less charitably, a concentration on the means in a deliberate attempt to obfuscate the ends.

Intended or not, the end of such "reform" would likely be darkly Hamiltonian: a powerfully strengthened and centralized government, able to act quickly and decisively without provision for the time or channels necessary for popular consultation. It would be an American political system whose rapidly dwindling openness has been entirely wrung out—and, as a further extension of the system of '96, a political economy that is stabilized, temporarily, in order to further rationalize and accommodate the needs of corporate capitalism. Like the two earlier Hamiltonian accomplishments, this one is also likely to be effective in (1) asserting and maintaining control of a depoliticized people and (2) giving the interests of capital an accommodating popular support, but only in the short run. Each has further narrowed the practice of democracy in order to unencumber the growth and hegemony of capital. This reform package suggests, once again, that democracy and capitalism are fundamentally contradictory and have indeed "reached a parting of the ways."[82]

But there is something askew in all of this. As has been shown, the Committee's authors provide a very shallow analysis upon which to base their proposals for reform. The Committee's recommendations, as well as the argument and analysis upon which they rest, are isolated from the larger political-economic and historical context. The authors never, for example, pose the question of the relationship between, on the one side, political parties and the constitutional structures they would reform and, on the other, the nature of the larger political-economic system within and through which they operate. They appear oblivious to the fact that, when the postwar boom ended, the growth coalition collapsed, the labor-capital accord guaranteeing industrial peace was terminated, and America's international hegemony was irreparably undermined. In the place of growth and boom, the struggle between capital and labor is increasingly becoming the central reality in American politics.

In fact, the Committee's proposals and the analysis that supports them appear light years away from this reality. Listen to C. Douglas Dillon, a founder and co-chair of the Committee:

> Our constitutional system worked as expected and served us well for over 150 years. It is only since World War II that serious strains began to appear. *The basic reasons for these strains lie in the technological developments that make life, and in particular political life, quite different today from what it was only fifty years ago.* These developments have annihilated time and distance. I refer to the airplane, in particular the jet airplane, and the development of television and inexpensive, instantaneous communications networks that cover our entire nation and, indeed, the globe.
>
> . . . Because of faster means of travel, members of Congress spent more time at home, in their districts, and, because of the telephone and the news media, they were in constant touch with constituents who were informed on a day to day, if not an hour to hour, basis as to developments in Washington. Gradually but steadily there was an erosion in party loyalty. Political parties began to lose their ideological identities.[83]

The constitutional problems the Committee points to are certainly real and serious, but they are not based in "technological developments" as Dillon argues, nor are they the result of minor weaknesses in political structures as other members of the Committee seem to believe. Rather, these problems are the manifestation of a fundamental political-economic transformation through which this country, as well as the world, has been moving since the end of World War II. This transformation has outstripped both the Hamiltonian structure and program as well as its refurbishment in the system of '96. Yet another reconfiguration, radical as it may be, and carefully cloaked in the dulcet tones of technical adjustment, will not save the system in the long run.

The authors do not seem to recognize that many of the needs of most citizens are *outside* the current parameters of the political system. Such needs go beyond what a two-party system dominated by the imperative of maintaining the profitability of corporate capitalism is willing or able to provide. The reconstructed party system envisioned by the Committee would only exacerbate the problem and drive even more citizens into the growing army of non-voters. Pressing but currently unmet needs would be further defined out of the political universe if the Committee's proposals were to be enacted. These needs include accessible and affordable health care, a clean and nontoxic environment, full employment at meaningful jobs producing a basic level of material well-being for all, and a decent education providing all members of the social order with the analytical skills and information necessary to make rational, considered decisions about the structures and practices that will shape their futures. These are issues that are pressing to get *in* the political system; to shut the door ever more firmly against them would, indeed, be to risk major constitutional crisis.

The Committee appears to assume that the enactment of its plan would make it possible to form a government commensurate to its responsibilities. They seem to think that all the impediments (seen as strictly political and largely structural) to decisive action would fall away, and the United States would sail with relative ease into the twenty-first century. Not only does the Committee refuse to acknowledge the breakdown of liberal capitalism and of the cross-party growth coalition that provided the basis for government during the twenty-five years following the war,[84] it does not allow that its proposals are being put forward in the midst of a powerful reaction to the collapse of the postwar boom. The two-party system has indeed faltered, as the Committee points out, but it has also simultaneously fractionalized *and* moved to the right. The proposals are coming in the midst of a skewed political system in which those who currently hold the initiative—the conservatives and new right, albeit in unhappy marriage—stand to be the primary beneficiaries of any change.

A NeoAntifederalism for the Twenty-first Century

Short of this worst-case scenario, we should seize the opportunity the bicentennial celebration affords to put forward a coherent alternative vision of what a democratic America could be as it enters the twenty-first century, of what the ends of social life should be and how to achieve them. Warren Burger's Bicentennial Commission will be celebrating a *status quo* that is in deep crisis. The Committee on the Constitutional System, in recognition of one somewhat narrow dimension of the crisis, will be recommending ways to tighten the constitutional system and strengthen political parties so as to better discipline an often restless and increasingly critical and cynical public. In so doing, it hopes to ease some of the accumulation problems of corporate capital. There is a pressing need for a third alternative that asks different questions and seeks different answers.

The Committee on the Constitutional System's proposals, in particular, provide an excellent point against which to begin expanding the terms of the debate and organizing such an alternative vision. The Committee has identified some serious problems endemic to postwar and particularly postboom politics—stalemated government, disintegrating political parties, voter apathy. But its solutions are not only inadequate to resolving the problems it has identified; they would actually move us further in the wrong direction. A thoughtful scrutiny of the Committee's proposals suggests that those who stand to lose from their implementation are those who have lost each time the system has been "reformed": small producers, the working class, women, blacks, Hispanics, and other minorities. Through their struggles, these groups have periodically gained access to and influence in political parties and the state apparatus. But they have also been either silenced or organized out of the policy-making arenas under the terms of "reform." The Committee's proposals suggest just such another reform.

For every one of the Committee's proposals it is possible to put forward a counter proposal, but this should happen only *after* the ends of social life—such as insuring substantive democracy and building a culture that will nurture it—have been fully discussed and agreed upon. We need to ask: What would democracy look and feel like in the twenty-first century? Does its realization require a constitutional restructuring? Should our constitution guarantee basic human rights such as meaningful work and an equitable share in the social product? Do we need a two-party system? To what degree is it feasible to shift the locus of decision-making power from the national to regional and local community governments? Perhaps it is time to give our government a new set of assignments.

At the outset, we need to push back the boundaries of debate, to return at least to the range of questions on the agenda before the system of '96 read them out of the discourse of American politics. But perhaps we should go even further back, before the Federalists carefully crafted their deliberately antidemocratic Constitution, before Hamilton, in the implementation of his program, formally separated political from economic life in the United States. What they did at the same time, of course, was wed wealth and power, detach the loyalties of the people from their state and local governments, and make national government the focus of power and the guarantor of accumulated private property.

If properly framed, these questions could generate widespread and energetic public debate and participation, putting the lie to the Committee's belief that the public is fundamentally disinterested, short of a paralyzing crisis. A substantive and thoughtful public dialogue would speak directly and concretely to the question of accountability, that all-but-ignored side of the Committee's professed dual purpose.

It would not be an easy task; it would not be an "efficient" process. But it would be substantive, programmatic, wide-ranging, and broadly participatory. It would be necessary to fight against generations of culturally induced passivity in the face of complex and "technical" questions, and the tendency toward deference to the more knowledgeable and more economically and politically powerful. It would raise hard questions about the ownership and use of private property and about the proper distribution of wealth and power. It would question the relationship between wealth and power in a society that calls itself democratic, ask about the proper quality of life for all, and query the measures that would be necessary to establish and insure that quality.

The Antifederalists understood these as political questions, as did the Populists. The 1787 Constitution took the first step toward separating and privatizing them, and in so doing it constricted the political universe. The system of '96 took the next major step. The Committee's proposals signify yet another step in this direction, one that would reinforce the principles of Hamiltonianism and 1896 by providing a set of structures through which many of the political-economic gains made by women, labor, and minorities during the recent boom years would be further diminished.

It is time to reset the agenda; and it is critical that a democratically grounded alternative begin to take form now, prior to the presentation of a well-articulated plan for elite reform such as that being developed by the Committee on the Constitutional System. If such a movement is not undertaken, the forces for a more broadly based participatory body politic may find themselves in the same position as the Antifederalists in the fall of 1787—outspent, outmaneuvered, disorganized, and on the defensive. This is one small way to begin building a democratic culture in which people can develop the confidence and skills to create their own society, one in which substantive as well as procedural democratic practices are extended to the larger political economy. If democracy in America is to be recovered, it will be from the grassroots. It will never come from committees of prominent citizens with close ties to corporate capitalism.

Notes

1. All of this will be led in magisterial style by former Chief Justice Warren Burger's Bicentennial Commission and lavishly underwritten at public expense.

2. Donald L. Robinson, ed., *Reforming American Government: The Bicentennial Papers of the Committee on the Constitutional System* (Boulder, Colo.: Westview Press, 1985). p. xv.

3. The Committee on the Constitutional System, "A Statement of the Problem," reprinted in Robinson, pp. 68–71.

4. This term and the analysis it implies comes from Alan Wolfe, *America's Impasse: The Rise and Fall of the Politics of Growth* (Boston: South End Press, 1981).

5. Robinson, p. xv.

6. James L. Sundquist, *Constitutional Reform and Effective Government* (Washington, D.C.: The Brookings Institution, 1986).

7. For a brief sketch of the major affiliations of the members of the Board of Directors, see Appendix.

8. Robinson, p. 1.

9. Ibid.

10. Ibid., p. xv.

11. The political scientists and their works that have been central to CCS thinking are: James MacGregor Burns, *The Deadlock of Democracy* (Englewood Cliffs, N.J.: Prentice Hall, 1963); Charles Hardin, *Presidential Power and Accountability* (Chicago: The University of Chicago Press, 1974); and James MacGregor Burns, *The Power to Lead* (New York: Simon & Schuster, 1984).

12. Sundquist, pp. 8–9; Lloyd Cutler, "To Form a Government," *Foreign Affairs*, 59 (Fall 1980), excerpted and reprinted in Robinson, pp. 11–23, and Douglas Dillon, address at Tufts University, May 30, 1982, reprinted in Robinson, pp. 24–29.

13. "A Statement of the Problem," Robinson, p. 69.

14. Co-chair C. Douglas Dillon, in an influential speech delivered in 1982, called for "a change to some form of parliamentary government." (Dillon in Robinson, p. 29.) The Committee, however, does not envision a parliamentary system fashioned strictly on the European model, but rather, a hybrid that would draw on the strengths of both European

parliamentarianism and American constitutionalism. Perhaps if the Committee's bundle of structural proposals was to become law, many of Hamilton's fondest hopes would be realized in the resulting practices.

15. Hamilton, Madison, Jay, *The Federalist*, with an introduction by Clinton Rossiter (New York: New American Library, 1961), No. 15, p. 106.

16. "A Statement of the Problem," in Robinson, p. 71.

17. Dillon, in Robinson, p. 26, and Robinson, *passim*.

18. Sundquist, p. 29, emphasis added.

19. Robinson, p. xv, emphasis added. However, Hardin, writing to a largely academic audience prior to the establishment of the Committee and without the necessary circumspection that such committee proposals require, clearly recognizes the fundamental departures entailed in such reforms: "The change will require *major surgery*. One cannot stop short of *bold and decisive departures*." Hardin in Robinson, p. 149, emphasis added.

20. For example, Sundquist tells us that:

> Structural amendments, in the absence of governmental breakdown that is indisputably traceable to institutional rather than individual failure, are inherently technical and abstract, not likely to arouse emotion. But the very fact that government has not broken down attests, in the popular mind, to the wisdom of the constitutional design. The absence of criticism surely reflects a faith that the structure that has survived so long without formal alteration must have served the country well since the beginning and can be counted on to serve it no less well in times to come. (Sundquist, p. 73.)

These "technical and abstract" amendments are thus best handled by experts (such as those who make up the membership of the Committee on the Constitutional System) who are more knowledgeable than the general public and, presumably, would be directly affected by the changes in ways that the proverbial man in the street would not. (Of the forty-one individuals who comprise the Committee's Board of Directors, nineteen are past or present members of Congress, the executive branch, or party officials. Most others have strong ties to one or more of these three categories.)

21. For example, Lyndon Johnson's 1966 proposal for four-year house terms, the four-four-four plan, and the six-six-three plan.

22. Robinson, pp. 175–76.

23. Sundquist, pp. 105–07.

24. Ibid., pp. 114–16; Robinson, pp. 175–77.

25. Hardin, in Robinson, p. 151.

26. The authors of the papers, however, appear to disagree on this point. Robinson devotes two sentences to what he clearly considers a non-problem: "The proposed amendment could. . . significantly handicap third-party presidential candidates, who would be required to assemble viable slates of candidates for Congress in order to compete against major party candidates. Third-party candidates for Congress would encounter similar difficulties." (Robinson, p. 179.) Sundquist, on the other hand, is of the opinion that the discipline required by a unified team ticket would likely cause dissenters to bolt the ticket, and therefore the party, and thus increase the likelihood of third party movements. Not to worry, though; Sundquist reassures us that "third parties in this country would tend to have short lives under the new electoral system just as under the present one." (Sundquist, p. 92.)

27. Ibid.

28. Ibid., p. 93.

29. For a thorough analysis of the rise and fall of agrarian populism see Lawrence Goodwyn, *The Populist Moment: A Short History of the Agrarian Revolt in America* (New York: Oxford University Press, 1978).

30. The term was developed by E.E. Schattschneider in *The Semisovereign People*

(New York: Holt, Rinehart and Winston, 1960), pp. 78–85, and has been given further historical depth and analytical rigor in the work of Walter Dean Burnham. See, in particular, "The System of 1896: An Analysis," Chapter 5 of Paul Kleppner et al., eds., *The Evolution of American Electoral Systems* (Westport, Conn.: Greenwood Press, 1981), pp. 147–202.

31. Goodwyn, p. 284.
32. Hardin, in Robinson, p. 150.
33. Ibid., p. 151.
34. Ibid., p. 182.
35. Ibid., p. 181.
36. Ibid.
37. Ibid.
38. Ibid.
39. Ibid., pp. 179–80.
40. Ibid., p. 182, emphasis added.
41. This is very similar to a constitutional amendment proposed in 1979 by then Congressman Henry Reuss, Democrat of Wisconsin. Reuss was also one of the founders of the Committee and is currently a member of its Board of Directors.
42. Robinson, pp. 183–85.
43. Ibid., pp. 185–86.
44. Robinson, p. 187.
45. Ibid., pp. 74–75.
46. *The Federalist*, No. 51, p. 322.
47. Robinson, Part 4.
48. Ibid., p. 189.
49. Robinson, pp. 256–57.
50. Ibid., p. 256.
51. Ibid., p. 258.
52. Sundquist, p. 236.
53. Robinson, p. 257.
54. Ibid., pp. 259–61.
55. *Immigration and Naturalization Service v. Chadha*, 103 U.S. 2764 (1983).
56. Robinson, p. 261; Sundquist, pp. 215–220.
57. Robinson, pp. 262–63.
58. Ibid., p. 263.
59. Robinson, p. 73.
60. Ibid., p. 74.
61. Sundquist, p. 177.
62. Ibid.
63. Robinson, p. 118.
64. Ibid., p. 119.
65. Ibid., p. 120.
66. Ibid.
67. Ibid., p. 121.
68. This act was largely dismantled in *Buckley v. Valeo*, 424 U.S. 1 (1976).
69. Robinson, pp. 122–24.
70. Ibid., p. 121.
71. Ibid., pp. 114–15.
72. Ibid., p. 116.
73. The formal title is The Committee on Party Structure and Delegate Selection.
74. Sundquist, p. 185.
75. Cutler, in Robinson, p. 20.

76. Thomas Edsall argues convincingly that the economic consequences of the Democratic Party reforms have not been to open access to previously excluded minorities, but rather to transfer much of the power to pick delegates to a new economic elite that is radically different from the traditional party base. He demonstrates that through the class-skewed primary turnout, a new and different elite, even less representative of the rank-and-file Democrats than the old party elite, has risen to power. For this important analysis see Thomas Edsall, *The New Politics of Inequality* (New York: W.W. Norton, 1947), pp. 51–57.

77. That there is some overlap and apparent contradiction in the package—for example, the statutory option to vote for party slates and the amendment requiring the team ticket, or the team ticket and the two-phase election—should not distract us from its overall thrust. These are alternate routes to the same end; the statutory provision for optional voting for a party slate is put forward to demonstrate a less arduous route than the team-ticket amendment. In this case, it is clear from the text that while the Committee prefers the amendment because of its compulsory requirements, it would settle for the less rigorous statute as second choice.

78. Robinson, p. 106.

79. Dillon, in Robinson, p. 29, and Robinson, *passim*.

80. Hardin is the only one to talk concretely about the importance of a viable opposition. He argues for the need for an "organized focused opposition with leadership centered in one person who will be continuously visible and vocal as the alternative to the President." Hardin, in Robinson, p. 5. Hardin would have the defeated presidential candidate designated leader of the opposition, given a seat in the House with all the privileges except voting, provided an official residence, offices, and necessary expenses. Ibid., pp. 150–51.

81. Sundquist, p. 240.

82. Samuel Bowles and Herbert Gintis, "The Invisible Fist: Have Capitalism and Democracy Reached a Parting of the Ways?" *American Economic Review*, 68 (May 1978), pp. 358–63.

83. Dillon, in Robinson, p. 25, emphasis added.

84. For three comprehensive and complementary analyses of the rise and fall of the postwar political economy see, Samuel Bowles, David M. Gordon, and Thomas E. Weisskopf, *Beyond the Waste Land: A Democratic Alternative to Economic Decline* (New York: Doubleday, 1983); Kenneth M. Dolbeare, *Democracy at Risk: The Politics of Economic Renewal*, revised ed. (Chatham, N.J.: Chatham House, 1986); and Alan Wolfe, *America's Impasse: The Rise and Fall of the Politics of Growth* (Boston: South End Press, 1981). These three books, particularly when taken together, demonstrate the nature of the systemic, long-term political-economic transformation and make it abundantly clear that the Committee's reforms are not aimed at the heart of the problem.

Appendix

Board of Directors of the Committee on the Constitutional System

Jonathan Bingham   (Former Congressman from New York; lawyer)
Richard Bolling   (Former Congressman from Missouri)
Nicholas Brady   (Former Senator from New Jersey; investment banker with Dillon, Read & Co.; Chairman, Purolator, Inc.; Director, Bessmer Securities Corp., Doubleday & Co., NCR Corp, Media General Inc.)
Janet Brown   (Chairperson, John F. Kennedy School Council, Harvard University)
James MacGregor Burns   (Co-Chairman, Project '87; Professor of Political Science, Williams College)

Gerhard Casper   (Dean, University of Chicago Law School; Board of Directors, ABA)

Douglas Cater   (Former Assistant to the President, 1964-68; President, Washington College)

William T. Coleman, Jr.   (Former Secretary of Transportation, 1975-77; lawyer; senior partner, O'Melveny & Meyers; member, Trilateral Commission; Director, IBM, Chase Manhattan Bank, Pepsi Co., AMAX Inc., American Can Co., Pennsylvania Mutual Life, INA Corp., Pan American World Airways; Board of Governors, Rand Corporation; Trustee, Brookings Institution)

LeRoy Collins   (Former Governor of Florida)

Lloyd Cutler, Co-chair   (Former Counsel to the President, 1979-80; lawyer, partner, Wilmer, Cutler & Pickering; member, Trilateral Commission; Director, American Cyanamind, Kaiser Industries, Alza Corp., Southeast Bank Corp.; Trustee, Brookings Institution; Director, Council on Foreign Relations, 1977-79)

Lynn Cutler   (Vice-Chairperson, Democratic National Committee)

C. Douglas Dillon, Co-chair   (Former Secretary of the Treasury, 1961-65; Director and President, U.S. & Foreign Securities Corp, and U.S. & International Securities Corp, 1937-53; President and Director, Dillon, Read & Co.; Chairman, Rockefeller Foundation, 1972-75, Brookings Institution, 1970-76)

Ruth Friendly   (Faculty member, Scarsdale New York School system)

J. William Fulbright   (Former Senator from Arkansas; of counsel, firm of Hogan & Hartson, Wash., D.C.)

W. Wilson Goode   (Mayor, city of Philadelphia)

Charles Hardin   (Professor of Political Science Emeritus, University of California, Davis)

Alexander Heard   (Chancellor Emeritus, Vanderbilt University; Director, Time, Inc.; Trustee, Ford Foundation, Robert A. Taft Institute of Government; Chm. President's Commission on Campaign Costs, 1961-62)

Betty Heitman   (Co-Chairperson, Republican National Committee; member advisory board, International Management and Development Institute)

Matthew Holden, Jr.   (Professor of Political Science, University of Virginia)

Linwood Holton   (Former Governor of Virginia; V.P., general counsel, American Council of Life Insurance; Chairman, Burket Miller Center Public Affairs, U. Va.)

A. E. Dick Howard   (Professor of Law, University of Virginia; counselor to Governor of Virginia; Executive Director, Virginia Commission on Constitutional Revision, 1968-69)

Nancy Landon Kassebaum, Co-chair   (Senator from Kansas)

Nancy Altman Lupu   (John F. Kennedy School of Government, Harvard University)

Bruce MacLaury   (President, Brookings Institution; President, Federal Reserve Bank of Minneapolis, 1971-77; Director, Dayton Hudson Corp.; American Express International Banking Corp.; Trustee, Joint Council Economic Education; Committee for Economic Development; member, Trilateral Commission)

Robert McClory   (Former Congressman from Illinois; private legal practice; of counsel Baker & McKenzie, Washington, D.C.)

Donald McHenry   (Former U.S. Ambassador to the United Nations; Research professor, Diplomacy & International Relations, Georgetown Univ.; Director, International Paper Corp., Coca-Cola Co., First Nat. Bank, Boston, Smith Kline Beckman Corp., First Nat. Boston Corp.; Board of Governors, American Stock Exchange; Trustee, Brookings Institution, Phelps-Stokes Fund, Ford Foundation)

Robert McNamara   (Former Secretary of Defense; Executive, Ford Motor Company, 1946-61; President, World Bank, 1968-81; Director, Royal Dutch Petroleum, The Washington Post, TWA, Corning Glass Works, Bank of America; Board of Directors, Ford Foundation, Brookings Institution, California Institute of Technology)

Martin Meyerson   (President Emeritus, University of Pennsylvania; Director, Real Estate Research Corp., 1961–67, Marine Midland Bank, 1966–70, Fidelity Bank, Scott Paper Co., Penn. Mutual Life, Certain Teed, Avatar)

Norman Ornstein   (Visiting Scholar, American Enterprise Institute)

Kevin Phillips   (President, American Political Research Corporation; editor and publisher, *The American Political Report, Business & Public Affairs*)

Jessie Rattley   (Past President, National League of Cities)

Henry Reuss   (Former Congressman from Wisconsin; legal practice, Wisconsin)

John Rhodes   (Former House Minority Leader from Arizona)

Dorothy Ridings   (President, National League of Women Voters)

Donna Shalala   (President, Hunter College; Governor, American Stock Exchange)

Rocco Siciliano   (Former Undersecretary of Commerce, 1969–71; Chairman of the Board & CEO, Ticor; Director, Pacific Lighting Corp., Penn. Mutual Life Insurance Co., American Medical International, Southern Pacific Co.; Trustee, J. Paul Getty Trust Mem.; member, California Roundtable; Vice Chairman, Trustee, Committee for Economic Development)

Mary Louise Smith   (Former Chairperson, Republican National Committee)

Elmer Staats   (Former Comptroller General, 1966–81; President, Harry S. Truman Scholarship Foundation; Director, Air Products & Chemicals, Inc., Metropolitan Life Insurance Co., Computer Data Systems, Inc., National Intergroup, Inc; Trustee, Committee for Economic Development, Kerr Foundation; Professor, Graduate School of Management, UCLA and Committee on Public Policy Studies, Univ. of Chicago)

James Sundquist   (Senior Fellow, The Brookings Institution; Secretary to Platform Committee, Democratic National Convention, 1960, 1968)

Dick Thornburgh   (Governor of Pennsylvania; Fellow, American Bar Foundation; Asst. Atty Gen., head of criminal division, Dept. of Justice, 1975–77)

Glenn Watts   (President, Communications Workers of America; Vice President, executive council, AFL-CIO; member Trilateral Commission, President's Comm. for a National Agenda for the 80s, Helsinki Watch; Trustee, Sec. Treasurer, American Institute for Free Labor Development; Trustee, Ford Foundation, George Meany Center for Labor Studies)

Source: Who's Who in America, 1984–85 (43rd ed.) Chicago, Marquis. The initial identification following each name is provided by Robinson, pp. 333–34.

Documents

The Declaration of Independence

When in the Course of human events, it becomes necessary for one people to dissolve the political bands which have connected them with another, and to assume among the Powers of the earth, the separate and equal station to which the Laws of Nature and of Nature's God entitle them, a decent respect to the opinions of mankind requires that they should declare the causes which impel them to the separation.

We hold these truths to be self-evident, that all men are created equal, that they are endowed by their Creator with certain unalienable Rights, that among these are Life, Liberty and the pursuit of Happiness. That to secure these rights, Governments are instituted among Men, deriving their just powers from the consent of the governed. That whenever any Form of Government becomes destructive of these ends, it is the Right of the People to alter or abolish it, and to institute new Government, laying its foundation on such principles and organizing its powers in such form, as to them shall seem most likely to effect their Safety and Happiness. Prudence, indeed, will dictate that Governments long established should not be changed for light and transient causes; and accordingly all experience hath shown, that mankind are more disposed to suffer, while evils are sufferable, than to right themselves by abolishing the forms to which they are accustomed. When a long train of abuses and usurpations, pursuing invariably the same Object evinces a design to reduce them under absolute Despotism, it is their right, it is their duty, to throw off such Government, and to provide new Guards for their future security.—Such has been the patient sufferance of these Colonies; and such is now the necessity which constrains them to alter their former Systems of Government. The history of the present King of Great Britain is a history of repeated injuries and usurpations, all having in direct object the establishment of an absolute Tyranny over these States. To prove this, let Facts be submitted to a candid world.

He has refused his Assent to Laws, the most wholesome and necessary for the public good.

He has forbidden his Governors to pass Laws of immediate and pressing importance, unless suspended in their operation till his Assent should be obtained; and when so suspended, he has utterly neglected to attend to them.

He has refused to pass other Laws for the accommodation of large districts of people, unless those people would relinquish the right of Representation in the Legislature, a right inestimable to them and formidable to tyrants only.

He has dissolved Representative Houses repeatedly, for opposing with manly firmness his invasions on the rights of the people.

He has refused for a long time, after such dissolutions, to cause others to be elected; whereby the Legislative Powers, incapable of Annihilation, have returned to the People at large for their exercise; the State remaining in the mean time exposed to all the dangers of invasion from without, and convulsions within.

He has endeavoured to prevent the population of these States; for that purpose obstructing the Laws of Naturalization of Foreigners; refusing to pass others to encourage their migration hither, and raising the conditions of new Appropriations of Lands.

He has obstructed the Administration of Justice, by refusing his Assent to Laws for establishing Judiciary Powers.

He has made Judges dependent on his Will alone, for the tenure of their offices, and the amount and payment of their salaries.

He has erected a multitude of New Offices, and sent hither swarms of Officers to harass our People, and eat out their substance.

He has kept among us, in times of peace, Standing Armies without the Consent of our legislature.

He has affected to render the Military independent of and superior to the Civil Power.

He has combined with others to subject us to a jurisdiction foreign to our constitution, and unacknowledged by our laws; giving his Assent to their acts of pretended legislation:

For quartering large bodies of armed troops among us;

For protecting them, by a mock Trial, from Punishment for any Murders which they should commit on the Inhabitants of these States;

For cutting off our Trade with all parts of the world;

For imposing taxes on us without our Consent;

For depriving us in many cases of the benefits of Trial by Jury;

For transporting us beyond Seas to be tried for pretended offences;

For abolishing the free System of English Laws in a neighbouring Province, establishing therein an Arbitrary government, and enlarging its Boundaries so as to render it at once an example and fit instrument for introducing the same absolute rule into these Colonies;

For taking away our Charters, abolishing our most valuable Laws, and altering fundamentally the Forms of our Governments;

For suspending our own Legislature, and declaring themselves invested with Power to legislate for us in all cases whatsoever.

He has abdicated Government here, by declaring us out of his Protection and waging War against us.

He has plundered our seas, ravaged our Coasts, burnt our towns, and destroyed the lives of our people.

He is at this time transporting large armies of foreign mercenaries to compleat the works of death, desolation and tyranny, already begun with circumstances of Cruelty & perfidy scarcely paralleled in the most barbarous ages, and totally unworthy the Head of a civilized nation.

He has constrained our fellow Citizens taken Captive on the high Seas to bear Arms against their Country, to become the executioners of their friends and Brethren, or to fall themselves by their Hands.

He has excited domestic insurrections amongst us, and has endeavoured to bring on the inhabitants of our frontiers, the merciless Indian Savages, whose known rule of warfare, is an undistinguished destruction of all ages, sexes and conditions.

In every stage of these Oppressions We have Petitioned for Redress in the most humble terms; Our repeated Petitions have been answered only by repeated injury. A Prince, whose character is thus marked by every act which may define a Tyrant, is unfit to be the ruler of a free People.

Nor have We been wanting in attention to our British brethren. We have warned them from time to time of attempts by their legislature to extend an unwarrantable jurisdiction over us. We have reminded them of the circumstances of our emigration and settlement here. We have appealed to their native justice and magnanimity, and we have conjured them by the ties of our common kindred to disavow these usurpations, which would inevitably interrupt our connections and correspondence. They too have been deaf to the voice of justice and of consanguinity. We must, therefore, acquiesce in the necessity, which denounces our Separation, and hold them, as we hold the rest of mankind, Enemies in War, in Peace Friends.

We, therefore, the Representatives of the United States of America, in General Congress, Assembled, appealing to the Supreme Judge of the world for the rectitude of our intentions, do, in the Name, and by Authority of the good People of these Colonies, solemnly publish and declare, That these United Colonies are, and of Right ought to be Free and Independent States; that they are Absolved from all Allegiance to the British Crown, and that all political connection between them and the State of Great Britain, is and ought to be totally dissolved; and that as Free and Independent States, they have full Power to levy War, conclude peace, contract Alliances, establish Commerce, and to do all other Acts and Things which Independent States may of right do. And for the support of this Declaration, with a firm reliance on the Protection of Divine Providence, we mutually pledge to each other our Lives, our Fortunes and our sacred Honor.

JOHN HANCOCK, President

Attested, Charles Thomson, Secretary

New Hampshire:
Josiah Bartlett
William Whipple
Matthew Thornton
Massachusetts Bay:
Samuel Adams
John Adams
Robert Treat Paine
Elbridge Gerry
Rhode Island, etc.:
Stephen Hopkins
William Ellery
Connecticut:
Roger Sherman
Samuel Huntington
William Williams
Oliver Wolcott
New York:
William Floyd
Philip Livingston
Francis Lewis
Lewis Morris
New Jersey:
Richard Stockton
John Witherspoon
Francis Hopkinson
John Hart
Abraham Clark
Delaware:
Caesar Rodney
George Read
Thomas McKean
Pennsylvania:
Robert Morris
Benjamin Rush

Pennsylvania (cont'd):
Benjamin Franklin
John Morton
George Clymer
James Smith
George Taylor
James Wilson
George Ross
Maryland:
Samuel Chase
William Paca
Thomas Stone
Charles Carroll of
Carrollton
Virginia:
George Wythe
Richard Henry Lee
Thomas Jefferson
Benjamin Harrison
Thomas Nelson, Jr.
Francis Lightfoot Lee
Carter Braxton
North Carolina:
William Hooper
Joseph Hewes
John Penn
South Carolina:
Edward Rutledge
Thomas Heyward, Jr.
Thomas Lynch, Jr.
Arthur Middleton
Georgia:
Button Gwinnett
Lyman Hall
George Walton

The Articles of Confederation and Perpetual Union

Whereas the Delegates of the United States of America, in Congress assembled, did, on the 15th day of November, in the Year of Our Lord One thousand Seven Hundred and Seventy seven, and in the Second Year of the Independence of America, agree to certain articles of Confederation and perpetual Union between the States of Newhampshire, Massachusetts-bay, Rhodeisland and Providence Plantations, Connecticut, New York, New Jersey, Pennsylvania, Delaware, Maryland, Virginia, North-Carolina, South-Carolina, and Georgia in the words following, viz. "Articles of Confederation and perpetual Union between the states of Newhampshire, Massachusetts-bay, Rhodeisland and Providence Plantations, Connecticut, New-York, New-Jersey, Pennsylvania, Delaware, Maryland, Virginia, North-Carolina, South-Carolina and Georgia."

ARTICLE I. The stile of this confederacy shall be "The United States of America."

ARTICLE II. Each State retains its sovereignty, freedom and independence, and every Power, Jurisdiction, and right, which is not by this confederation expressly delegated to the United States, in Congress assembled.

ARTICLE III. The said states hereby severally enter into a firm league of friendship with each other, for their common defence, the security of their Liberties, and their mutual and general welfare, binding themselves to assist each other, against all force offered to, or attacks made upon them, or any of them, on account of religion, sovereignty, trade, or any other pretence whatever.

ARTICLE IV. The better to secure and perpetuate mutual friendship and intercourse among the people of the different states in this union, the free inhabitants of each of these states, paupers, vagabonds, and fugitives from justice excepted, shall be entitled to all privileges and immunities of free citizens in the several states; and the people of each State shall have free ingress and regress to and from any other state, and shall enjoy therein all the privileges of trade and commerce, subject to the same duties, impositions, and restrictions, as the inhabitants thereof respectively, provided that such restriction shall not extend so far as to prevent the removal of property, imported into any state, to any other state, of which the Owner is an inhabitant; provided also that no imposition, duties or restrictions shall be laid by any State, on the property of the United States, or either of them.

If any person guilty of, or charged with treason, felony, or other high misdemeanor in any State, shall flee from justice, and be found in any of the United States, he shall, upon demand of the governor or executive power, of the State from which he fled, be delivered up and removed to the State having jurisdiction of his offence.

Full faith and credit shall be given in each of these states to the records, acts, and judicial proceedings of the courts and magistrates of every other State.

ARTICLE V. For the more convenient management of the general interests of the United States, delegates shall be annually appointed, in such manner as the legislature of each State shall direct, to meet in Congress, on the 1st Monday in November in every year, with a power reserved to each State to recall its delegates, or any of them, at any time within the year, and to send others in their stead for the remainder of the year.

No State shall be represented in Congress by less than two, nor more than seven members; and no person shall be capable of being a delegate for more than three years in any term of six years; nor shall any person, being a delegate, be capable of holding any office under the United States, for which he, or any other for his benefit, receives any salary, fees, or emolument of any kind.

Each State shall maintain its own delegates in a meeting of the states, and while they act as members of the committee of the states.

In determining questions in the United States, in Congress assembled, each State shall have one vote.

Freedom of speech and debate in Congress shall not be impeached or questioned in any court or place out of Congress, and the members of Congress shall be protected in their persons from arrests and imprisonments, during the time of their going to and from, and attendance on Congress, except for treason, felony, or breach of the peace.

ARTICLE VI. No State, without the consent of the United States, in Congress assembled, shall send any embassy to, or receive any embassy from, or enter into any conference, agreement, alliance, or treaty with any king, prince, or state; nor shall any person, holding any office of profit or trust under the United States, or any of them, accept of any present, emolument, office or title, of any kind whatever, from any king, prince, or foreign state; nor shall the United States, in Congress assembled, or any of them, grant any title of nobility.

No two or more states shall enter into any treaty, confederation, or alliance, whatever, between them, without the consent of the United States, in Congress assembled, specifying accurately the purposes of which the same is to be entered into, and how long it shall continue.

No State shall lay any imposts or duties which may interfere with any stipulations in treaties entered into by the United States, in Congress assembled, with any king, prince, or state, in pursuance of any treaties already proposed by Congress to the courts of France and Spain.

No vessels of war shall be kept up in time of peace by any State, except such number only as shall be deemed necessary by the United States, in Congress assembled, for the defence of such State or its trade, nor shall any body of forces be kept up by any State, in time of peace, except such number only as, in the judgment of the United States, in Congress assembled, shall be deemed requisite to garrison the forts necessary for the defence of such State; but every State shall always keep up a well regulated and disciplined militia, sufficiently armed and accoutred, and shall provide, and constantly have ready for use, in public stores, a due number of field pieces and tents, and a proper quantity of arms, ammunition and camp equipage.

No State shall engage in any war without the consent of the United States, in Congress assembled, unless such State be actually invaded by enemies, or shall have received certain advice of a resolution being formed by some nation of Indians to invade such State, and the danger is so imminent as not to admit of a delay till the United States, in Congress assembled, can be consulted; nor shall any State grant commissions to any ships or vessels of war, nor letters of marque or reprisal, except it be after a declaration of war by the United States, in Congress assembled, and then only against the kingdom or state, and the subjects thereof, against which war has been so declared, and under such regulations as shall be established by the United States, in Congress assembled, unless such State be infested by pirates, in which case vessels of war may be fitted out for that occasion, and kept so long as the danger shall continue, or until the United States, in Congress assembled, shall determine otherwise.

ARTICLE VII. When land forces are raised by any State for the common defence, all officers of or under the rank of colonel, shall be appointed by the legislature of each State respectively, by whom such forces shall be raised, or in such manner as such State shall direct; and all vacancies shall be filled up by the State which first made the appointment.

ARTICLE VIII. All charges of war and all other expences, that shall be incurred for the common defence or general welfare, and allowed by the United States, in Congress assembled, shall be defrayed out of a common treasury, which shall be supplied by the several states, in proportion to the value of all land within each State, granted to or surveyed for any person, as such land and the buildings and improvements thereon shall be estimated according to such mode as the United States, in Congress assembled, shall, from time to time, direct and appoint.

The taxes for paying that proportion shall be laid and levied by the authority and direction of the legislatures of the several states, within the time agreed upon by the United States, in Congress assembled.

ARTICLE IX. The United States, in congress assembled, shall have the sole and exclusive right and power of determining on peace and war, except in the cases mentioned in the 6th article; of sending and receiving ambassadors; entering into treaties and alliances, provided that no treaty of commerce shall be made, whereby the legislative power of the respective states shall be restrained from imposing such imposts and duties on foreigners as their own people are subjected to, or from prohibiting the exportation or importation of any species of goods or commodities whatsoever; of establishing rules for deciding, in all cases, what captures on land or water shall be legal, and in what manner prizes taken by land or naval forces in the service of the United States, shall be divided or appropriated; of granting letters of marque and reprisal in times of peace; appointing courts for the trial of piracies and felonies committed on the high seas, and establishing courts for receiving and determining, finally, appeals in all cases of captures; provided, that no member of Congress shall be appointed a judge of any of the said courts.

The United States, in Congress assembled, shall also be the last resort on appeal in all disputes and differences now subsisting, or that hereafter may arise between two or more states concerning boundary, jurisdiction or any other cause whatever; which authority shall always be exercised in the manner following: whenever the legislative or executive authority, or lawful agent of any State, in controversy with another, shall present a petition to Congress, stating the matter in question, and praying for a hearing, notice thereof shall be given, by order of Congress, to the legislative or executive authority of the other State in controversy, and a day assigned for the appearance of the parties by their lawful agents, who shall then be directed to appoint, by joint consent, commissioners or judges to constitute a court for hearing and determining the matter in question; but, if they cannot agree, Congress shall name three persons out of each of the United States, and from the list of such persons each party shall alternately strike out one, the petitioners beginning, until the number shall be reduced to thirteen; and from that number not less than seven, nor more than nine names, as Congress shall direct, shall, in the presence of Congress, be drawn out by lot; and the persons whose names shall be so drawn, or any five of them, shall be commissioners or judges to hear and finally determine the controversy, so always as a major part of the judges who shall hear the cause shall agree in the determination; and if either party shall neglect to attend at the day appointed, without shewing reasons which Congress shall judge sufficient, or, being present, shall refuse to strike the Congress shall proceed to nominate three persons out of each State, and the secretary of Congress shall strike in behalf of such party absent or refusing; and the judgment and sentence of the court to be appointed, in the manner before prescribed, shall be final and conclusive; and if any of the parties shall refuse to submit to the authority of such court, or to appear or defend their claim or cause, the court shall nevertheless proceed to pronounce sentence or judgment, which shall, in like manner, be final and decisive, the judgment or sentence and other proceedings being, in either case, transmitted to Congress, and lodged among the acts of Congress for the security of the parties concerned: provided, that every commissioner, before he sits in judgment, shall take an oath, to be administered by one of the judges of the supreme or superior court of the State where the cause shall be tried, "well and truly to hear and determine the matter in question, according to the best of his judgment, without favour, affection, or hope of reward;" provided, also, that no State shall be deprived of territory for the benefit of the United States.

All controversies concerning the private rights of soil, claimed under different grants of two or more states, whose jurisdictions, as they may respect such lands and the states which passed such grants, are adjusted, the said grants, or either of them, being at the same time claimed to have originated antecedent to such settlement of jurisdiction, shall, on the petition of either party to the Congress of the United States, be finally determined, as near as may be, in the same manner as is before prescribed for deciding disputes respecting territorial jurisdiction between different states.

The United States, in Congress assembled, shall also have the sole and exclusive right and power of regulating the alloy and value of coin struck by their own authority, or by that of the respective states; fixing the standards of weights and measures throughout the United States; regulating the trade and managing all affairs with the Indians not members of any of the states; provided that the legislative right of any State within its own limits be not infringed or violated; establishing and regulating post offices from one State to another throughout all the United States, and exacting such postage on the papers passing through the same as may be requisite to defray the expences of the said office; appointing all officers of the land forces in the service of the United States, excepting regimental officers; appointing all the officers of the naval forces, and commissioning all officers whatever in the service of the United States; making rules for the government and regulation of the said land and naval forces, and directing their operations.

The United States, in Congress assembled, shall have authority to appoint a committee to sit in the recess of Congress, to be denominated "a Committee of the States," and to consist of one delegate from each State, and to appoint such other committees and civil officers as may be necessary for managing the general affairs of the United States, under their direction; to appoint one of their number to preside; provided that no person be allowed to serve in the office of president more than one year in any term of three years; to ascertain the necessary sums of money to be raised for the service of the United States, and to appropriate and apply the same for defraying the public expences; to borrow money or emit bills on the credit of the United States, transmitting, every half year, to the respective states, an account of the sums of money so borrowed or emitted, to build and equip a navy; to agree upon the number of land forces, and to make requisitions from each State for its quota, in proportion to the number of white inhabitants in such State; which requisitions shall be binding; and, thereupon, the legislature of each State shall appoint the regimental officers, raise the men, and cloathe, arm, and equip them in a soldier-like manner, at the expence of the United States; and the officers and men so cloathed, armed, and equipped, shall march to the place appointed and within the time agreed on by the United States, in Congress assembled; but if the United States, in Congress assembled, shall, on consideration of circumstances, judge proper that any State should not raise men, or should raise a smaller number than its quota, and that any other State should raise a greater number of men than the quota thereof, such extra number shall be raised, officered, cloathed, armed, and equipped in the same manner as the quota of such State, unless the legislature of such State shall judge that such extra number cannot be safely spared out of the same, in which case they shall raise, officer, cloathe, arm, and equip as many of such extra number as they judge can be safely spared. And the officers and men so cloathed, armed, and equipped, shall march to the place appointed and within the time agreed on by the United States, in Congress assembled.

The United States, in Congress assembled, shall never engage in a war, nor grant letters of marque and reprisal in time of peace, nor enter into any treaties or alliances, nor coin money, nor regulate the value thereof, nor ascertain the sums and expences necessary for the defence and welfare of the United States, or any of them; nor emit bills, nor borrow money on the credit of the United States, nor appropriate money, nor agree upon the number of vessels of war to be built or purchased, or the number of land or sea forces to be raised, nor appoint a commander in chief of the army or navy, unless nine states assent to the same; nor shall a question on any other point, except for adjourning from day to day, be determined, unless by the votes of a majority of the United States, in Congress assembled.

The Congress of the United States shall have power to adjourn to any time within the year, and to any place within the United States, so that no period of adjournment be for a longer duration than the space of six months, and shall publish the journal of their proceedings monthly, except such parts thereof, relating to treaties, alliances or military operations, as, in their judgment, require secrecy; and the yeas and nays of the delegates of each State on any question shall be entered on the journal, when it is desired by any delegate; and the delegates of a State, or any of them, at his, or their request, shall be furnished with a transcript of the said journal, except such parts as are above excepted, to lay before the legislatures of the several states.

ARTICLE X. The committee of the states, or any nine of them, shall be authorized to execute, in the recess of Congress, such of the powers of Congress as the United States, in Congress assembled, by the consent of nine states, shall, from time to time, think expedient to vest them with; provided, that no power be delegated to the said committee, for the exercise of which, by the articles of confederation, the voice of nine states, in the Congress of the United States assembled, is requisite.

ARTICLE XI. Canada acceding to this confederation, and joining in the measures of the United States, shall be admitted into and entitled to all the advantages of this union; but no other colony shall be admitted into the same, unless such admission be agreed to by nine states.

ARTICLE XII. All bills of credit emitted, monies borrowed and debts contracted by, or under the authority of Congress before the assembling of the United States, in pursuance of the present confederation, shall be deemed and considered as a charge against the United States, for payment and satisfaction whereof the said United States and the public faith are hereby solemnly pledged.

ARTICLE XIII. Every state shall abide by the determinations of the United States, in Congress assembled, on all questions which, by this confederation, are submitted to them. And the articles of this confederation shall be inviolably observed by every State, and the union shall be perpetual; nor shall any alteration at any time hereafter be made in any of them, unless such alteration be agreed to in a Congress of the United States, and be afterwards confirmed by the legislatures of every State.

These articles shall be proposed to the legislatures of all the United States, to be considered, and if approved of by them, they are advised to authorize their delegates to ratify the same in the Congress of the United States; which being done, the same shall become conclusive.

And Whereas it hath pleased the Great Governor of the World to incline the hearts of the legislatures we respectively represent in congress, to approve of, and to authorize us to ratify the said articles of confederation and perpetual union. Know Ye that we the undersigned delegates, by virtue of the power and authority to us given for that purpose, do by these presents, in the name and in behalf of our respective constituents, fully and entirely ratify and confirm each and every of the said articles of confederation and perpetual union, and all and singular the matters and things therein contained: And we do further solemnly plight and engage the faith of our respective constituents, that they shall abide by the determinations of the united states in congress assembled, on all questions, which by the said confederation are submitted to them. And that the articles thereof shall be inviolably observed by the states we respectively represent, and that the union shall be perpetual. In Witness whereof we have hereunto set our hands in Congress. Done at Philadelphia in the state of Pennsylvania the ninth day of July, in the Year of our Lord one Thousand seven Hundred and Seventy-eight, and in the third year of the independence of America.

On the part & behalf of the State of New Hampshire.
 Josiah Bartlett
 John Wentworth, Jr.
 August 8th, 1778
On the part and behalf of the State of Massachusetts Bay.
 John Hancock
 Samuel Adams
 Elbridge Gerry
 Francis Dana
 James Lovell
 Samuel Holten
On the part and behalf of the State of Rhode-Island and Providence Plantations.
 William Ellery
 Henry Marchant
 John Collins
On the part and behalf of the State of Connecticut.
 Roger Sherman
 Samuel Huntington
 Oliver Wolcott
 Titus Hosmer
 Andrew Adams
On the part and behalf of the State of New York.
 Jas. Duane
 Fra. Lewis
 Wm. Duer
 Gouvr. Morris
On the Part and in behalf of the State of New Jersey, November 26th, 1778.
 Jno. Witherspoon
 Nathl. Scudder
On the part and behalf of the State of Pennsylvania.
 Robert Morris
 Daniel Roberdeau
 Jon. Bayard Smith
 William Clingar
 Joseph Reed
 22nd July, 1778

On the part & behalf of the State of Delaware.
 Thos. McKean
 Feby. 22d, 1779
 John Dickinson
 May 5th, 1779
 Nicholas Van Dyke
On the part and behalf of the State of Maryland.
 John Hanson
 March 1, 1781
 Daniel Carroll
On the Part and Behalf of the State of Virginia.
 Richard Henry Lee
 John Banister
 Thomas Adams
 Jno. Harvie
 Francis Lightfoot Lee
On the part and behalf of the State of North Carolina
 John Penn
 July 21st, 1778
 Corns. Harnett
 Jno. Williams
On the part and on behalf of the State of South Carolina.
 Henry Laurens
 William Henry Drayton
 Jno. Mathews
 Richd. Hutson
 Thos. Heyward, Jr.
On the part and behalf of the State of Georgia
 Jno. Walton
 24th July, 1778
 Edwd. Telfair
 Edwd. Langworthy

The Constitution of the United States

We the people of the United States, in Order to form a more perfect Union, establish Justice, insure domestic Tranquility, provide for the common defense, promote the general Welfare, and secure the Blessings of Liberty to ourselves and our Posterity, do ordain and establish this CONSTITUTION for the United States of America.

Article I

SECTION 1. All legislative Powers herein granted shall be vested in a Congress of the United States which shall consist of a Senate and House of Representatives.

SECTION 2. The House of Representatives shall be composed of Members chosen every second Year by the People of the several States, and the Electors in each State shall have the Qualifications requisite for Electors of the most numerous Branch of the State Legislature.

No Person shall be a Representative who shall not have attained to the Age of twenty-five Years, and been seven Years a Citizen of the United States, and who shall not, when elected, be an inhabitant of that State in which he shall be chosen.

Representative and direct Taxes shall be apportioned among the several States which may be included within this Union, according to their respective Numbers, which shall be determined by adding to the whole Number of free Persons, including those bound to Service for a Term of Years and excluding Indians not taxed, three fifths of all other persons. The actual Enumeration shall be made within three Years after the first Meeting of the Congress of the United States, and within every subsequent Term of ten Years, in such Manner as they shall by Law direct. The Number of Representatives shall not exceed one for every thirty Thousand, but each State shall have at Least one Representative; and until such enumeration shall be made, the State of New Hampshire shall be entitled to chuse three, Massachusetts eight, Rhode-Island and Providence Plantations one, Connecticut five, New-York six, New Jersey four, Pennsylvania eight, Delaware one, Maryland six, Virginia ten, North Carolina five, South Carolina five, and Georgia three.

When vacancies happen in the Representation from any State, the Executive Authority thereof shall issue Writs of Election to fill such Vacancies.

The House of Representatives shall chuse their Speaker and other Officers; and shall have the sole Power of Impeachment.

SECTION 3. The Senate of the United States shall be composed of two Senators from each State, chosen by the Legislature thereof, for six Years; and each Senator shall have one Vote.

Immediately after they shall be assembled in Consequence of the first Election, they shall be divided as equally as may be into three Classes. The Seats of the Senators of the first Class shall be vacated at the Expiration of the second Year, of the second Class at the Expiration of the fourth Year, and of the third Class at the Expiration of the sixth Year, so that one-third may be chosen every second Year; and if Vacancies happen by Resignation, or otherwise, during the Recess of the Legislature of any State, the Executive thereof may make temporary Appointments until the next Meeting of the Legislature, which shall then fill such Vacancies.

No Person shall be a Senator who shall not have attained to the Age of thirty Years, and been nine Years a Citizen of the United States, and who shall not, when elected, be an Inhabitant of that State in which he shall be chosen.

The Vice-President of the United States shall be President of the Senate, but shall have no vote, unless they be equally divided.

The Senate shall chuse their other Officers, and also a President pro tempore, in the absence of the Vice-President, or when he shall exercise the Office of the President of the United States.

The Senate shall have the sole Power to try all Impeachments. When sitting for that purpose, they shall be on Oath or Affirmation. When the President of the United States is tried, the Chief Justice shall preside; And no person shall be convicted without the Concurrence of two thirds of the Members present.

Judgment in Cases of Impeachment shall not extend further than to removal from office, and disqualification to hold and enjoy an Office of honor, Trust, or Profit under the United States; but the Party convicted shall nevertheless be liable and subject to Indictment, Trial, Judgment, and Punishment, according to law.

SECTION 4. The Times, Places and Manner of holding Elections for Senators and Representatives, shall be prescribed in each state by the Legislature thereof; but the Congress may at any time by Law make or alter such Regulations, except as to the Places of Chusing Senators.

The Congress shall assemble at least once in every year, and such meeting shall be on the first Monday in December unless they shall by Law appoint a different Day.

SECTION 5. Each House shall be the Judge of the Elections, Returns and Qualifications of its own Members, and a Majority of each shall constitute a Quorum to do Business from day to day, and may be authorized to compel the Attendance of absent Members, in such Manner, and under such Penalties, as each House may provide.

Each House may determine the Rules of its Proceedings, punish its Members for disorderly Behavior, and, with the Concurrence of two thirds, expel a Member.

Each House shall keep a Journal of its Proceedings, and from time to time publish the same, excepting such Parts as may in their Judgment require Secrecy; and the Yeas and Nays of the Members of either House on any question shall, at the Desire of one fifth of those Present, be entered on the Journal.

Neither House, during the Session of Congress, shall, without the Consent of the other, adjourn for more than three days, nor to any other Place than that in which the two Houses shall be sitting.

SECTION 6. The Senators and Representatives shall receive a Compensation for their Services, to be ascertained by Law, and paid out of the Treasury of the United States. They shall in all Cases, except Treason, Felony, and Breach of the Peace, be privileged from Arrest during their Attendance at the Session of their respective Houses, and in going to and returning from the same; and for any Speech or Debate in either House, they shall not be questioned in any other Place.

No Senator or Representative shall, during the Time for which he was elected, be appointed to any civil Office under the Authority of the United States, which shall have been created, or the Emoluments whereof shall have been increased, during such time; and

188 CONSTITUTION OF THE UNITED STATES

no Person holding any Office under the United States shall be a Member of either House during his continuance in Office.

SECTION 7. All Bills for raising Revenue shall originate in the House of Representatives; but the Senate may propose or concur with Amendments as on other bills.

Every Bill which shall have passed the House of Representatives and the Senate, shall, before it become a Law, be presented to the President of the United States. If he approve he shall sign it, but if not he shall return it, with his Objections, to that House in which it shall have originated, who shall enter the Objections at large on their Journal, and proceed to reconsider it. If after such Reconsideration two thirds of that House shall agree to pass the bill, it shall be sent, together with the objections, to the other House, by which it shall likewise be reconsidered, and if approved by two thirds of that House, it shall become a Law. But in all such Cases the Votes of both Houses shall be determined by Yeas and Nays, and the Names of the Persons voting for and against the Bill shall be entered on the Journal of each House respectively. If any Bill shall not be returned by the President within ten Days (Sundays excepted) after it shall have been presented to him, the Same shall be a Law, in like Manner as if he had signed it, unless the Congress by their Adjournment prevent its Return, in which Case it shall not be a Law.

Every Order, Resolution, or Vote to which the Concurrence of the Senate and House of Representatives may be necessary (except on a question of Adjournment) shall be presented to the President of the United States; and before the Same shall take Effect, shall be approved by him, or being disapproved by him, shall be repassed by two thirds of the Senate and House of Representatives, according to the Rules and Limitations prescribed in the Case of a Bill.

SECTION 8. The Congress shall have Power to lay and collect Taxes, Duties, Imposts and Excises, to pay the Debts and provide for the common defence and general Welfare of the United States; but all Duties, Imposts and Excises shall be uniform throughout the United States;

To borrow money on the credit of the United States;

To regulate Commerce with foreign Nations, and among the several States, and with the Indian Tribes;

To establish an uniform Rule of Naturalization, and uniform Laws on the subject of Bankruptcies throughout the United States;

To coin Money, regulate the Value thereof, and of foreign Coin, and fix the Standard of Weights and Measures;

To provide for the Punishment of counterfeiting the Securities and current Coin of the United States;

To establish Post Offices and post Roads;

To promote the Progress of Science and useful Arts, by securing for limited Times to Authors and Inventors the exclusive Right to their respective Writings and Discoveries;

To constitute Tribunals inferior to the Supreme Court;

To define and punish Piracies and Felonies committed on the high Seas, and offences against the Law of Nations;

To declare War, grant Letters of Marque and Reprisal, and make Rules concerning Captures on Land and Water;

To raise and support Armies, but no Appropriation of Money to that Use shall be for a longer Term than two Years;

To provide and maintain a Navy;

To make Rules for the Government and Regulation of the land and naval forces;

To provide for calling forth the Militia to execute the Laws of the Union, suppress Insurrections and repel Invasions;

To provide for organizing, arming, and disciplining the Militia, and for governing such Part of them as may be employed in the Service of the United States, reserving to the States respectively, the Appointment of the Officers, and the Authority of training the Militia according to the discipline prescribed by Congress;

To exercise exclusive legislation in all Cases whatsoever, over such District (not exceeding ten miles square) as may, by Cession of particular States, and the acceptance of Congress, become the Seat of Government of the United States, and to exercise like Authority over all Places purchased by the Consent of the Legislature of the States in which the Same shall be, for the Erection of Forts, Magazines, Arsenals, dock-Yards, and other needful Buildings; —And

To make all Laws which shall be necessary and proper for carrying into Execution the foregoing Powers, and all other Powers vested by this Constitution in the Government of the United States, or in any Department or Officer thereof.

SECTION 9. The Migration or Importation of such Persons as any of the States now existing shall think proper to admit, shall not be prohibited by the Congress prior to the Year one thousand eight hundred and eight, but a tax or duty may be imposed on such Importation, not exceeding ten dollars for each Person.

The privilege of the Writ of Habeas Corpus shall not be suspended, unless when in Cases of Rebellion or Invasion the public Safety may require it.

No Bill of Attainder or ex post facto Law shall be passed.

No capitation, or other direct, Tax shall be laid unless in Proportion to the Census or Enumeration herein before directed to be taken.

No Tax or Duty shall be laid on Articles exported from any State.

No Preference shall be given by any Regulation of Revenue to the Ports of one State over those of another; nor shall Vessels bound to, or from, one State, be obliged to enter, clear, or pay Duties in another.

No Money shall be drawn from the Treasury, but in Consequence of Appropriations made by Law; and a regular Statement and Account of the Receipts and Expenditures of all public Money shall be published from time to time.

No Title of Nobility shall be granted by the United States; And no person holding any Office of Profit or Trust under them, shall, without the Consent of the Congress, accept of any present, Emolument, Office or Title, of any kind whatever, from any King, Prince, or foreign State.

SECTION 10. No State shall enter any Treaty, alliance, or Confederation; grant Letters of Marque and Reprisal; coin Money; emit Bills of Credit; make any Thing but gold and silver Coin a Tender in Payment of Debts; pass any Bill of Attainder, ex post facto Law, or Law impairing the Obligation of Contracts, or grant any Title of Nobility.

No State shall, without the Consent of the Congress, lay any Imposts or Duties on Imports or Exports, except what may be absolutely necessary for executing its inspection Laws; and the net Produce of all Duties and Imposts, laid by any State on Imports or Exports, shall be for the Use of the Treasury of the United States; and all such Laws shall be subject to the Revision and Control of the Congress.

No State shall, without the Consent of Congress, lay any duty of Tonnage, keep Troops, or Ships of War in time of Peace, enter into any Agreement or Compact with another State, or with a foreign Power, or engage in War, unless actually invaded, or in such imminent Danger as will not admit of delay.

Article II

SECTION 1. The executive Power shall be vested in a President of the United States of America. He shall hold his Office during the Term of four years, and, together with the Vice-President, chosen for the same Term, be elected, as follows:

Each State shall appoint, in such Manner as the Legislature thereof may direct, a Number of Electors, equal to the whole Number of Senators and Representatives to which the State may be entitled in the Congress; but no Senator or Representative, or Person holding an Office of Trust or Profit under the United States, shall be appointed an Elector.

The Electors shall meet in their respective States, and vote by Ballot for two persons, of whom one at least shall not be an Inhabitant of the same State with themselves. And they shall make a List of all the Persons voted for, and of the Number of Votes for each; which list they shall sign and certify, and transmit sealed to the Seat of the Government of the United States, directed to the President of the Senate. The President of the Senate shall, in the Presence of the Senate and House of Representatives, open all the Certificates, and the Votes shall then be counted. The Person having the greatest Number of Votes shall be the President, if such Number be a Majority of the whole Number of Electors appointed; and if there be more than one who have such Majority, and have an equal Number of Votes, then the House of Representatives shall immediately chuse by Ballot one of them for President; and if no Person have a Majority, then from the five highest on the List the said House shall in like Manner chuse the President. But in chusing the President, the Votes shall be taken by States, the Representation from each State having one Vote; a quorum for this Purpose shall consist of a Member or Members from two-thirds of the States, and a Majority of all the States shall be necessary to a Choice. In every Case, after the Choice of the President, the Person having the greatest Number of Votes of the Electors shall be the Vice-President. But if there should remain two or more who have equal votes, the Senate shall chuse from them by Ballot the Vice-President.

The Congress may determine the Time of chusing the Electors, and the Day on which they shall give their Votes; which Day shall be the same throughout the United States.

No person except a natural-born Citizen, or a Citizen of the United States, at the time of the Adoption of this Constitution, shall be eligible to the Office of President; neither shall any Person be eligible to that Office who shall not have attained to the Age of thirty-five years, and been fourteen Years a Resident within the United States.

In Case of the Removal of the President from Office, or of his Death, Resignation, or Inability to discharge the Powers and Duties of the said Office, the same shall devolve on the Vice-President, and the Congress may by Law provide for the Case of Removal, Death, Resignation, or Inability, both of the President and Vice-President, declaring what Officer shall then act as President, and such officer shall act accordingly, until the disability be removed, or a President shall be elected.

The President shall, at stated Times, receive for his Services a Compensation, which shall neither be increased nor diminished during the Period for which he shall have been elected, and he shall not receive within that Period any other Emolument from the United States, or any of them.

Before he enter on the execution of his Office, he shall take the following Oath or Affirmation: — "I do solemnly swear (or affirm) that I will faithfully execute the Office of President of the United States, and will, to the best of my Ability, preserve, protect, and defend the Constitution of the United States."

SECTION 2. The president shall be Commander in Chief of the Army and Navy of the United States, and of the Militia of the several States, when called into the actual Service of the United States; he may require the Opinion, in writing, of the principal Officer in each of the executive Departments, upon any subject relating to the Duties of their respective Offices, and he shall have Power to Grant Reprieves and pardons for Offences against the United States, except in Cases of Impeachment.

He shall have Power, by and with the Advice and Consent of the Senate, to make Treaties, provided two thirds of the Senators present concur; and he shall nominate, and by and with the Advice and Consent of the Senate, shall appoint Ambassadors, other public Ministers and Consuls, Judges of the Supreme Court, and all other Officers of the United States, whose Appointments are herein otherwise provided for, and which shall be established by Law: but the Congress may by Law vest the Appointments of such inferior Officers, as they think proper, in the President alone, in the

Courts of Law, or in the Heads of Departments.

The President shall have Power to fill up all Vacancies that may happen during the Recess of the Senate, by granting Commissions which shall expire at the End of their next Session.

SECTION 3. He shall from time to time give to the Congress Information of the State of the Union, and recommend to their Consideration such Measures as he shall judge necessary and expedient; he may, on extraordinary occasions, convene both Houses, or either of them, and in Case of Disagreement between them, with respect to the Time of Adjournment, he may adjourn them to such Time as he shall think proper; he shall receive Ambassadors and other public Ministers; he shall take Care that the Laws be faithfully executed, and shall Commission all the Officers of the United States.

SECTION 4. The President, Vice-President and all civil Officers of the United States, shall be removed from Office on Impeachment for, and Conviction of, Treason, Bribery, or other high Crimes and Misdemeanors.

Article III

SECTION 1. The judicial power of the United States shall be vested in one supreme Court, and in such inferior Courts as the Congress may from time to time ordain and establish. The Judges, both of the supreme and inferior Courts, shall hold their Offices during good Behaviour, and shall, at stated Times, receive for their Services, a compensation, which shall not be diminished during their Continuance in office.

SECTION 2. The judicial Power shall extend to all Cases, in Law and Equity, arising under this Constitution, the Laws of the United States, and treaties made, or which shall be made, under their Authority; —to all Cases affecting ambassadors, other public ministers and consuls; —to all cases of admiralty and maritime Jurisdiction; —to Controversies to which the United States shall be a Party; —to Controversies between two or more States; —between a State and Citizens of another State; —between Citizens of different States; —between Citizens of the same State claiming Lands under Grants of different States, and between a State, or the Citizens thereof, and foreign States, Citizens or Subjects.

In all cases affecting Ambassadors, other public Ministers and Consuls, and those in which a State shall be a Party, the supreme Court shall have original Jurisdiction. In all the other Cases before mentioned, the supreme Court shall have appellate Jurisdiction, both as to law and Fact, with such Exception, and under such Regulations as the Congress shall make.

The trial of all Crimes, except in Cases of Impeachment, shall be by Jury; and such Trial shall be held in the State where the said Crimes shall have been committed; but when not committed within any State, the Trial shall be at such Place or Places as the Congress may by Law have directed.

SECTION 3. Treason against the United States, shall consist only in levying War against them, or in adhering to their Enemies, giving them Aid and Comfort. No Person shall be convicted of Treason unless on the Testimony of two Witnesses to the same overt Act, or on Confession in open Court.

The Congress shall have power to declare the Punishment of Treason, but no Attainder of Treason shall work Corruption of Blood, or Forfeiture except during the Life of the Person attained.

Article IV

SECTION 1. Full Faith and Credit shall be given in each State to the public Acts, Records, and judicial Proceedings of every other State. And the Congress may by general Laws prescribe the Manner in which such Acts, Records and Proceedings shall be proved, and the Effect thereof.

SECTION 2. The Citizens of each State shall be entitled to all Privileges and Immunities of Citizens in the several States.

A Person charged in any State with Treason, Felony, or other Crime, who shall flee from Justice, and be found in another State, shall on demand of the executive Authority of the State from which he fled, be delivered up, to be removed to the State having Jurisdiction of the crime.

No Person held to Service or Labour in one State, under the Laws thereof, escaping into another, shall, in Consequence of any Law or Regulation therein, be discharged from such Service or Labour, but shall be delivered up on Claim of the Party to whom such Service or Labour may be due.

SECTION 3. New States may be admitted by the Congress into this Union; but no new State shall be formed or erected within the Jurisdiction of any other State; nor any State be formed by the Junction of two or more States, or parts of States, without the Consent of the Legislatures of the States concerned as well as of the Congress.

The Congress shall have Power to dispose of and make all needful Rules and Regulations respecting the Territory or other Property belonging to the United States; and nothing in this Constitution shall be so construed as to Prejudice any Claims of the United States, or of any particular State.

SECTION 4. The United States shall guarantee to every State in this Union a Republican Form of Government, and shall protect each of them against Invasion; and on Application of the Legislature, or the Executive (when the legislature cannot be convened) against domestic Violence.

Article V

The Congress, whenever two-thirds of both Houses shall deem it necessary, shall propose Amendments to this Constitution, or, on the Application of the Legislatures of two-thirds of the several States, shall call a Convention for proposing Amendments, which, in either Case, shall be valid to all Intents and Purposes, as part of this Constitution, when ratified by the Legislatures of three-fourths of the several States, or by Conventions in three-fourths thereof, as the one or the other Mode of Ratification may be proposed by the Congress; Provided that no Amendment which may be made prior to the Year One thousand eight hundred and eight shall in any Manner affect the first and fourth Clauses in the Ninth Section of the First Article; and that no State, without its Consent, shall be deprived of its equal Suffrage in the Senate.

Article VI

All Debts contracted and Engagements entered into, before the Adoption of this Constitution, shall be as valid against the United States under this Constitution, as under the Confederation.

This Constitution, and the Laws of the United States which shall be made in Pursuance thereof; and the Treaties made, or which shall be made, under the Authority of the United States, shall be the supreme Law of the Land; and the Judges in every State shall be bound thereby, any Thing in the Constitution or Laws of any State to the Contrary notwithstanding.

The Senators and Representatives before mentioned, and the Members of the several State Legislatures, and all executive and judicial officers, both of the United States and of the several States, shall be bound by Oath or Affirmation to support this Constitution; but no religious Test shall ever be required as a qualification to any office of public trust under the United States.

Article VII

The Ratification of the Conventions of nine States shall be sufficient for the Establishment of this Constitution between the States so ratifying the same.

Done in Convention by the Unanimous Consent of the States present the Seventeenth

Day of September in the Year of our Lord one thousand seven hundred and Eighty seven, and of the Independence of the United States of America the Twelfth. In Witness whereof We have hereunto subscribed our names.

G°. Washington—President and Deputy from Virginia

New Hampshire:
John Langdon
Nicholas Gilman

Massachusetts:
Nathaniel Gorham
Rufus King

Connecticut:
Wm. Saml. Johnson
Roger Sherman

New York:
Alexander Hamilton

New Jersey:
Wil. Livingston
David Brearley
Wm. Paterson
Jona. Dayton

Pennsylvania:
B. Franklin
Thomas Mifflin
Robt. Morris
Geo. Clymer
Thos. FitzSimons
Jared Ingersoll
James Wilson
Gouv. Morris

Delaware:
Geo. Read
Gunning Bedford, Jr.
John Dickinson
Richard Bassett
Jaco. Broom

Maryland:
James McHenry
Dan of St. Thos. Jenifer
Danl. Carroll

Virginia:
John Blair
James Madison, Jr.

North Carolina:
Wm. Blount
Richd. Dobbs Spaight
Hu Williamson

South Carolina:
J. Rutledge
Charles Cotesworth
  Pinckney
Charles Pinckney
Pierce Butler

Georgia:
William Few
Abr. Baldwin

AMENDMENTS TO THE CONSTITUTION

Amendment I (1791)

Congress shall make no law respecting an establishment of religion, or prohibiting the free exercise thereof; or abridging the freedom of speech, or of the press; or the right of the people peaceably to assemble, and to petition the Government for a redress of grievance.

Amendment II (1791)

A well regulated Militia, being necessary to the security of a free State, the right of the people to keep and bear Arms shall not be infringed.

Amendment III (1791)

No Soldier shall, in time of peace, be quartered in any house, without the consent of the Owner, nor in time of war, but in a manner to be prescribed by law.

Amendment IV (1791)

The right of the people to be secure in their persons, houses, papers, and effects, against unreasonable searches and seizures, shall not be violated, and no Warrants shall issue, but upon probable cause, supported by Oath or affirmation, and particularly describing the place to be searched, and the persons or things to be seized.

Amendment V (1791)

No person shall be held to answer for a capital or otherwise infamous crime, unless on a presentment or indictment of a Grand Jury, except in cases arising in the land or naval forces, or in the Militia, when in actual service in time of war or public danger; nor shall any person be subject for the same offence to be twice put in jeopardy of life or limb; nor shall be compelled in any criminal case to be a witness against himself, nor be deprived of life, liberty, or property, without due process of law; nor shall private property be taken for public use, without just compensation.

Amendment VI (1791)

In all criminal prosecutions, the accused shall enjoy the right to a speedy and public trial, by an impartial jury of the State and district wherein the crime shall have been committed, which district shall have been previously ascertained by law, and to be informed of the nature and cause of the accusation; to be confronted with the witnesses against him; to have compulsory process for obtaining witnesses in his favor, and to have the Assistance of Counsel for his defense.

Amendment VII (1791)

In suits at common law, where the value in controversy shall exceed twenty dollars, the right of trial by jury shall be preserved, and no fact tried by a jury, shall be otherwise reexamined in any Court of the United States, than according to the rules of the common law.

Amendment VIII (1791)

Excessive bail shall not be required, nor excessive fines imposed, nor cruel and unusual punishments inflicted.

Amendment IX (1791)

The enumeration in the Constitution, of certain rights, shall not be construed to deny or disparage others retained by the people.

Amendment X (1791)

The powers not delegated to the United States by the Constitution, nor prohibited by it to the States, are reserved to the States respectively, or to the people.

Amendment XI (1798)

The Judicial power of the United States shall not be construed to extend to any suit in law or equity, commenced or prosecuted against one of the United States by Citizens of another State, or by Citizens or Subjects of any Foreign State.

Amendment XII (1804)

The Electors shall meet in their respective States and vote by ballot for President and Vice-President, one of whom, at least, shall not be an inhabitant of the same State with themselves; they shall name in their ballots the person voted for as President, and in distinct ballots the person voted for as Vice-President, and they shall make distinct lists of all persons voted for as President, and of all persons voted for as Vice-President, and of the number of votes for each, which lists they shall sign and certify, and transmit sealed to the seat of the government of the United States, directed to the President of the Senate; —The President of the Senate shall, in the presence of the Senate and House of Representatives, open all the certificates and the votes shall then be counted; —The person having the greatest number of votes for President, shall be the President, if such number be a majority of the whole number of Electors appointed; and if no person have such majority, then from the persons having the highest numbers not exceeding three on the list of those voted for as President, the House of Representatives shall choose immediately, by ballot, the President. But in choosing the President, the votes shall be taken by states, the representation from each state having one vote; a quorum for this purpose shall consist of a member or members from two-thirds of the States, and a majority of all the States shall be necessary to a choice. And if the House of Representatives shall not choose a President whenever the right of choice shall devolve upon them, before the fourth day of March next following, then the Vice-President shall act as President, as in the case of the death or other constitutional disability of the President. —The person having the greatest number of votes as Vice-President, shall be the Vice-President, if such number be a majority of the whole number of Electors appointed, and if no person have a majority, then from the two highest numbers on the list, the Senate shall choose the Vice-President; a quorum for the purpose shall consist of two-thirds of the whole number of Senators, and a majority of the whole number shall be necessary to a choice. But no person constitutionally ineligible to the office of President shall be eligible to that of Vice-President of the United States.

Amendment XIII (1865)

SECTION 1. Neither slavery nor involuntary servitude, except as a punishment for crime whereof the party shall have been duly convicted, shall exist within the United States, or any place subject to their jurisdiction.

SECTION 2. Congress shall have power to enforce this article by appropriate legislation.

Amendment XIV (1868)

SECTION 1. All persons born or naturalized in the United States, and subject to the jurisdiction thereof, are citizens of the United States and of the State wherein they reside. No State shall make or enforce any law which shall abridge the privileges or immunities of citizens of the United States; nor shall any State deprive any person of life, liberty, or property, without due process of law; nor deny to any person within its jurisdiction the equal protection of the laws.

SECTION 2. Representatives shall be apportioned among the several States according to their respective numbers, counting the whole number of persons in each State, excluding Indians not taxed. But when the right to vote at any election for the choice of electors for President and Vice-President of the United States, Representatives in Congress, the Executive and Judicial officers of a State, or the members of the Legislature thereof, is denied to any of the male inhabitants of such State, being twenty-one years of age, and citizens of the United States, or in any way abridged, except for participation in rebellion, or other crime, the basis of representations therein shall be reduced in the proportion which the number of such male citizens shall bear to the whole number of male citizens twenty-one years of age in such State.

SECTION 3. No person shall be a Senator or Representative in Congress, or elector of President and Vice-President, or hold any office, civil or military, under the United States, or under any State, who, having previously taken an oath, as a member of Congress, or as an officer of the United States, or as a member of any State legislature, or as an executive or judicial officer of any State, to support the Constitution of the United States, shall have engaged in insurrection or rebellion against the same, or given aid or comfort to the enemies thereof. But Congress may by a vote of two-thirds of each House, remove such disability.

SECTION 4. The validity of the public debt of the United States, authorized by law, including debts incurred for payment of pensions and bounties for services in suppressing insurrection or rebellion, shall not be questioned. But neither the United States nor any

State shall assume or pay any debt or obligation incurred in aid of insurrection or rebellion against the United States or any claim for the loss or emancipation of any slave; but all such debts, obligations, and claims shall be held illegal and void.

SECTION 5. The Congress shall have the power to enforce, by appropriate legislation, the provisions of this article.

Amendment XV (1870)

SECTION 1. The right of citizens of the United States to vote shall not be denied or abridged by the United States or by any State on account of race, color, or previous condition of servitude.

SECTION 2. The Congress shall have power to enforce this article by appropriate legislation.

Amendment XVI (1913)

The Congress shall have power to lay and collect taxes on incomes, from whatever source derived, without apportionment among the several States, and without regard to any census or enumeration.

Amendment XVII (1913)

The Senate of the United States shall be composed of two Senators from each State, elected by the people thereof, for six years; and each Senator shall have one vote. The electors in each State shall have the qualifications requisite for electors of the most numerous branch of the State legislatures.

When vacancies happen in the representation of any State in the Senate, the executive authority of such State shall issue writs of election to fill such vacancies; *Provided*, That the legislature of any State may empower the executive thereof to make temporary appointments until the people fill the vacancies by election as the legislature may direct.

This amendment shall not be so construed as to affect the election or term of any Senator chosen before it becomes valid as part of the Constitution.

Amendment XVIII (1919)

SECTION 1. After one year from the ratification of this article the manufacture, sale, or transportation of intoxicating liquors within, the importation thereof into, or the exportation thereof from the United States and all territory subject to the jurisdiction thereof for beverage purposes is hereby prohibited.

SECTION 2. The Congress and the several States shall have concurrent power to enforce this article by appropriate legislation.

SECTION 3. This article shall be inoperative unless it shall have been ratified as an amendment to the Constitution by the legislatures of the several States, as provided in the Constitution, within seven years from the date of the submission hereof to the States by the Congress.

Amendment XIX (1920)

The right of citizens of the United States to vote shall not be denied or abridged by the United States or by any State on account of sex.

Congress shall have power to enforce this article by appropriate legislation.

Amendment XX (1933)

SECTION 1. The terms of the President and Vice-President shall end at noon on the 20th day of January, and the terms of Senators and Representatives at noon on the 3d day of January, of the years in which such terms would have ended if this article had not been ratified; and the terms of their successors shall then begin.

SECTION 2. The Congress shall assemble at least once in every year, and such meeting shall begin at noon on the 3d day of January, unless they shall by law appoint a different day.

SECTION 3. If, at the time fixed for the beginning of the term of the President, the President elect shall have died, the Vice-President elect shall become President. If a President shall not have been chosen before the time fixed for the beginning of his term, or if the President elect shall have failed to qualify, then the Vice-President elect shall act as President until a President shall have qualified; and the Congress may by law provide for the case wherein neither a President elect nor a Vice-President elect shall have qualified, declaring who shall then act as President, or the manner in which one who is to act shall be selected, and such person shall act accordingly until a President or Vice-President shall have qualified.

SECTION 4. The Congress may by law provide for the case of the death of any of the persons from whom the House of Representatives may choose a President whenever the right of choice shall have devolved upon them, and for the case of the death of any of the persons from whom the Senate may choose a Vice-President whenever the right of choice shall have devolved upon them.

SECTION 5. Sections 1 and 2 shall take effect on the 15th day of October following the ratification of this article.

SECTION 6. This article shall be inoperative unless it shall have been ratified as an amendment to the Constitution by the legislatures of three-fourths of the several States within seven years from the date of its submission.

Amendment XXI (1933)

SECTION 1. The eighteenth article of amendment to the Constitution of the United States is hereby repealed.

SECTION 2. The transportation or importation into any State, Territory, or possession of the United States for delivery or use therein of intoxicating liquors, in violation of the laws thereof, is hereby prohibited.

SECTION 3. This article shall be inoperative unless it shall have been ratified as an amendment to the Constitution by conventions in the several States, as provided in the Constitution, within seven years from the date of the submission hereof to the States by the Congress.

Amendment XXII (1951)

No person shall be elected to the office of the President more than twice, and no person who has held the office of President, or acted as President, for more than two years of a term to which some other person was elected President shall be elected to the office of the President more than once.

But this Article shall not apply to any person holding the office of President when this Article was proposed by the Congress, and shall not prevent any person who may be holding the office of President, or acting as President, during the term within which this Article becomes operative from holding the office of President or acting as President during the remainder of such term.

Amendment XXIII (1961)

SECTION 1. The District constituting the seat of Government of the United States shall appoint in such manner as the congress may direct:

A number of electors of President and Vice President equal to the whole number of Senators and Representatives in Congress to which the District would be entitled if it were a State, but in no event more than the least populous State; they shall be in addition to those appointed by the States, but they shall be considered, for the purposes of the election of President and Vice President, to be electors appointed by a State; and they shall meet in the

District and perform such duties as provided by the twelfth article of amendment.

SECTION 2. The Congress shall have power to enforce this article by appropriate legislation.

Amendment XXIV (1964)

SECTION 1. The right of citizens of the Untied States to vote in any primary or other election for President or Vice President, for electors for President or Vice President, or for Senator or Representative in Congress, shall not be denied or abridged by the United States or any State by reason of failure to pay any poll tax or other tax.

SECTION 2. The Congress shall have the power to enforce this article by appropriate legislation.

Amendment XXV (1967)

SECTION 1. In case of the removal of the President from office or his death or resignation, the Vice President shall become President.

SECTION 2. Whenever there is a vacancy in the office of the Vice President, the President shall nominate a Vice President who shall take the office upon confirmation by a majority vote of both houses of Congress.

SECTION 3. Whenever the President transmits to the President pro tempore of the Senate and the Speaker of the House of Representatives his written declaration that he is unable to discharge the powers and duties of his office, and until he transmits to them a written declaration to the contrary, such powers and duties shall be discharged by the Vice President as Acting President.

SECTION 4. Whenever the Vice President and a majority of either the principal officers of the executive departments, or of such other body as Congress may by law provide, transmit to the President pro tempore of the Senate and the Speaker of the House of Representatives their written declaration that the President is unable to discharge the powers and duties of his office, the Vice President shall immediately assume the powers and duties of the office as Acting President.

Thereafter, when the President transmits to the President pro tempore of the Senate and the Speaker of the House of Representatives his written declaration that no inability exists, he shall resume the powers and duties of his office unless the Vice President and a majority of either the principal officers of the executive departments, or of such other body as Congress may by law provide, transmit within four days to the president pro tempore of the Senate and the Speaker of the House of Representatives their written declaration that the President is unable to discharge the powers and duties of his office. Thereupon Congress shall decide the issue, assembling within 48 hours for that purpose if not in session. If the Congress, within 21 days after receipt of the latter written declaration, or, if Congress is not in session, within 21 days after Congress is required to assemble, determines by two-thirds vote of both houses that the President is unable to discharge the powers and duties of his office, the Vice President shall continue to discharge the same as Acting president; otherwise, the President shall resume the powers and duties of his office.

Amendment XXVI (1971)

SECTION 1. The right of citizens of the United States, who are 18 years of age or older, to vote shall not be denied or abridged by the United States or by any state on account of age.

SECTION 2. The Congress shall have power to enforce this article by appropriate legislation.

About the Editors

JOHN F. MANLEY, professor of political science at Stanford University, is the author of *The Politics of Finance* and *American Government and Public Policy*.

KENNETH M. DOLBEARE is study director at the Institute for Public Policy at The Evergreen State College in Olympia, Washington. He is the author of many books, including *Neopolitics: American Political Ideas in the 1980s*, *Democracy at Risk: The Politics of Economic Renewal*, and *American Politics: Policies, Power, and Change*.